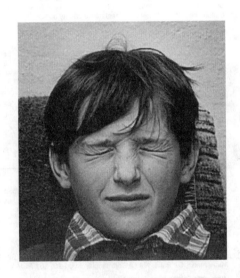

# INDEX ON CENSORSHIP 5 1996

Volume 25 No 5 September/October 1996 Issue 172

**Editor & Chief Executive**
Ursula Owen

**Director of Administration**
Philip Spender

**Deputy Editor**
Judith Vidal-Hall

**Production Editor**
Rose Bell

**Fundraising Manager**
Elizabeth Twining

**News Editor**
Adam Newey

**Fundraising Assistant**
Joe Hipgrave

**Editorial Assistants**
Anna Feldman
Philippa Nugent

**Africa**
Adewale Maja-Pearce

**Eastern Europe**
Irena Maryniak

**Circulation & Marketing Director**
Louise Tyson

**Subscriptions Manager**
Kelly Cornwall

**Accountant**
Suzanne Doyle

**Volunteer Assistants**
Michaela Becker
Laura Bruni
Kate Cooper
Ian Franklin
Nicholas McAulay
Mansoor Mirza
Albert Opoku
Grazia Pelosi
Dagmar Schlüter
Kate Smith
Sarah Smith
James Solomon
Katheryn Thal
Melissa Twyford
Tara Warren

**Directors** Louis Blom-Cooper, Ajay Chowdhury, Caroline Moorehead, Ursula Owen, Peter Palumbo, Jim Rose, Anthony Smith, Philip Spender, Sue Woodford (Chair)

**Council** Ronald Dworkin, Amanda Foreman, Thomas Hammarberg, Clive Hollick, Geoffrey Hosking, Michael Ignatieff, Mark Littman, Pavel Litvinov, Robert McCrum, Uta Ruge, William Shawcross, Suriya Wickremasinghe

**Patrons** Chinua Achebe, David Astor, Robert L Bernstein, Harold Evans, Richard Hamilton, Stuart Hampshire, Yehudi Menuhin, Iris Murdoch, Philip Roth, Tom Stoppard, Michael Tippett, Morris West

*Index on Censorship* (ISSN 0306-4220) is published bi-monthly by a non-profit-making company: Writers & Scholars International Ltd, Lancaster House, 33 Islington High Street, London N1 9LH

Tel: 0171-278 2313
Fax: 0171-278 1878
E-mail: indexoncenso@gn.apc.org
http://www.oneworld.org/index_oc/

Index *on Censorship* is associated with Writers & Scholars Educational Trust, registered charity number 325003

Periodicals postage (US subscribers only) paid at Newark, New Jersey. Postmaster: send US address changes to *Index on Censorship* c/o Mercury Airfreight Int/ Ltd Inc, 2323 Randolph Avenue, Avenel, NJ 07001, USA

**Subscriptions 1996**
(6 issues p.a.)
Individuals: UK £36, US $50, rest of world £42
Institutions: UK £40, US $70, rest of world £46
Students: UK £25, US $35, rest of world £31

© This selection Writers & Scholars International Ltd, London 1996
© Contributors to this issue, except where otherwise indicated

Printed by Martins, Berwick upon Tweed, UK

Cover design: Senate

**Australian committee** Philip Adams, Blanche d'Alpuget, Bruce Dawe, Adele Horin, Angelo Loukakis, Ken Methold, Laurie Muller, Robert Pullan and David Williamson c/o Ken Methold, PO Box 825, Glebe NSW 2037, Australia

**Danish committee** Paul Grosen, Niels Barfoed, Claus Sønderkøge, Herbert Pundik, Nils Thostrup, Toni Liversage and Björn Elmquist, c/o Claus Sønderkøge, Utkaervej 7, Ejerslev, DK-7900 Nykobing Mors, Denmark

**Dutch committee** Maarten Asscher, Gerlien van Dalen, Christel Jansen, Chris Keulemans, Wieke Rombach, Mineke Schipper and Steven de Winter, c/o Gerlien van Dalen and Chris Keulemans, De Balie, Kleine-Gartmanplantsoen 10, 1017 RR Amsterdam

**Norwegian committee** Trond Andreassen, Jahn Otto Johansen, Alf Skjeseth and Sigmund Strømme, c/o NFF, Bydøy allé 21, N-0262 Oslo, Norway

**Swedish committee** Gunilla Abrandt and Ana L Valdés, c/o Dagens Nyheter, Kulturredaktionen, S-105 15 Stockholm, Sweden

**USA committee** Rea Hederman, Peter Jennings, Harvey J Kaye, Susan Kenny, Jane Kramer, Radha Kumar, Jeri Laber, Gara LaMarche, Anne Nelson, Faith Sale, Michael Scammell

*Photo credits: (Front cover) Child survivor of a massacre by Muslims and Croats of a Serb village, Serdari, near Banja Luka, March 1993 (Michael Walter/Panos Pictures); (Back cover) Madres de Plaza de Mayo, Argentina, February 1991 (Hugo Fernandez/Andes Press Agency)*

**Former Editors:** Michael Scammell (1972-81); Hugh Lunghi (1981-83); George Theiner (1983-88); Sally Laird (1988-89); Andrew Graham-Yooll (1989-93)

# EDITORIAL

## Some truth, a little justice

'To forgive and forget we should know what actually happened,' said Nelson Mandela on the first day of South Africa's Truth Commission, which is hearing harrowing evidence from victims and torturers under apartheid (p45). This issue of *Index* reminds us that questions of truth, justice and reconciliation are not esoteric academic debates: they lie at the heart of what happens next in countries like South Africa, former Yugoslavia, Rwanda.

The transition from totalitarian government to democracy, from war to peace, is fraught with practical, moral and political dilemmas. War crimes tribunals establish criminal accountability; but can the trials of a few individuals be justice enough when thousands have been implicated in horrific human rights abuses? Truth commissions try to create conditions for forgiveness through accountability, amnesty and reparation. But, as Michael Ignatieff asks (p110), 'can a nation be reconciled to its past as individuals can, by replacing myth with fact, lies with truth?'

The question is how memory might serve reconciliation rather than perpetuate old grievances. For Ntsiki Biko in South Africa the imperative is that justice be done first (p67). Alberto Manguel, arguing with Mario Vargas Llosa over Argentina's history, is adamant that pardon — 'the victim's prerogative' — requires the truth to be told first (p123); and here agreement comes from an unlikely quarter, Gerrie Hugo, who organised torture in South Africa (p61). Meanwhile, in Ireland and Israel the process of reconciliation has not even begun. And 50 years after Nuremberg, war criminals are again on trial in Europe, but many of those found guilty will be convicted *in absentia* and not actually punished for their crimes (p137).

And what does reparation actually mean for the countless people whose lives have been destroyed by unspeakable suffering — the child, now an old woman, who lost her sanity after seeing a man's head split in two, 'like a cabbage', the men whose limbs were systematically broken by their torturers, the women whose husbands or children have been 'disappeared'? On the whole, our contributors agree that the best we can do is at least to try and deal with the dark past, 'look the beast in the eye'. Then, with a bit of luck, there might be some truth and a little justice. ❑

# contents

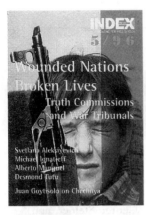
*Index on Censorship* and
**Writers and Scholars Educational Trust**

depend on donations to guarantee their independence
and to fund research

The Trustees and Directors would like to thank all those whose
donations support *Index* and WSET, including

**The Bromley Trust
The European Commission
Pearson plc
The Reuter Foundation**

# LETTERS

## Give reason a little chance

**From Nicolas Walter, Rationalist Press Association, London**

THE feature 'God is not dead' [*Index* 4/1996] was spoilt by the introductory material. In particular, John Tusa's introduction ['They say God is dead. Why won't He lie down?'] was vitiated by errors and omissions about past critics of religion. Thus it isn't true that Nietzsche pronounced it dead, that Marx derided it as a delusion, or that Freud regarded it as immature delusion; all three said much more intelligent and interesting things about it. Nor is it true that scientists dismissed it as unverifiable fantasy or humanists as evasion of grown-up confrontation with life; many biologists, anthropologists, sociologists, psychologists, philosophers who rejected religion also said subtle and significant things about it. In fact, is it true that anyone at the beginning of this century said that religion was dead or dying? As for the situation today, some forms of religion may now be reviving in some places — as is documented by your feature, and much other material — but most forms of religion are still declining in most places (certainly in Britain). Anyway, what evidence is there that religion continues to offer an alternative set of explanations for human life and behaviour, that rationality is one of the ideas which has been found wanting, or that the science and secularism of our age are more harmful than the magic and mysticism of the past? What has religion ever explained, or irrationality ever solved, or prayer ever granted? Reference is made to Jonathan Sacks, Hans Küng, Eli Cohen, Desmond Tutu, George Steiner, and Patrick Collinson, but not to any of the many non-religious theorists or activists of the past half-century. Nor indeed is any reference made to the organised free thought movement, which has been saying throughout the present century as well as the last one that religion, far from being dead or dying, is a living and continuing threat to human thought and welfare, and that the modernisers within religion, however welcome they may be, can't settle the real issue — that religion isn't true. Anyway, what have secular states got to do with Nazi Germany? Most Nazi leaders were Roman Catholics, most German Christians supported the Nazi regime and Hitler himself invoked God to the very end! If anything, Nazism is a good example of what irrational belief can lead to. Indeed Communism and Fascism should surely be seen not as simple opposites but as complex parodies of the Judaeo-Christian tradition. ❏

# Short memories

**From Clare Hartley, London**

DURING the Soviet era and the 'atheistic' state, Moscow could get away with religious persecution. The persecutions included the Russian Orthodox Church. But now it is the Russian Orthodox Church which is pushing for government intolerance towards other 'non-local' religions.

If they get their way, the Russians would have problems co-sponsoring peace processes where ethnic or religious conflict dominate. They would not be able to continue to co-sponsor the peace process between the Israelis and the Palestinians because if they deny the Jews the right to worship in Russia, many right-wing Jews including the Russian immigrants would reject Russia's role and Israel would be forced to break diplomatic relations with Moscow. The Vatican would also break diplomatic relations with Russia if Roman Catholics were banned from practising in Russia.

Religious extremists in America might burn down Russian Orthodox churches in retaliation for the banning of their own religions in Russia. As for the 'fringe' cults and sects, there would be many reminders of Waco and mass suicides like the 'Jones' cult in Guyana if the Russian authorities pursue repressive measures against them. And the more one persecutes people because of their religion, the stronger they become. Persecution with rewards of the 'afterlife' is an attractive prospect for fresh recruitments. Religious persecution has always failed in the past. One has only to look back in history. It would also fail in Russia just as it has done during the Communist era. The Russian Orthodox Church should understand this. Many of their own priests were murdered following the Russian Revolution. The problem is they appear to have short memories as they have now proved themselves as intolerant as the Soviet Communist Party before them. ❏

# Addresses, please

**From Michael Schmidt**
**Carcanet Press Ltd**
**402/406 Corn Exchange**
**Manchester M4 3BY**

THE offices of Carcanet Press Ltd and of *PN Review* were destroyed in the Manchester bomb of 15 June and only a portion of the records have been recovered. The editors would be grateful if authors, contributors, subscribers and members of the mailing list could write in providing address, telephone and fax numbers so that the operation can be fully restored as soon as possible. ❏

# news
## in the

- **With friends like these** Death threats continue against Khalid Lodhi, former London bureau chief for the Pakistan People's Party (PPP) daily *Musawaat*. He lost his job after providing the British *Sunday Express* with information on the multi-million-pound sale of a Surrey mansion to Asif Zardawi, husband of PPP leader and prime minister Benazir Bhutto. Zardawi has threatened to sue the *Sunday Express;* Lodhi receives threatening telephone calls in the middle of the night; and back in Faisalabad, his parents have been warned that 'your son's dead body will return to Pakistan very soon.'

- **It's good to talk** In August, the Pakistan government lifted its year-long ban on mobile phones and pagers, imposed to prevent members of the Mohajir Qaumi Movement keeping in touch with its exiled leaders in the UK. Anyone wishing to buy such equipment henceforth must provide proof of identity and two references.

- **No sex please, we're Polish** An anti-pornography drive was launched in Bialystok, Poland, at the end of July. Shops that refuse to stock pornographic magazines are rewarded with a sign depicting a *Playboy*-style bunny symbol crossed out. The names of shopkeepers who co-operate will be displayed in the city's Catholic churches.

- **Picture this** Hong Kong's Obscene Articles Tribunal ruled the July edition of *Cosmopolitan* indecent because it featured a good sex guide. 'There are no nude pictures,' commented a bemused editor, 'just some illustrations.'

- **Talk of the devil** The British Labour Party is rejoicing in what could prove to be a pyrrhic victory: the Advertising Standards

Authority has upheld its complaints on the Tory ad 'satanising' its leader Tony Blair; ads of a 'personally vindictive nature' are condemned under ASA guidelines. While Labour itself has not been above such practises in the past, their current squeamishness threatens one of the better traditions in British journalism. For centuries, the press was enlivened by the likes of Steele, Addison, Cruikshank and a host of other scribblers whose scurrilous pens spared no-one.

• **Porn free** Delegates to Unicef's Stockholm conference (27-31 August) on the sexual exploitation of children, were surprised by the array of child pornography and assorted paedophilia openly displayed in the capital's bookshops. Sweden has possibly the most liberal laws in the world on this: ban nothing. Old objection: is the action furthered by the image?

• **Patriot games** Franjo Tudjman's grip on the Croatian media tightens daily. His latest target is the top-rated Radio 101, a station devoted to 'western music not patriotic songs'. Not without a touch of irony, Radio 101's director Zeljko Matic observes, 'When the Communists wanted to keep Tudjman's Croat sentiments under wraps, we were the station who gave him a chance to air his views. At that time he was all for political freedom and human rights...'

• **The big sleep** After a resounding success with the general public, breaking box office records in Cairo and Alexandria, the film *Noum el Assal* (Fast Asleep) has fallen foul of the puritans who claim it is insulting to Christianity as well as Islam. A plague of impotence among Arab men is used metaphorically to comment on the political apathy that afflicts most Arab populations in the face of dictatorial regimes.

• **Jumping on the banned wagon** Palestinian writer Edward Said has run foul of Yasser Arafat. Two of his books — compilations of his regular column in *Al-Hayat* — have been banned from Gaza and the West Bank. He has also been vilified by the official Voice of Palestine radio. Said, who in his own words has become a 'non-person' in the Palestinian media, has been consistently critical of what he calls a 'fraudulent peace process' and of Arafat's 'dictatorial, profoundly corrupt and visionless attempt to rule his people'. 'Like every despot before him, he thinks that by confiscating books, banning articles, imprisoning people who seem too independent, he can blot out dissent and dissatisfaction.'

• **In Colombia** a casual remark made in an interview by the US ambassador — that a group of civilians had approached him in August 1995 to see how he felt about supporting 'a small coup' against President Samper — set off shock waves in a country whose relations with the *yanquis* are not at their warmest. Washington thinks Samper has been obstructive in their fight against the drugs trade, and endorses the long-standing accusation that Samper's election campaign was financed in part by the cartels.

A follow-up investigation by the news weekly *Semana* reveals that a group of opposition politicians and army officers were ready to take power at 2am on 11 November 1995; negative reactions in the US were to be avoided by immediately handing over leaders of the Calí drugs cartel to Washington. The plotters saw no need to muzzle a media that was highly critical of Samper and were thwarted only by the assassination of their candidate, veteran Samper critic Alvaro Gómez Hurtado, nine days before zero hour.

Since then, Samper has been cleared by Congress of any suspicion of involvement with drugs money, and is threatening to sue journalists who repeat the allegations. But relations with the US have deteriorated further since a senior official was quoted as saying, 'As is often the case with the Colombian government, they're lying.' And the Gómez murder, meanwhile, remains unsolved.

• **Bosnian elections** When the Dayton peace agreement was signed in November 1995, few believed that the West would put in an intervening force of some 60,000 troops only to ratify through peace what the war was fought for: ethnic states. Yet this, it seems, will be the case. In the past few months, Bosnia-watchers have warned that the September elections will be a de facto ratification of partition; many now recognise that the Dayton agreement, with its formal recognition of Republika Srpska, is essentially a partition agreement with an exit clause: that if the Bosnian electorate (including the Bosnian Serbs) vote out their nationalist and in some cases criminal leaders, the West will make serious moves towards reintegration. If, on the other hand, the Bosnian electorate remandates ethno-nationalist leaders, then the international community will be in a position to accept partition as the 'democratically expressed will of the people'.

Whether anyone seriously expected the Bosnian electorate to vote out their nationalist leaders is debatable. The stubborn push for early elections in a country which is still reeling from war, where ethnic cleansing, gang rule, intimidation and police terror continue, where refugees are pawns in ethno-territorial consolidation and which still does not know whether it will be a country at all, would indicate otherwise. What the West does seem to have hoped for, if US envoy Richard Holbrooke is anyone to go by, is that the elections would mark a peaceful transition to partition. Appearing on US television on the eve of the Dayton agreement Mr Holbrooke was asked if this was partition. 'I would prefer to use the Czechoslovak example of voluntary dissolution,' he said.

The run-up to elections, however, shows that partition is more likely to continue conflict than usher in peace. President Izetbegovic has been using the run-up to warn of an impending Croat-Bosniak war; as the recent kerfuffle over local election results in Mostar indicate, affairs do not march, nor even limp, in the Federation. A third partition always hovered in Dayton's wings: if a two-way partition is acceptable, then why not a three-way one? Unsurprisingly, the answer to this — that a tiny land-locked Muslim Bosnia would perpetuate Islamic resentment, and that Croatia was more amenable to pressure than Serbia — does not satisfy Hercegovinians. The Mostar problem has now been put on hold as a result of President Clinton's intervention. So far, all this has achieved is to stave off the problem: President Tudjman

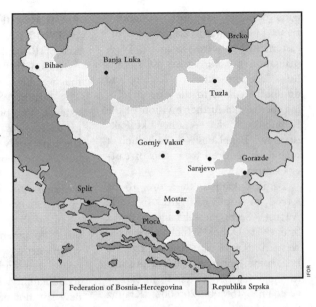

Federation of Bosnia-Hercegovina ☐ Republika Srpska

*The Dayton agreement map, November 1995*

has agreed that the 'Republic of Herceg-Bosna' (the rogue Croat statelet) will be dismantled from 31 August, but his control over the Hercegovinian mafias has always been in question and without their arrest the Federation cannot work.

Yet it is not Mostar but Banja Luka that may bring the simmering partition war to a head. One look at the map of Republika Srpska shows why. The Serb entity is in two parts, connected only by the narrow Posavina corridor to which the disputed town of Brcko is key. Serb attempts to rig elections there have been a major factor in the agreement to postpone local elections, possibly until next year. Additionally, the two parts lean in opposite directions, Banja Luka towards Zagreb and the eastern strip towards Belgrade. Normalisation would again pull Banja Luka economically to Zagreb and diminish its links to the east, involving, perhaps, a further division of the Republika Srpska — rather like Pakistan and Bangladesh — in which it would be reduced to a strip of eastern Bosnia.

Banja Luka has, therefore, to be forced to look eastward. In early August, Serb radicals blew up a bridge at Doboj which connected western Republika Srpska to the Federation, and it is still not possible to telephone Banja Luka from Sarajevo. The 150,000-200,000 Krajina Serb refugees, most of whom are stateless because Croatia will not let them return, actively contribute to these efforts; they need Banja Luka to be isolated if they are to hope for support. But the isolation of Banja Luka can only be maintained artificially, through keeping it in a state of anarchy and under mafia rule, like Mostar.

To this extent, while any elections at this point are likely to ratify partition at the political level, efforts to consolidate partition on the ground will not only continue conflict but will eventually show that Bosnia can only be successfully divided into two if the Republika Srpska is further partitioned, which would make a nonsense of partition altogether and entail a prolonged international presence in the region. ❏

### • On Her Majesty's Secret Service

A short but Orwellian Act of Parliament was given Royal Assent on 18 July, seemingly without much public debate, fuss or bother. The Security Services Act of 1996 extends the powers of the intelligence services to carry out surveillance not only on known criminals, but also on people suspected of criminal acts or conspiracy. Broadly speaking the security services can break in and enter private property to plant all sorts of spying devices, seize documents and bug phones when acting 'in support of the police' but with none of the public accountability of the police. This new law not only offends the guidelines and judgements laid down by the European Court, it also overturns centuries-old English case law.

The Act says the intelligence services and other law enforcement agencies (which include the Inland Revenue and Customs and Excise) 'shall act in support of the police forces in the prevention and detection of crime'. The Act sets no limits to this support. The Act also gives the secretary of state exceptionally wide powers, uncontrolled by judicial review, to issue warrants permitting all manner of surveillance. The scope is broad, the only limitation being that the suspected offence consists of violence, or results in financial gain, or (most significantly) is conducted by a large number of persons in pursuit of a common purpose. If, for example, you are a member of a trade union, engaged in a group intending to demonstrate in Trafalgar Square, or under investigation by Customs and Excise because of your tax return, the secretary of state may issue a warrant to seize your documents, secretly watch your home, observe your comings and goings, and tap your phones, without any limitation as to the manner of surveillance, or the activity under surveillance. There is no way you can obtain access to the information held about your private life (unlike the Freedom of information Act in the USA) and you have no right to be notified when the surveillance has ceased (if you ever knew about it in the first place).

In Britain, no right of privacy has ever been ensured, except in cases where interference with property is concerned, making trespass illegal. However, as far back as 1765, a case was brought by a Mr Entick, whose house had been turned upside down for four hours by the King's messengers looking for seditious papers under a warrant issued by a minister of state. Mr Entick's counsel pleaded: 'If they [the search warrants] have been granted [by the minister] then it is high time to put an end to them; for if they are held to be legal, the liberty of the country is at an end. Ransacking a man's secret drawers and boxes to come at evidence against him, is like racking his body to come at his secret thoughts...' The judge decided that such warrants authorising intrusion into property were illegal. This was the rule of law and an accepted part of Britain's constitutional practice for over two centuries until it was overturned in July.

The European Convention on Human Rights goes much further and guarantees respect for private life. In two recent French cases the European Court decided that telephone tapping and bugging of all sorts represents interference in private life. Any law allowing it must be clear and foreseeable, that is, understood to relate to a defined category of people (such as suspected terrorists and organised crime), defined offences (such as conspiracy to hijack a plane), include a procedure of summary reports of intercepted conversations, and also define the circumstances in which the recording is erased or destroyed when no longer necessary. The Act contains none of these elements and is therefore in contravention of the European Convention.

In the aftermath of Atlanta, Pan Am 103 and the possibility of terrorism on board TWA 800, there is a feeling that the security services need sufficient powers to act quickly and effectively. But this Act was passed just before the parliamentary recess, and not long before a general election. It will not have gone unnoticed that the Labour Party could theoretically be subject to the executive warrant under this new Act. If the events of Watergate had taken place in Britain today, they would have been entirely legal. ❑

## JUAN GOYTISOLO

# Urbicides, massacres, common graves

**As Chechnya becomes the platform on which the Kremlin's political power struggle is being fought out, peace hangs in the balance. There is no certainty that the Chechen leadership will play along with one more broken promise from Moscow. A distinguished Spanish journalist, who travelled through the region in June describes scenes of devastation and remembers the long history of Chechen-Russian wars**

O N 11 DECEMBER 1994, the Russian army invaded the Republic of Chechnya 'in order to restore constitutional order' and eliminate a regime of 'bandits and criminals'. According to the ex-minister of defence, Pavel Grachov, the operation was to last a few hours: a simple victory parade. Seventeen months later, the 'parade' has brought some 40,000 civilian victims, including numerous Russians installed in Grozny; the losses of the army of occupation stand at around 13,000 dead and posted missing and the devastation of the capital, smaller settlements and hamlets can only be compared, in dimension and intensity, to that caused in some Russian and German cities during World War II. In little more than a year and a half of conquest, the army has suffered greater losses than in the 12 years of its disastrous adventure in Afghanistan.

As in Afghanistan, the new Kremlin leaders first tried to cover up the

MARTIN ADLER/PANOS PICTURES

*(Left) Presidential palace, Grozny: Valentina Krasnentiya (82) with picture of her missing daughter*

operation as the work of a group of 'patriots' resolved to rid themselves of Dudayev's tyranny and corruption. In November 1994, the tanks entered Grozny for the first time under cloak of 'fraternal help' to honest Chechens but the incursion ended catastrophically. The armoured cars were destroyed by grenade-throwers and, in spite of official disclaimers from Moscow, attributing the outburst to mysterious mercenaries, the Russian military leaders had to swallow the bitter pill of taking charge of the prisoners generously handed back by Dudayev. Neither the painful reminder of the defeat in Afghanistan which contributed so much to the fall of the Soviet regime nor the successive wars against the Chechens from the time of Imam Mansur helped Yeltsin or Pavel Grachov foresee the likelihood their troops would gradually be bogged down in a quagmire, sucked into mess they would escape with difficulty. Hence the pathetic efforts of state television and press to conceal the wretched truth, to cover up the barbarism, clumsiness and disorganisation of military operations, transmuting disasters into heroic actions, rehearsing the ritual litany of the 'imminent liquidation of the last bandit hide-outs'. Despite so much fabrication and self-deception — a legacy of the defunct regime of the USSR — Shamil Basayev's incursions in Budennovsk and Raduyev's in Kiliar with the victorious return of both to Chechnya in the face of intense army fire that inflicted more losses in their own ranks than in the enemy's, opened the eyes of a sector of public opinion and upped the number of citizens opposed to the war. Few, very few reinforcements or undernourished, badly paid officers or petty-officers now want to risk their lives and meet a glorious end on the field of honour. Chechnya, clearly, isn't worth the candle.

THE proclamation of the independence of this autonomous republic of 13,000 square metres on 27 October 1991 by the general of the Soviet Airforce Dzhokhar Dudayev is reminiscent in many ways of that made by the *naqshbandiya* Nadjmuddin from Gotso in August 1917, then led militarily by Sheik Uzun Hadji: in both cases their authors took advantage of the opportunities opened up by the collapse of Tsarism and the foreseeable break-up of the USSR. A significant precursor of Dudayev, Kaitmas Alichanov, a colonel of Chechen stock in Nicholas II's army, participated actively in the struggle for independence, first against the Cossacks and white Russians of Denikin and then against the Bolsheviks. The war was exceptionally savage and the *murids*, led by Mohammed of

Balkani, whose tomb or *mazar* in Daghestan is the object of pilgrimages in less harsh times than ours, annihilated a whole brigade of the Red Army in the valley of Arkhan, very close to the place where on 15 April this year a convoy of the 245th Motorised Infantry Regiment was wiped out and its complement of tanks burnt. The war ended, provisionally, in 1925 with the capture of Imam Nadjmuddin and his lieutenants in their mountain fastnesses in the Caucasus. Both today and in the era of Imam Shamil, the villages of Vedeno and Bamut surrendered after a merciless, bitterly fought siege.

BUT unlike Imam Shamil and the religious leaders of the Emirate in the Northern Caucasus, Dudayev did not succeed in winning over to his leadership a clear-cut, determined majority of Chechens. His patrimonial concept of the state, the fragmentation of clans and his passivity — some say complicity — in relation to the local Mafia aroused discord and set it at odds with various sectors of the independence movement. During the three years of his presidency, Chechnya was thrown into turmoil: accounts were settled and corruption flourished. As Osman Imaiev, the Republic's former public prosecutor and member of the delegation which discussed with the Russians the ceasefire of 30 July 1995, admitted to me, a number of files passed through his hands of those 'disappeared' in confrontations between rival clans. The laying of the oil pipeline from the Caspian to the Black Sea through Chechen territory equally aroused the greed and latent war of conflicting interests. But what Dudayev failed to achieve via personal manoeuvring and weakness, the Russians created in a few days by their brutal intervention in December and devastation of the capital: almost total Chechen unity in defence of their independence.

It is not at all exaggerated to speak of Leningrad or Dresden, and those black and white images of desolation etched in the memory for ever. The centre of Grozny was literally flattened by the joint action of heavy artillery and tank-fire, missiles and bombs launched from aeroplanes and helicopters. The Presidential Palace from whose cellars Dudayev resisted, Parliament, the Institute of Pedagogical Sciences, National Bank of the Republic, Higher Institute for Oil Studies, Abdelrrahman Avturkhanov Museum, Lermontov Theatre, Fine Arts Museum, Caucasus Hotel etc all vanished from the face of the earth. To conceal the magnitude of the urbicide, mountains of debris were heaped up and thrown on rubbish tips and pits around Grozny. The infill work proceeds and the authors of the 'feat' have cast a veil of metal fences around the affected area to ward off prying eyes. Through cracks and holes one can glimpse even today the incessant activity of bulldozers and crushers. Only a handful of wild shrubs and small trees survive the devastation. On the horizon, two plumes of black smoke atop the blazing oil wells on the outskirts: their burning still darkens the gloomy atmosphere and, now and then, the voracious, blazing flames reach up as a living symbol of the hell which descended on the city like a bird of prey.

In neighbouring areas, the spectacle is, if possible, more desolate: hollowed-out buildings, blackened eye-sockets, toothless mouths; wrinkled, half-melted houses, facades pitted by smallpox; derisory traffic signals; ghostly cranes suspended in the void. A pink block of flats, once occupied by the local nomenklatura, shows off slightly twisted Doric, Ionic and Corinthian columns, balconies with singed balustrades, small opera-boxish balconies mushy as meringues. My companion tells me a Russian family survives, crouched in one of the back cellars. We go to have a look: a half-crippled man with disturbed mother and 19-year-old daughter live in a dingy room exposed to the elements: no work, no wages, no help. They subsist like many old and infirm Russians on Chechen charity. Whilst the Caucasians keep alive the bonds of family and clan solidarity, the Russians suffer a more tragic destiny, abandoned by the indifference of their compatriots responsible for their plight. The old women begging in the area of the market show that the invaders' destructive fury didn't even spare their compatriots.

In a park by the fenced-off area, among trees and rose borders, I discover the incongruous statue of a bear on a bicycle in what two years ago must have been a children's park. The small monument had had better luck than the one erected to Lenin a hundred metres further on, which only preserves its pedestal. (Days later, in an abandoned plot by the battered railway station, I found the leader of the Soviets' enormous statue, hidden under thick undergrowth, Vladimir Illich Ulyanov seemed to be preaching fiercely and energetically at the leafy vegetation on behalf of new, equally implacable ecological revolution.)

The rest of the city offers the same scenario of rage and decrepitude: ruined buildings, burnt-out tanks, skeleton roofs, hanging beams, entire districts abandoned by their inhabitants. Sometimes, in the remnant of a building, a sign warns off possible marauders 'People living here' or even more laconically, 'People alive'. The new city centre, with the pro-Russian

Presidency building and army barracks, is a veritable entrenched battleground: fortified posts, tanks at every corner, nests of machine-guns on the roofs of main buildings, endless soldiers and policemen on a war footing. All the places I have visited — the press centre, the offices where I obtained first my Russian press credentials and, second, those from Zavgaiev's puppet administration — are protected by sandbags and guards with machine-guns. Despite such an imposing array of firepower, the capital conquered in two months of blood and fire fell in a few hours on 6 March to several hundred independence fighters armed with grenade-throwers. As the success of their lightening incursion demonstrates, the much heralded Russian pacification is quite illusory. As I saw for myself days later, night belongs to the Chechens and the innumerable control posts and military bases set up in the theoretically pacified zone are frequently transformed into besieged islets, exposed to sudden thrusts from an invisible enemy force.

To the indeterminate number of civilian deaths caused by the war — Russian and Chechen commentators and experts estimate a figure of 40,000 — must be added the number of people who disappear in regular round-ups and are sent to the sinister filter points. Together with Ricardo Ortega, Antena 3's Moscow correspondent, I interviewed the Red Cross president in Grozny, Hussein Khamidov. This civil aviation pilot's life abruptly changed direction the day he found the corpses of two of his children in a common grave, a few weeks after they 'vanished' at the end of January 1995. Since then, Khamidov, elegantly dressed in grey suit and tie, has devoted himself entirely to the task of uncovering the slaughter-houses and ossuaries scattered throughout Chechen territory and to photographing the victims. Seated in his tiny office, he shows us sheaves of cards with carefully appended photographs. Each dead person appears marked with a number to the provisional figure of 1313. Four hundred and twenty-six have been identified and numerous people come to his office to search out and identify their relatives. As we talk, a man appears who has 11 disappeared in his family: he comes daily, hopeful new 'finds' will allow him to bury one of them.

Identification is difficult: in many cases, they are skulls scalped or incinerated by flame-throwers, corpses stacked in munitions boxes in foetal position. Almost all bear signs of torture and summary execution: shot at close range in eyes, forehead, neck, hands tied by rope or wire. In a pitiless succession of horror prints, I gaze at victims with empty eye-sockets, hollow nasal orifices, skulls set in a cast howling, gasping from asphyxiation, protesting indignation, signs of shock, unspeakable pain, sometimes surprised innocence, rarely serenity. Despite the insistence of the Red Cross, the Russian military authorities have opened no investigation of the wells and ditches replete with corpses. No court will judge the architects of such slaughter.

While we were at the Red Cross, a Chechen cameraman showed us a video of images of the bombing of Kadir Yurt on 28 March: 12 children were killed. The Russian High Command denied the attack occurred and blamed the disinformation on a propagandistic manoeuvre by the 'bandits'.

Although the majority of the executions date back to March and April 1995, the round-ups and arbitrary arrests continue. At the filter point in the Staro-Promislovi district, dependent on the Russian Federation Ministry of the Interior in Chechnya, hundreds of detainees were interned at the beginning of June and each barracks is provided with dungeons for interrogation and torture. A youth called Salman related before the camera his journey and stay in one of them. In the lorry which carried him packed with dozens of suspects, the Russian soldiers killed eight of his companions who had protested against the conditions of their transportation and they then drank vodka sitting on the corpses. The Military Command issued a communique to the effect that the murdered were victims of bullets from independence guerrilla fighters.

The second protocol of the agreements signed on 10 June in Nazran stipulates the creation of a commission comprising six Russians and six Chechens to search out and identify those who have disappeared or been arrested in the 17 months of war. Another clause indicates the definitive closure of the filter points. But after so many broken promises and unkept pacts, the Chechens awaited the results of the Russian elections without forging too many illusions as to Zyuganov and Yeltsin's real intentions. Everything may continue as before and the desire for revenge on the part of military commanders like Vladimir Shamanov and Viachesvav Tikomirov, humiliated by the failure of their brutal pacification and the disorganisation and low morale of their troops, inevitably augurs nothing different. 'The war', one of the leaders of the independence struggle later interviewed by me said without boasting, 'has lasted for two centuries. Who knows whether it will last another 40 or 50 years?' ❑

*Downtown Grozny 1996: Russian conscript*

# To the mountains

AT THE END of May, on the eve of the meeting between Yeltsin and the Chechen president Zelijman Yanarbiev, the army blocked all access to the town of Shali, some 30 kilometres from Grozny: the leadership had detected the presence of a large concentration of *guerrilleros* set on stymieing the electoral farce of pro-Russian chief Doku Zavgaiev. The response of the besieged in their turn was to lay siege to the barracks of the police and military command, paying back the occupying force in kind: siege for siege.

The tension mounted on 30 May, with the assassination of the independence leader sent to negotiate, an outrage that frustrated the projected peace conversations in Daghestan, that were initiated days later in Ingushetia. On 2 June, hardline General Shamanov, the right-hand man of the recently 'resigned' Russian defence minister of Chechnya, demanded that the district 'elders' surrender the rebels on pain of prolonging the siege and submitting the city to exemplary punishment. There was no punishment, no surrender, but the siege continued. Shali was an area from which foreigners and journalists were banned.

On Thursday 6 June, my attempt to reach there failed. After negotiating innumerable road controls with the help of magazines, lighters and packets of cigarettes, we fell at the last hurdle: an officer inspected my papers and my companion's and we were ordered back.

We repeated our attempt the following day: the officer on duty had changed and, thanks to the efficient safe-pass of some bottles of vodka, he stamped our entry: the battered car in which we were travelling drove masterfully into no-man's land, a strip of two or three kilometres where life was apparently being lived normally: stalls and sales pitches for petrol and refreshments were established at regular intervals to Shali.

On our entry into the city, we heard the dull thud of explosions, passed without problems the independence fighters' control barrier and emerged on to an esplanade or main square dominated by a frenzy of activity incomprehensible at first sight.

Dozens of armed *guerrilleros* mounted guard on street corners or perched in windows or on roofs in neighbouring buildings. Next to the mosque, a group of women and old men defiantly waved a framed photograph of Dudayev decorated with images of Imam Shamil and Kunta Hadj. Sorrowful cries go up of *allahu akbar* (God is the greatest). We are in the place where on 18 January 1864, 4,000 unarmed *murids*, disciples of Kunta Hadj were victims of the firepower of the blue uniforms apostrophised by Lermontov: an evil act that caused 200 dead and a thousand wounded. Almost 130 years have gone by but the situation remains identical, the protagonists the same. But, what do Shamanov, Tikomirov, and the other colonisers from the Kremlin know of the sad 'deeds' of their predecessors, noted by Baddely in *The Russian Conquest of the Caucasus?*

In spite of the ceasefire signed 11 days earlier, a helicopter has just bombed the Chechen security headquarters. The anger of the people packed into the square is the anger admirably described by Tolstoy. When they realise a foreign journalist — an outside witness — is there, he is surrounded by women and old men. Here is my transcription of their chorus of voices, as translated for me by Volodia, my companion.

'Zavgaiev talked about coming here, but he'd better clear off to Russia. We don't want his illegal government! They've been killing us for the last two years. Why? Just because we demand our Republic' (a woman wearing a headscarf).

'We demonstrate peacefully yet they shoot at us. The Russians say we are criminals. Look: there are no criminals or bandits here, only people who want their freedom' (an old lady).

'The Uzbeks, Tajiks, Kazakhs have their own countries. We are like them. We don't want to be Russian serfs. Freedom and independence!' (an older man, wearing a hat, carrying a shotgun).

'The Russians won't allow the press to come so the world doesn't know what's happening. Tell people we'd rather starve to death or die of cold than accept slavery' (an old man who looks like a peasant).

There are bursts of machine-gun fire and we are ordered to disperse. My companion takes me to a pompous, colonnaded building, the Home of Culture, now bristling with *guerrilleros*. Soon Abu Movsaiev appears, security chief of the Chechen Republic of Ichkeria (that is how the Chechens describe their country), flanked by Aslanbel Ismailov, the man who orchestrated and participated in Shamil Basayev's daring incursion into Budennovsk, in the heartland of Russia. Abu Movsaiev wears a tracksuit and bullet-proof jacket and carries a sub-machine-gun over his shoulder. I notice two women fighters in his escort.

'Zavgaiev and his men wanted to call a "council of ministers" here and couldn't,' he explains. 'That's why the Russians have taken retaliatory action. A few minutes ago they bombarded my headquarters and we returned fire.

'Our fighters are besieging the military command and police barracks. We won't attack: we want to negotiate the raising of the siege. But I think they're preparing a revenge attack.'

Abu Movsaiev apologised to us for the rushed exchanges and, for a few minutes, I walk round the square noting down the slogans which Volodia translates for me: 'Long live Ichkeria! Death to the traitors!', insults directed at Yeltsin and the Russians.

ON OUR return to Grozny along a deserted road — they allow no vehicles to pass and only women, the aged and children to walk through — we cross army controls and stop at one flying the usual red flag adorned by an eye-catching image of Brezhnev. Volodia enters the precinct protected by sandbags, and, thanks to the usual safe-pass, we are welcomed by the soldiers with open arms.

They are volunteers, deceived by the official discourse about defending the endangered homeland and, according to which, those who fall on the field of honour, 'do so with a smile on their lips' (thus spake Pavel Grachov). They live miserably. They show us a table protected from the sun by a makeshift awning: their daily food ration is reduced to a hunk of bread and lard, with a little pepper and salt: except for one Lebed supporter, the sympathies of the rest are split between Zyuganov and Zhirinovsky. Vodka loosens their tongues and emotional expansiveness: they like Spain and dream of the Canary Islands. One who is tall and thin, with one tooth missing, defends Zhirinovsky and wants to know my opinion of him. I don't mince my words and mention his 'original' proposal of a new division of Poland and his promise that 'Russian soldiers will clean their boots on the beaches of the Indic Sea.'

'Why not?' he replies. 'Poland has always been a country divided between Germany and our Tsars. Without the traitors in power, we'd already be on the shores of India and in the Persian Gulf.'

'Our commanders here are worthless. It's their fault we've lost more. They're to blame for more than 10 thousand. Can you imagine how many there'll be if the war lasts 10 years? Zhirinovsky says: for every dead Russian, kill a hundred Chechens; for each ambush, raze to the ground a hundred villages. And, if they don't learn, we'll use nuclear weapons.'

I mention the lessons of Vietnam, but he won't be persuaded.

'The Americans aren't as tough as we are. Can you imagine them living in these conditions?' We say goodbye, leave the post, abandoning them to a half nostalgic, half wild-eyed stupor, beneath the flag with the resurrected countenance of Brezhnev.

THE EXPLOSIVE mixture of ultranationalism, imperial dreams and the desire to revenge military defeats, their hatred for the Chechens — who 'should be destroyed like wild animals', as shown by those interviewed by Nevzorov, the Duma deputy — illustrates the depths of confusion into which a great sector of the Russian population and intelligentsia has fallen, including Solzhenitsyn. It is a breeding ground for salvation-bringing Messiahs, the identification of Stalin and Christ and the flourishing of Nazi groups like the 'Russian Order', whose slogan, as communicated by its spokesman, Alexander Barkashov, is 'the earliest possible elimination of Jews and gypsies'.

The low morale of the army as evidenced in Chechnya lays bare the tensions existing between the commanders who support the defenestrated defence minister Pavel Grachov and those who oppose him: the breach opened between the swagger of a handful of generals and racist volunteers and the raw recruits, witnesses to the incompetence, barbarism and unlimited corruption of a war which they endure like a jail sentence, in conditions of penury, worthy of compassion.

If officers and petty-officers are satisfied with vodka, as in the times of Nicholas I, the appetites of their superiors, comfortably installed in Moscow are much more voracious. 'The newspaper *Izvestia*', wrote *El País* correspondent Pilar Bonet on 26 May 96, 'has revealed enormous losses in the Commercial Office of the Defence Ministry that, according to tax investigators, has spent thousands of millions of roubles on the purchase of alcoholic drinks.' According to the same correspondent, the man responsible for Ministry finances, Vasili Vorovev, was sacked for 'crass irregularities' while General Zherebtsov, architect of the most unpopular levy and others of his rank have constructed 'luxury *dachas* on the strength of the Defence Budget'.

In these circumstances, I do not find it strange that, as Alexander Lebed the 'new-for the moment-saviour of the fatherland' stated, 30 per cent of the soldiers were openly wondering 'whether it wasn't time to point their guns in the other direction' and another 30 per cent were thinking the same, but saying nothing.

In the brittle end of reign and permanent atmosphere of conspiracy around Yeltsin, everything is possible: the Mafia and corrupt functionaries are ready to sacrifice whatever lives are necessary to preserve their fortunes and privileges, oblivious to the spectacle of the recruits in the high-risk, regions of Chechnya begging a crust of bread from passing vehicles. On Sunday 9 June, in torrential rain, we head south. My aim is to reach the fractious area of Vedeno and Bamut and interview the military leader of the sector, Shamil Basayev. But the blocked roads and unusable, mud-bound tracks prevent us getting beyond Shatoi, despite the skills of our driver.

After the first road controls, and corresponding distribution of American cigarettes, the road winds down towards the broad, impetuous flow of the river Argun. A splendid panorama: the jagged mountains of the Caucasus push forward their wooded flanks veiled at intervals by strips of fog. In abrupt contrast with this natural beauty, the soldiers in the fortified stations and control posts dotting the route offer a picture of incredible poverty and dereliction: they stop the few cars there are not to inspect the documentation of local villagers but to ask for loose cigarettes, bread, for something to eat. They ask my companion whether anyone talks of demobilisation, is interested in the conversations which Aslan Maschadov, head of the pro-Independence Command, in Ingushetia. They all talk not of victory but of peace.

After we have crossed the bridge, we confront the remains of the mortar bomb ambush of 16 April: more and more burnt-out tanks, rusty artillery pieces scattered over the hillside, a small cross planted by the soldiers, in a silent but eloquent protest against the futility of their immolation. The road is a succession of control posts, damp, down-at-heel encampment, nests of machine-guns manned by youths numb with cold, vistas of poorly clothed, underfed recruits, warming their hands around miserable fires. From time to time, we have to stop and give way to a long column of T90 combat vehicles each serviced by a crew of a dozen tanks. The rain is relentless and soaks the ferns and the climbing plants like water lilies that prosper by the roadside. They are the landscapes wonderfully described by Lermontov and Tolstoy: slopes dotted in firs, scarps, mists, a strange watch tower, that probably acted as a look-out post for the *murids* of Mansur and Shamil. The evidence of the scorched-earth policy is also the same: the burnt houses near Zonaj, draped in sadness and rancour.

Shatoi is equally desolate: in its central market constructed by the Tsars, half a dozen stalls survive against a backcloth of ruins. The central square, the town hall, all has been fodder for the flames. A slogan in Arabic characters cries out in desperation: *allahu akbar.*

My indignation at the devastation and atrocities inflicted by the Occupying Forces merge at the end of my stay with feelings of anxiety and sorrow at the fate of Russia. The executioners are, after all, the victims of broken dreams and utopias, of ancestral resignation to the arbitrary ways of their despots and Messiahs.

As the film director Andrei Konshalkovski wrote recently, 'the Orthodox mentality shapes a collective consciousness. People don't feel individually responsible for their acts. They always find someone else to be responsible: God, the government, the Tsar, Stalin, Brezhnev. Nobody wants to admit they are partly to blame.'

Will Russians one day accept their overwhelming responsibility for the brutal crushing of Chechnya? ❑

*Juan Goytisolo is a Spanish writer and journalist. His most recent novel to be published in English is* The Marx Family Saga *(Translated by Peter Bush, Faber & Faber, 1996)*

© *Juan Goytisolo 1996* © *English translation by Peter Bush*

# MARTIN SHORT

# Shooting the messenger

**Veronica Guerin was murdered for daring to investigate where other journalists feared to tread. Few of her investigative colleagues in Britain step outside boardroom scandals and the sex lives of politicians into the violent world of organised crime**

I N THE early afternoon of Wednesday 26 June this year Veronica Guerin, crime reporter for Ireland's *Sunday Independent*, was driving along the Naas dual carriageway at Clondalkin on the outskirts of Dublin. When she stopped her car at traffic lights, a heavy white motorcycle drew alongside. Off jumped the helmeted pillion passenger, raised a handgun and, from just two feet away, shot Veronica five times in the chest and neck. He then climbed back on the bike which sped ahead and turned down a side road. By the time the police arrived, a most remarkable investigative reporter was dead.

Paying tribute, her editor Aengus Fanning wrote of this darkest day in Irish newspaper history. 'For the first time a journalist has been murdered for daring to write about our criminal underworld and daring to chronicle the lives of the brutal people who inhabit it.' This was 'a blatant and terrifying attack on a free press and on freedom of speech'. Dick Spring, Ireland's foreign minister, said her killing was 'an attack on all of us and on the values on which democracy and democratic politics are based.'

On the day after her death she was due to speak in London on the theme, 'Dying to tell a story: journalists at risk'. This formed part of a conference highlighting the increasing threat to journalists throughout the world. The organisers, Freedom Forum, have recently erected a memorial in Arlington, Virginia, listing 934 journalists killed in the course of work. Of these, 194 have died in Europe. Veronica's name will now be added to that roll.

She had been asked to speak because her relentless inquiries into organised crime in Dublin had already precipitated two violent attacks on her. In 1994 shots were fired into her home after she had revealed a particular thug's role in the murder of the notorious Martin Cahill, 'the General' of Dublin gangland. And in 1995, after she wrote a story identifying the prime suspect for a £3 million robbery, a man called at her home, raised a gun to her head, then ostentatiously shot her in the thigh. So clear a sign to 'lay off' would have deterred most journalists but not Veronica. Still on crutches, she visited several ganglords and told them she would not be intimidated.

The attacks did not stop. In September 1995 she visited the £4 million equestrian centre and fortress home of 'the Warehouse Man', whose criminal activities and extravagant lifestyle had placed him very near the top of the national crime rankings. According to her subsequent statement, she had asked this John Gilligan for an interview when suddenly he 'grabbed me violently about the upper part of the body. He then struck me violently about the head and face with his fists and shouted, "I'll fucking kill you, your husband, your fucking son, your family, everyone belonging to you."' Next day, she said, she received a call from the same man in which he not only repeated his threat against her but announced, 'I am going to kidnap your son and ride [bugger] him.'

An assault charge was brought against Gilligan but this had still not been heard by the time Veronica was killed. As she was the only witness against him, the case has now been dropped.

For investigative journalists in Britain, Veronica Guerin's death has serious implications. It should warn us that while most victims of an increasing number of hit killings on our slightly larger island have been criminals themselves, it may only be a matter of time before our own drug dealers, armed robbers, fraudsmen and international money launderers target those few folk who embarrass them in the press or on television. With many more guns in the hands of gangsters far more willing to use them than even the Kray twins 30 years ago, we have been misled into believing we have a charmed life or some mystical immunity from the contagion slaughtering journalists, photographers and TV crew members by the dozen in recent years in countries such as Bosnia, Algeria, Somalia, Rwanda and Colombia.

*Veronica Guerin 1960-1996: murdered on the streets of Dublin*

The main reason why journalists in Britain feel less threatened by the gun than our colleagues in Ireland is a negative one. Few investigative reporters here ever seek to confront major criminals face to face as Veronica Guerin felt driven to do. This partly reflects an editorial bias against in-depth crime investigations in favour of inquiries into cover-ups by ministers and public officials, into the sex lives of politicians and now, for example, into the fatcat salaries of privatised utility bosses. None of these target categories are known to hire hitmen to wipe out journalists. That may yet come. They hire public relations firms, a far more effective way of diverting most scribblers away from the truth.

The British media's reluctance to probe major criminals prior to them going to jail owes something to the heavy caution of libel lawyers, due partly to the humiliating defeat which Ronnie Kray and Lord Boothby inflicted on the *Sunday Mirror* in the 1960s. In addition, some crime reporters have a firm belief — justified or not — that our police forces are generally capable of catching the Mr Bigs of crime, and are more or less dedicated to doing so. If true, this might absolve us from acting as a surrogate law enforcement agency, or a stalking-horse for police or customs. But it is not always true.

Some British tabloids and TV shows do investigate drug dealers and gun suppliers, before confronting them with photographers or even two camera crews: one to film the villains, the other to film our intrepid but thoroughly protected star reporter under attack. Yet on closer study it usually emerges that such targets are low-level operators and that the journalists are not working alone. Often they have tipped off a specialist police squad in advance, to legalise the drug or gun 'buy' and to pounce as soon as the minnow malefactors have been caught on camera.

There is a stronger and more honourable tradition in British investigative journalism: the exposure of bent detectives, whether their corruption lies in the areas of drugs, robbery, prostitution or pornography or just plain old graft. The media's application of the principle, 'Who guards the guardians?' has itself helped maintain reasonably honest police forces, by obliging them to expel their corrupt elements from time to time and so become more capable of combating other forms of organised crime than would have been possible without such adversarial scrutiny. This in turn may have reduced our obligation to do their criminal investigations for them.

**[Veronica's killing was] a blatant and terrifying attack on a free press and on freedom of speech... on all of us and on the values on which democracy and democratic politics is based**

We have yet to see if the vast profits generated by the drug business will eventually overwhelm British law enforcement. But if that ever happens, we shall probably be too late to do much about it. It may already have happened in Ireland, which accounts for Veronica's relentless pursuit of her country's drug millionaires. She received much of her information from Ireland's national police force, the Garda, who felt unable to attack such targets directly themselves. On Veronica's death the *Irish Times* portrayed the Garda as resigned to a 'condition of marginal relevance'. The paper argued that 'senior Gardai have largely ceased to call for additional resources in equipment or manpower... What they lack are the legal instruments to elicit evidence and secure convictions.'

During those breast-beating days of near-national mourning for Veronica, Irish politicians uttered dire threats against organised crime, promising to step up Garda recruitment and to use a non-jury criminal court for major drug trials. There would be curbs on bail and on the right of silence. The government also promised to strike the godfathers where they would most hurt — in their pockets — with enhanced asset-seizure laws. More recently, the Garda's own Criminal Assets Bureau has announced it will focus on the criminals' white-collar financial advisers.

For all this hue and cry such resolve is inconsistent. In 1993 many leading criminals took advantage of a tax amnesty which allowed anyone to declare their ill-gotten earnings in return for a no-questions-asked levy of 15 per cent. This way the government legitimised their hot money for them! And in July this year the Revenue Commissioners were forced to abandon an operation against the sale of cigarette packets that do not display excise tax stamps. A Revenue source said gangsters were abusing their officers verbally and physically: 'We were hurting them. Then the intimidation started and we had just no protection.'

The story illustrates exactly why Veronica Guerin felt so driven. 'Do they think they're untouchable', she used to say, 'just because governments have not had the guts to stand up to them? The media won't let go because that's what our job is. The only thing that will influence a good reporter is the story. If there are lies, it is our job as reporters to highlight them.'

The American broadcaster Walter Cronkite said: 'Freedom of the press is not just important to democracy, it *is* democracy.' We may all proudly stand up to oppose the destruction of free speech by bully-boys in far-off tyrannies, but meantime we must not ignore the similar threat posed here at home by bully-boy crime bosses whom both politicians and press appear too lazy or too aloof to combat. Investigative reporting is a lonely, painstaking, painful and usually thankless area of journalism. Sometimes specialists in the exposure of organised crime wonder if they are merely baying at the moon. They certainly don't deserve to die because of apathy in Westminster, Whitehall, Scotland Yard or even in the new marble palaces of our media conglomerates. ❑

*Martin Short* is the author of five books on organised crime, the Mafia, Scotland Yard, police corruption and Freemasonry. His most recent publication is The Krays' Lieutenant. He is also a prolific producer of television documentaries on crime and policing

# OPINION

## BILL ROLSTON

# Turning the page without closing the book

**A truth commission in the North of Ireland would be premature at this point, but the debate on truth and justice should precede any negotiations if the new society is to prosper**

IN AUGUST 1996, as part of the West Belfast Festival, *Féile an Phobail*, Paula McBride, a South African human rights activist, spoke about the Truth and Reconciliation Commission currently operating in South Africa. She conceded that there had been problems in its operation, but emphasised that at its best the Commission was giving a voice to people who previously had had none.

Her audience included republican ex–prisoners and many people — victims, relatives and others — who had struggled for years against the state's abuse of human rights in the North of Ireland. No audience could have listened more avidly, knowledgeably and sympathetically to what McBride had to say. Yet, there was an apparent paradox: no-one instantly demanded such a commission for the North of Ireland. On the contrary, the audience was sceptical: almost unanimously they agreed that calls for a truth commission in Ireland would be premature.

The paradox would be easier to explain if the audience had consisted of British government ministers, civil servants and members of the British army and Royal Ulster Constabulary (RUC). Such an audience would have argued that there is no need for a truth commission because, as a democratic state, Northern Ireland has all the mechanisms necessary to ensure truth — courts, inquests, independent inquiries, an active human rights lobby, a free press. Moreover, within such a democratic framework, the security forces are subject to the rule of law and are therefore incapable of systematic human rights abuses such as occur in military dictatorships.

Yet major atrocities have been committed by state forces and covered up by the state as the killings on Bloody Sunday, 30 January 1972, when 14 civil rights demonstrators were killed by British paratroopers in Derry; or the assassination of three unarmed IRA members in Gibraltar on 6 March 1988 and of three men robbing a bookmaker's shop on the Falls Road on 13 January 1990, both by British undercover agents; or the killing of 26 civilians in Dublin and a further seven in Monaghan on 17 May 1974 by loyalist bombs with the help, it has frequently been alleged since, of British agents, amply demonstrate.

And there are questions on Britain's conduct during the war against insurgency in the North of Ireland that remain unanswered: how high in the British administration did authorisation for various policies go? For instance, the shoot-to-kill policy carried out by undercover British army and police in the 1980s. The killing of six people in 1982 was the subject of an independent investigation by a senior British police officer, John Stalker, who was himself later dismissed from his job for being too eager to pursue the truth; his report was never made public, even though Stalker himself concluded that there was clear evidence of unlawful killing in all six cases. Also, the miscarriages of justice that led to many innocent people spending long terms in prison, most notably the Birmingham Six, the Guildford Four, the Maguire family and Judith Ward. The Belfast-based Committee on the Administration of Justice believes that there are currently over 50 prisoners serving long sentences who are in the same category. And the collusion between British forces and loyalist paramilitary groups; this included the involvement of a British intelligence agent in the loyalist Ulster Defence Association, Brian Nelson, in the procurement of large quantities of arms from South Africa, the use of these arms in the assassination of nationalist civilians in the late 1980s and early 1990s, and the leaking of confidential security files on republican activists and sympathisers to help the loyalist assassination squad. The report of the official investigation into collusion by British police officer John Stevens has not been made public. The authorised use of plastic and rubber bullets by the British army and RUC, resulted in the deaths of 17 people, eight of whom were under 16 years of age.

State forces have acted with virtual impunity, particularly where killing is concerned. Despite 357 deaths caused between 1969 and 1994 by members of the British forces — approximately 10 per cent of all deaths in the conflict — the number of prosecutions has been low, and only seven military or police personnel have been convicted, four for murder, one for attempted murder and two for manslaughter. Moreover, on the few occasions when British soldiers have been sentenced to life imprisonment, they have been released in less than four years. Impunity is further underwritten by the hobbling of the various mechanisms that exist to ensure accountability: for example, evidence is withheld in court cases and inquests (such as that at Gibraltar) through the use of 'public interest immunity certificates', and so–called independent tribunals are in fact little more than staged public relations exercises for the state.

Given the record, it is not difficult to see why those who have long opposed the actions of the British state in Ireland should have little faith in another state–sponsored mechanism supposedly guaranteeing the pursuit of the truth. They have struggled through the years for truth and justice. The odds against them have been great and they have frequently suffered for their pains: human rights lawyer Pat Finucane was assassinated in February 1989; other activists have been imprisoned, beaten, stigmatised and marginalised. Opposition is not to seeking the truth as such, but to the involvement of the British state.

Whether or not a truth commission occurs in a society in transition from a previously repressive regime depends on the balance of political forces at the point of that transition. Ireland is not as yet at that point. The IRA ceasefire of August 1994 did not lead to major concessions on the part of the British, nor to inclusive negotiations, a point emphasised by the IRA as the reason for their partial breaking of the ceasefire in February 1996. In this situation, there is little doubt that the British authorities are under no pressure to reveal the truth of past human rights abuses. Moreover, there

COLMAN DOYLE/CAMERA PRESS

*'Bloody Sunday' in Derry, 30 January 1972: British paratroopers confront civil rights demonstrators moments before the troops stormed the barricade and began the slaughter*

is little doubt that, if they were to establish a truth commission now, it would only be because it fitted their own interests and not those of victims and their relatives in Ireland. It is also beyond doubt that such a commission would be constructed in such a way that it would guarantee neither truth nor justice.

Yet the concept of a genuine truth commission — one with the authority, legitimacy and support to unearth the truth — should not be rejected out of hand. For the sake of the victims and their relatives and to ensure a clean bill of health for the new society, the human rights abuses of the past cannot be swept under the carpet. It is easy to say that Irish negotiators are principled and will not let this happen. But, even with the strongest of principles and the best of will, it has happened elsewhere. Paradoxically, the fact that the scale of past human rights abuses in Ireland has been small compared with, say, Chile or Rwanda, could make it more likely that negotiations would focus on 'more important' items relating to the future, such as the constitution, the economy, etc.

Certainly, there will be many liberal voices at that point stating with great plausibility that it is time to move forward rather than to keep dwelling in the past. And negotiators will be facing skilled and wily opponents with a long imperial history of dividing and conquering and of creating victories from apparent defeats. If the negotiating position in relation to past human rights abuses is not worked out in advance, it is not beyond the realms of possibility that the issue will be lost or reduced in the flurry of negotiations. The trick, as Sergio Hevia Larenas, Chilean human rights lawyer, puts it, is to turn the page without closing the book: a trick that requires a great deal of preparatory practice. In learning this trick, there are lessons for Ireland in the experience of other societies.

Any temptation to separate truth and justice must be resisted. Seeking truth is not an end in itself for victims; they need to feel that in some way or other the wrong done to them has been at least partially righted. At the same time, the pursuit of truth and justice does not necessarily mean show trials or endless vengeance. It is possible to separate justice and the judicial system, to have investigation and prosecution, but to stop short of punishment.

It is not necessary that in the pursuit of truth and justice the violations of the oppressor and those of the oppressed be judged in the same light. In South Africa, this 'tyranny of equality' is seen as a problem by some former insurgents. In the Philippines, however, it was decided that the truth commission would deal with the abuses of army personnel only, on the grounds that the violence of insurgents had already been dealt with during the previous military regime.

It may make sense to separate truth and reconciliation. In South Africa, the emphasis on forgiveness can be a loaded weapon easily turned on the oppressed and less easily on their oppressors. In the North of Ireland the emphasis on forgiveness has been used as an ideological onslaught on victims. It focuses on the psychological state of victims rather than on the material causes of their condition and serves as one more denial of the reality of their victimhood. Emphasis on the causes acknowledges the wrong that has been done to them. As victims here have often remarked, they have no difficulty forgiving as long as they know who it is they have to forgive.

As they discovered in Brazil, there is more than one way to document the truth. There, despite the absence of an official truth commission, a systematic account of the truth and acknowledgement of the wrongs done to victims (*Brasil: Nunca Mais*) was compiled under the auspices of the Cardinal of São Paulo, Cardinal Arns, and a Presbyterian minister, Jaime Wright.

This last may not be as far-fetched a scenario for the Irish situation as may at first appear. In 1990, when it was clear that the authorities were not prepared to charge any of the soldiers concerned nor to institute a public inquiry into the event, the Cullyhanna Justice Group held a tribunal into the killing by British soldiers of a local man, Fergal Caraher, and the wounding of his brother, Micheál. The tribunal of international lawyers heard carefully prepared evidence and produced a report in 1992. The Group was also active in lobbying the US Congress. As a result of its activity, two soldiers were charged with the murder of Fergal Caraher. Even though they were subsequently found not guilty, it is clear that the interests of truth and justice would not have been served at all without the Justice Group.

S WEEPING the concerns of victims under the carpet would not only be a Trojan horse imported into the heart of the new society, but would add insult to their injury.

At the end of her lecture, Paula McBride made an impassioned plea. Pointing to the anomaly of ANC prisoners held by a government dominated by the ANC, she urged the republicans in her audience who were waiting the chance to begin their period of negotiations to 'leave no prisoners behind, no matter how fast or how slow you move'.

The same should be said about victims of past human rights abuses. ❑

*Bill Rolston is a senior lecturer in sociology at the University of Ulster in Jordanstown. He is the author of* Turning the Page Without Closing the Book: The Right to Truth in the Irish Context *(Dublin, Irish Reporter Publications, 1996)*

# INTERVIEW

## DESMOND TUTU

**Archbishop Desmond Tutu, chairman of South Africa's Truth and Reconciliation Commission, talks to James Brittain of the need to deal with the country's dark past before 'concentrating on the future'**

# Healing a nation

*Let me begin by asking you what you hope to achieve with the Truth Commission?*

WELL, the law that sets us up says it is the Promotion of National Unity and Reconciliation Act and that is ultimately the goal: to assist in the healing of a traumatised, divided, wounded, polarised people.

*How deep are those wounds in South Africa?*

DEEP, very deep, on all sides, but I suppose especially on the side of those who were the victims of one of the most vicious systems. Many people will survive whose loved ones were detained without trial, probably died mysteriously in detention. People were banned to a twilight existence, others went into exile and, of course, epitomised by Madiba [Mandela], people were in jail for very, very, very long terms.

*So how important is it that the Commission addresses these scars?*

ABSOLUTELY crucial. You see there are some people who have tried to be very facile and say let bygones be bygones: they want us to have a national amnesia. And you have to keep saying to those people that to pretend that nothing happened, to not acknowledge that something horrendous did happen to them, is to victimise the victims yet again. But even more important, experience worldwide shows that if you do not deal with a dark past such as ours, effectively look the beast in the eye, that beast is not going to lie down quietly; it is going, as sure as anything, to come back and haunt you horrendously. We are saying we need to deal with this past as quickly as possible — acknowledge that we have a disgraceful past — then close the door on it and concentrate on the present and the future.

This is the purpose of the Commission; it is just a small part of a process in which the whole nation must be engaged.

*Are you confident the Commission can address the hurt of all those unknown people throughout the country as well as the high-profile cases like Steve Biko, Griffith and Victoria Mexenge and others? How effective can it be in dealing with a national problem?*

THERE ARE, indeed, those who oppose the setting up of the Truth and Reconciliation Commission. Forgiveness and reconciliation are not cheap, they are costly, and it is important that that effect is registered by the opposition of these people like the Ribeiros, for instance. But you see you've also got opposition from another quarter — the quarter which says this Truth Commission is not really about reconciliation if it is going to become a witch-hunt, seeking out perpetrators. And most of those perpetrators, because of the kind of situation out of which we come, will be mainly from the white community, the Afrikaner community. And when those perpetrators come forward, or when we have victims who say the people who violated their rights are so and so and so and so, people will say that we, the Truth Commission, are engaging in an orgy of witch-hunting.

But, quite crucially, the majority, the vast majority of the people of this country want the Commission: most of the religious community — the major churches, the Jewish community, the Muslims, the Indians — have come out in support of the Commission. And those people we are talking about, the people not of high profile, will be going into townships and want to be able to tell their story and to know that the nation at the very least, and perhaps the international community, knows their story. It is very moving to be in Guguletu, for instance, and hear the mother of a boy who was one of the so-called Guguletu Seven, who was shot by the police, saying, 'I just want someone to be able to say, not as the inquest magistrate said "no-one was to blame"; I want someone to say that this was done by so and so. And this will be enough for me.' She's not looking for revenge. It's an incredible and very deeply moving thing.

One of my problems is going to be whether I will be able to survive listening to harrowing accounts. I laugh easily, but I cry easily as well. And I was telling my colleagues on the Commission, 'I don't know...you are going to have to live with a chairperson who may break down in the course of listening to testimony.' You don't programme yourself, and as you listen — and especially listening to people who have sometimes been regarded as of not much consequence — you experience their dignity in the pain that they have experienced, and you hear too that they don't want revenge. And then you say thank you God.

*There's a deep anger about this whole question of amnesty for crimes. What do you say to people like Mrs Biko, who, almost 20 years after Steve Biko's death, is still angry and hurt and upset and just does not accept that the people or persons who murdered her husband should be allowed to walk free if they tell her what they did?*

AS I'VE SAID, the one thing that it does underline is that forgiveness and reconciliation has a price tag attached to it. We've got to where we are, a democratic dispensation, by negotiation. And the heart of that negotiation was compromise. And people have got to acknowledge that yes, we were on the brink of civil war in 1994, and we saw a bit of the mayhem that could be sown by the explosions at the airport in Johannesburg. It indicated the kind of thing which we might have experienced in this country. And it was because people sat down and said let's agree that it can't be winner take all, there is no clear winner, you've got to have give and take, that you have a government of National Unity instead of one political party.

You say we then have to say what happens to people who perpetrated atrocities. Now, some people would have said let's give a blanket amnesty. Here they said no, let it be amnesty applied for on an individual basis, people making full disclosures. But that's part of the cost. And you say to those who say we want justice, that if there were no amnesty, then we would have had justice and ashes.

*Do you not feel it is dangerous to bring all this into people's consciousnesses but then not to fulfil that desire for justice?*

THE POINT again is that we are talking about a small group of people. The vast majority are saying I just want an acknowledgement; some say I hope I receive a reparation — which is part of the possibility available in the Truth Commission which has been set up. And reparation, not compensation. We will never be able to compensate people for the loss of loved ones. But it will mean that the nation says: one, yes, something happened to you; two, we are sorry; three, we want symbolically to show this by this reparation — which may be a scholarship for your children, which may be an augmentation of your pension, which may be, in some instances, putting up a clinic in a community that suffered.

Yes, there are going to be people who are not satisfied, I mean there are people who are not satisfied that we have a government of National Unity rather than one party being the government. There are people who are upset that you have 11 official languages — but that is part of the negotiation, part of the compromise that has enabled even these people to claim certain rights.

*I've talked to quite a few people — the likes of Eugene de Kock, Dirk Coetzee — who say they are sitting on a wealth of dirt that could bring down South Africa. Do you have a sense that we are about to unleash some kind of orgy?*

THE THING is we are going to have to take that risk: if you do not open up and examine that can of worms now, in a controlled environment, that can of worms is going to open some day. And we shall remain in an unstable environment because you will never know when some revelation is going to happen. You will always be on tenterhooks — what are we going to hear today against whom? Let it all come out now man, and let's try and see how we can deal with it.

Take the Malan* trial. Isn't it interesting that the court trial has revealed some extraordinary things. I am not aware that it has provoked people into seeking revenge. I mean people have read, have heard on television that murders were committed left, right and centre in an unbridled fashion. But it has not actually — remarkably — made people say in a kind of blood thirsty way, we want to get our own back. There are things that have been revealed there that ought by right to have filled people with a deep, deep anger, an explosive anger. People read these accounts and you could almost say that they are blasé. In a way they are saying, 'We always knew.' Now, at last, it is coming out as truth.

*What about senior politicians, say, for example, Deputy President F W de Klerk. If some astonishing revelation were to come to light as a result of the Truth Commission, is he untouchable?*

NOBODY is untouchable. If Madiba is involved and we get evidence, that evidence is going to be set forward and it will be part of the report that we give. We can subpoena anybody starting from the president of this country. Nobody is untouchable. We hope obviously that it won't be necessary, but we have powers of seizure: any document we want we can demand and, fortunately, at the stage at which we are, nobody has said in government, the police, the security forces, nobody has said that they are going to deny us documents. Whether some of these things have been destroyed is a different matter.

I would say most people are serious about this exercise, but they want it to happen quickly, a maximum of two years — which is important. We hope it can be done in 18 months, so that we don't keep mulling over and raking over the past. We are concentrating, it is this period, and then we're finished. And once we've done it effectively we close that chapter and open a new chapter: say now we, South Africans, can go together into the future.

*One final question. The Truth Commission has been criticised as being victim friendly; designed to encourage people to go through a cathartic experience to heal themselves. Can you reassure people that the Commission is not just for the victims of apartheid, that it applies to both sides: that neither camp has the moral ground?*

THE ACT is quite clear. We are first of all enjoined to be independent and impartial. Second, a victim is a victim is a victim. There is no distinction between someone who is a victim of human rights violations, perpetrated by, say, the liberation movements, or one who is a victim of violations perpetrated by the apartheid dispensation. Once someone comes before the Commission and we say yes, a gross human rights violation has happened, we don't ask what is your political affiliation. In the matter of amnesty, no moral distinction is going to be made between acts perpetrated by the liberation movements and acts perpetrated by the apartheid dispensation. We can make that distinction, as most human beings would, but the act itself makes that moral distinction superfluous. ❑

© *Interviewed in South Africa by James Brittain for ITN, May 1996*

*\*Magnus Malan, former Minister of Defence, currently on trial with other senior military officials for the murder of 10 persons in KwaMakutha outside Durban in the mid-1980s*

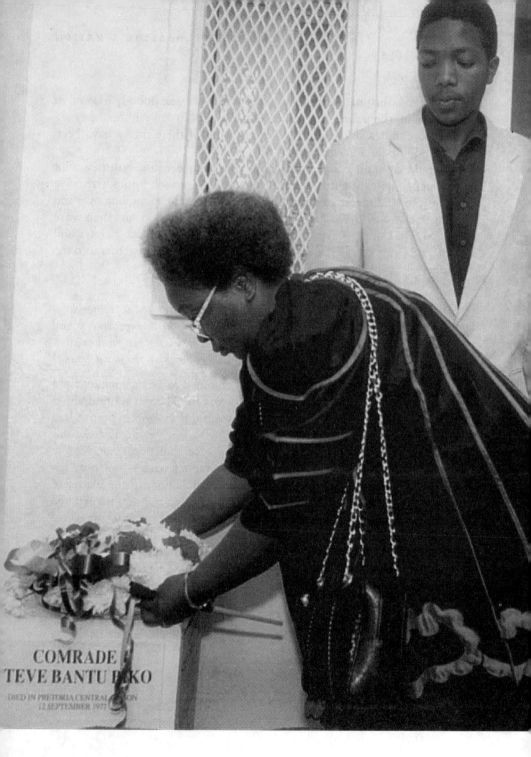

COMRADE
TEVE BANTU BIKO
DIED IN PRETORIA CENTRAL PRISON
12 SEPTEMBER 1977

# Tears, anger, forgiveness

As South Africa seeks publicly through its Truth and Reconciliation Commission to come to terms with its tormented past, voices on all sides contest the Commission's ability to bring justice as well as truth; to satisfy the need for revenge as well as the desire for forgiveness

NICKY DE BLOIS/AP

*(Left) Pretoria Central Prison, 1995: Mrs Ntsiki Biko, with her son Nkosinathi, lays a wreath in the cell where her husband, Steve, died in 1977*

# PIETER-DIRK UYS

# The truth, the whole truth and nothing but...

FIFTY YEARS after the Nuremberg Trials, South Africans stand on the eve of their Truth and Reconciliation Commission. The search for the truth about the past. The demand for the guilty to step forward. To be forgiven? To be punished? A former apartheid minister takes the stand. He peers at the watching Commissioners.

'Comrades,' he says, his moustache twitching. 'I have a clear conscience. I have never used it!'

On the other side of the political spectrum, the former terrorists and tired ANC rebels who now rest in the armchairs of power, seek the truth with all their might. Just to hide it deeper?

A Truth and Reconciliation Commission sounds as silly as John Cleese's Ministry for Funny Walks! Of course it's not; it's probably the only way that some of our people will find out what happened to them and their loved ones during a time of great darkness and fear. So there's nothing funny about having a Truth Commission.

Happily we have a man with a great sense of humour leading it. And knowing that Archbishop Desmond Tutu is the only person in the land who can sit in a glass house and throw stones, one also hopes that if he thinks the dirty washing of the past will damage our fragile reconciliation, he'll pull the plug and let it all gurgle away down the drain.

What is funny about a Truth Commission are the people now accused of crimes against humanity, who are all determined to be seen telling the truth their way! They're queuing up to get into the stand, where they can passionately admit to pulling triggers, hiding bombs, cutting up bodies. But only because someone else told them to.

'We were only obeying orders!' they will mutter, sounding like a Mel Brooks comedy. There are just too many clever people around, those jackbooted survivors of the shadowlands of apartheid, who now *toyi-toyi* with clenched fists in the air. They all have blood up to their elbows, but keep referring to it as 'long red gloves'. And we believe them for the sake of peace.

Of course they'll not be packed off in disgrace with the facts of their folly branded across their faces. They'll get away with murder, like so many of their bloody brothers have done all over the world. It's the poor clerk who pushed a pen for 46 years, doing his dreary job without question, who'll get the finger.

'You are responsible!' the Commission will thunder. That's us, the people. The 'you'. And they're probably right. And yet, how can we whites be guilty of anything, if we were all anti-apartheid? I haven't met anyone in South Africa lately who had anything to do with those years of oppression. The white policeman says he fought the System secretly. The black teacher insists he subverted the bad policies with a smile. The Indian doctor swears he sewed up broken terrorists with love. The mixed-race, coloured journalist admits to quoting banned words with guts. The parents all told their children the truth.

Of course they did. After all, we were all in the Struggle! So how can a Truth Commission find any truth, when we have no-one who admits to the lies? How can we find guilt when all the evidence has been destroyed? Files have been shredded, names have been changed. A past has been forgotten. A nation stares into the future, lobotomised by soccer fever and embracing amnesia like a child a fluffy toy.

There will be much anger and many tears during the sessions of the Truth Commission. Terrible realities will take the place of the frightful rumours. But I think there will also be much bitter laughter, as we see those who parade their designer innocence trip over their own nooses of deception. Every generation has its fools who will speak the truth as they see it. If we have 11 official languages, surely we can also find 11 million official truthsayers.

When we look back to those bad years when the lights of our civilisation seemed to be out forever, one can see how Truth, as we think we know it today, passed through three stages. First it was ridiculed and as a result the bearers of that truth were imprisoned, banned and killed. Then it was opposed as being the Lie, the subversion of goodness, the Satan! And now it is regarded as self-evident!

It is said the man who fears no truths has nothing to fear from lies. But then it also takes two to speak the truth. One to utter it and one to hear. A sinister minister of police during the 1980s said it all, as only they could: 'The public is entitled to know what is happening around it. But at the same time, it is equally entitled to the Truth.' We look forward to seeing this man on the stand, eyes filled with crocadile-tears as he repeats again and again: 'This is the pure and simple truth, Your Honour. I just didn't know what was going on!'

Same old story. Truth is rarely pure and never simple! And 50 years after the Nuremberg Trials, will we see history not just repeating itself, but taking tragedy and turning it into farce? ❑

**Pieter-Dirk Uys** *is a South African broadcaster, writer and performer*

# ADEWALE MAJA-PEARCE

*Testifying before the Truth and Reconciliation Commission, 3 May 1996*

# Binding the wounds

**Resentment, anger and the desire for revenge threaten to undermine the Truth Commission's attempt to reconcile victims and oppressors**

PRESIDENT Nelson Mandela's uncanny instinct for the telling symbolic act was again on display on the first day of the Truth and Reconciliation Commission hearings in Johannesburg, which were held from 29 April to 3 May. I was in the basement of the Central Methodist Church, where the South Africa Communications Service had set up a Media Centre for the attendant journalists, when I became aware of a commotion on the ground floor. I went upstairs in time to see Madiba, as he is fondly called, emerge from a black BMW, wave to the small crowd that had begun to gather as word of his presence spread, and then make his way to the first floor, where the Commission was sitting.

It so happened that Mandela arrived just as one of his fellow political detainees on Robben Island, Gerald Thebe, was coming to the end of his own harrowing testimony concerning his torture in detention. Archbishop Desmond Tutu, the chair of the Commission, immediately called a halt to the proceedings and invited the President to say a few words. Mandela obliged readily enough but kept his speech short and to the point. He said that, in appointing the 17 commissioners, he had been careful to ensure that all political parties were represented as well as 'eminent South Africans who enjoyed the confidence and the support of the entire population'. He said that it was a great source of comfort to him to have been able 'to bring together these men and women who were doing such a marvellous job because until we know what offences, what crimes were committed against the innocent people, there will never be reconciliation in the proper sense of the word'. He said that 'to forgive and forget means that we should know what actually happened', and that 'those who were tortured and are still alive would like the criminals to be brought to book.' He said, finally, that he had come today because he thought he should see for himself the 'vital service' that the Commission was doing. Then he thanked everybody present and took his seat in the public gallery.

It was all very moving and all very typical of Mandela, and it had the effect, among other things, of lifting the proceedings from the threatened torpor occasioned by having to listen to the seemingly endless catalogue of human suffering: the mother whose son had been blown to bits by a parcel bomb; another mother whose son had been shot dead by the security forces; a woman whose brother had also been killed by the security forces; two fathers whose sons had died in detention; and, finally, a man who had been permanently maimed by a bomb delivered to his

NATASHA PINCUS/THE STAR

house by a person he had never met before or seen since. There was a limit, in other words, to how much of this it was possible to absorb at the high emotional level demanded by those for whom the reality of their loss continued to be a daily event, in some cases stretching back many years; and I wondered, even then, how the commissioners, who were brought face to face with each of the witnesses in the unrelenting glare of the television cameras so that there was no possibility of escape, however briefly, could possibly cope with a week of this without collapsing from nervous exhaustion. And some of the commissioners, including Archbishop Tutu, had just come from two weeks of such hearings, first in East London and then in Cape Town; after Johannesburg, they were off to Durban, and so on for the next 18 months, traversing the country from north to south, east to west.

At any rate, Mr Thebe, an immensely dignified man in his late 30s, concluded his own testimony, answered a few questions from some of the commissioners who wanted elucidation on this or that point, then stood up and turned to Mandela and gave his fellow ex-prisoner the clench-fisted salute, which was duly returned. This was, indeed, the new South Africa, whereupon the good Archbishop, knowing very well that Mandela's time was limited, but wanting to give visible demonstration of the immense distance travelled in the two short years since the country's first ever democratic elections, announced a change in the programme and called ahead of time a former activist with the African National Congress (ANC), George Dube, who claimed to have been tortured by his and Mandela's own liberation movement between 1980 and 1983 in a camp established for that purpose in Angola, apparently on suspicion of being a spy.

It's worth pointing out that the ANC had already accepted responsibility for 'serious abuses and irregularities' (to use Mandela's own words) in their camps in Zambia and Tanzania as well as Angola as far back as 1993 following charges to that effect by the then ruling National Party as part of its own desperate but doomed attempt to claw back some of the moral high ground that was being daily eroded as more and more revelations of their own less than salubrious activities over four and a half decades came to light. It was a pity — and an irony — that George Dube, the victim in question, failed to seize the dramatic moment afforded by the present occasion. The man simply couldn't tell a story. By the end of his allotted 30 minutes, and despite much gentle prodding by the commissioner allocated to him to lead him through his testimony, Mr

Dube was still stuck somewhere in Mozambique, having taken us on a tour of Zambia, Zimbabwe and Tanzania. By the time we finally arrived in Angola his main grouse appeared to be the poor quality of the food that he and his fellow inmates were forced to endure, with claims of his torture — 'I was beaten and kicked and we were made to do hard labour from morning to sunset. There was no water to wash' — only briefly sketched in as a sort of incidental backdrop. It was just as well, perhaps, that he also provided us — unintentionally, no doubt — with the opportunity to release some of our nervous tension when he complained that after his release and return to South Africa he had asked the ANC to send him to school to learn how to cook, but to no avail. That said, however, Mandela, along with the commissioners, did their best to take Mr Dube's testimony as seriously as it deserved given the Commission's own brief of 'establishing as complete a picture as possible of the causes, nature and extent of the gross violations of human rights' committed against *all* the people of South Africa between 1 March 1960 and 5 December 1993, that is to say from the beginning of the armed struggle following the Sharpeville Massacre to the installation of the Transitional Executive Council in the run-up to the multi-party elections.

The decision to be seen to apportion blame across the board, which underpinned the setting up of the Commission in the first place, was especially important given the very real possibility, inescapable under the circumstances, that the hearings would simply degenerate into a catalogue of abuse inflicted by the white minority against the black, coloured and Indian majority. In this context, one of the most moving testimonies that first day came from an Afrikaner by the name of Johan Smit, whose eight-year-old son, Cornio Smit, was killed in a bomb blast in the Sanlam Centre in Natal in 1985, just two days before Christmas. Mr Smit explained in calm, measured Afrikaans how he had later met the parents of the ANC guerrilla hanged for the bombing and told them that he bore no grudge in his heart because, he said, as a small shopkeeper he had daily seen men and women denied their democratic rights struggling to pay for essentials and had understood why they had been forced to go to war. He said, finally, that his son had died for the country's freedom because without his death many of the whites he knew would not have grasped the evil nature of apartheid, and that 'in war things happen which no-one plans. Troops are overzealous and start doing what was not ordered'.

Not that everyone was so forgiving. 'Would you believe that I still hate whites?' was the parting shot of one woman, Rokaya Salojee, whose husband, Suliman Salojee, an ANC activist, died in detention in 1964 under the usual mysterious circumstances associated with the apartheid years. Another woman, Hawa Timol, whose son, Ahmed Timol, died in detention under similarly mysterious circumstances, voiced the same sentiments: 'I told the police it was impossible for him to have jumped... I still need to know who killed my son. I cannot be expected to forgive at this stage,' but as her other son led her away it was easy to believe that she would take her hatred to the grave and even beyond. Indeed, as the week unfolded with its tortures and killings and disappearances of husbands and wives and daughters and sons, there were times when it began to seem that we were faced not so much with the lofty and doubtless worthy desire for reconciliation but with the far more understandable, because all too human, need for retribution. And why, come to that, should the *boere* escape the consequences of their actions especially when they seem less than willing to travel even half the distance traversed by so many of the victims of their inhumanity?

Even I could see the *boere*'s intransigence and general lack of seriousness regarding the new dispensation when I arrived at the airport and announced to the Afrikaner immigration officers, all of whose jobs were guaranteed under the terms of the political settlement that ended the country's international isolation, that I was a journalist come to cover the hearings. I may as well have announced that I was a terrorist. 'No way are you coming in,' one of them said as he pointed a blunt finger at my chest and proceeded to give me a long story about a new law, passed earlier that month, which required journalists with British passports to obtain a visa from the High Commission in London before they were permitted to enter the country. I showed him my other entry stamps but in vain. It took six hours and a phone call from the deputy minister of home affairs before they saw their way to revoke my suddenly acquired 'Prohibited Person' status (in 1996!); and then it turned out, when I made some enquiries among those who should know, that no such law in fact existed, and that the entire exercise had been a pathetic because doomed display of power by men who were still trying to come to terms with their own impotence. One wouldn't have wanted to be in their clutches when they were able to throw people from tenth-floor windows with impunity.

Conversely, I understood something of the trepidation of the *boere* when I happened to catch an impromptu interview with Tokyo Sexwale, the premier of Gauteng Region (of which Johannesburg is the capital), outside the Central Methodist Church. The contrast with Mandela's appearance at the very same spot four days earlier couldn't have been starker. 'Somebody killed Steve Biko,' he demanded with barely suppressed rage. 'Somebody killed...' he continued, and reeled off a list of his former comrades who hadn't been as fortunate as he, having survived 13 years on Robben Island and living to tell the tale. Then he urged the culprits to come and testify, now, 'while our hearts are still open,' because if they didn't, he said, 'they will be hunted down...' He was a charismatic man and a good speaker, easily carried away by his own rhetoric, but at that point he checked himself and simply added, 'otherwise they will not enjoy a peaceful old age.' Even so, the message was clear enough, and it had little to do with fancy ideas about truth and reconciliation, still less any biblical notion about who is and who isn't entitled to exact vengeance; and never mind the claims of the Archbishop, who was at that moment helping yet another victim relive the nightmare that would not go away, that would never go away because it simply isn't possible to heal the maimed or bring back a loved one from the dead.

And, yet, it was difficult to dismiss the Archbishop's own faith in the possibility of miracles, even in South Africa, even in the late twentieth century. It was Desmond Tutu, after all, following his appointment as the first black Anglican Dean of Johannesburg in 1975, who immediately wrote an open letter to Prime Minister John Vorster (the man who, as minister of justice, passed a law allowing for indefinite detention in solitary confinement without charge or trial) expressing his desire for 'real reconciliation with justice for all, and to peaceful change to a more just and open society'. Few indeed would have dared hope that such was possible in their lifetime: Mandela still had another 15 years to serve, and the children of Soweto were yet to be murdered in order that their parents might present themselves to the Truth and Reconciliation Commission to tell the world about their abiding grief.

But the miracle did happen, and may yet happen again, at least if the Archbishop has anything to do with it; in his own words: 'Ubuntu [African communalism] says I am human only because you are human. If I undermine your humanity, I dehumanise myself. You must do what you can to maintain this great harmony, which is perpetually undermined by resentment, anger, desire for vengeance. That's why African jurisprudence is restorative rather than retributive.' ❏

## PRISCILLA GAMA

# 'They have killed my son'

'I would like to talk about him joining the struggle. It was sometime in the 80s, I don't remember when exactly, the police came at night. We were still asleep. We heard the windows being hit, they said, "Open up, we're police." I went to my son and woke him and said, "What's happening?" and he said, "Please, mama, don't be afraid, open for them." I said, "Shouldn't I just hide you?", and he said, "No, don't hide me, but if you're scared of opening, let me open." He opened. There were three white policemen and one black person but this black person's face was covered so I could only see his eyes. They called out, "Where's Cosmas? Where's Cosmas?" and Cosmas said, "Here I am," so they said, "Let's go, let's go." He said, "Please wait, I want to get dressed."

'I know that day it was very cold; it was the winter. As he dressed they were opening up cupboards, these white police, asking, "Where is the gun?" Cosmas said, "Did you give me any gun?" And then he got up and they left with him. When they left I took a pen and a paper so that I could write the number plate of the Caspar but one of the white guys blocked the number plate and I was crying and one of them asked me, "Why aren't you going to sleep?" and I said, "I'm so worried, I can't sleep because I don't know where you're taking my child." He said, "You know, these children have taken the law into their hands, they know so much." That's all what they said to me and they left. I went back into the house. As I was still sitting there I heard some noise outside in the street and I went out and I saw a lot of people at the corner and I heard this voice and I could see that it was him and he said, "Mama, I'm back." I said to him, "How

*Miners' strike, Johannesburg, July 1987: the dying days of apartheid*

did you come back?" He said, "They went to another house looking for another boy and I managed to escape." I said, "Have you run away?" and he just laughed, he didn't answer me.

'Okay, from then I knew that my child was involved in the struggle. He was about 13 years old at the time, and we spoke one day together with his father, and I said, "Can't you just avoid being involved in the struggle? It doesn't look as if you will live long"; and my child said, "No, I will not stop being involved, even if they kill us." So things continued, he was very strong in the struggle, going to ANC rallies, organising transport, and people used to come around to my place to get transport to rallies. At the beginning of 1993, before he died, he used to be very well known.

'As things went on there were a lot of eyes on the house and one day he said, "Mama" — he had dreadlocks on his hair, he was like a rasta — he said, "Mama, I know that these police are identifying me by my dreadlocks, could you please make me a hat that I can use." I said, "But is it not better for you to go away, go to Soweto or to Natal?" He said, "No, I will not leave you alone, mama." This was very bad. His other brother went to Soweto and the last born also went to Soweto so it was only him, my husband and myself who remained behind. Even when he went to school — he really liked school — things were very difficult for me because sometimes he would phone me and say, "Mama, I'm not able to come home, things are very bad, but don't be worried." And then he told me that some men would come to school and say they were looking for a rasta from our location but many people at school don't know what is rasta.

'On 1 October 1993 there was a reception behind our house. He left the house about eight in the evening. He said, "Please, mama, don't lock, I will come back and sleep here," and I closed the door but I didn't lock and I went to sleep. In the morning I didn't realise that he had come back and left again and I went to my neighbour, and while I was still talking with my neighbour I saw many women in the street, they were covering their shoulders, and I said, "What is happening to these women who are wearing shawls, they are coming towards us?" During that time the boers were killing our children quite a lot and there was such chaos and confusion. My neighbour said, "Let us check where these women are going to; it looks as if they are coming towards us," but it looked as if they were coming towards my house and I said, "Look at them, they are coming to me." I left my neighbour and came back home, but it didn't occur in my mind what was happening. The last woman said, "Please, come inside," and I said, "Please, tell me what are you looking for?" They said, "Please, come inside." As I came in I went to the bedroom, I found my husband on top of the bed crying and the women they were crying and they were saying, "No, Cosmas has been killed by the boers," and I said, "No, that simply isn't possible, don't start crying, you haven't seen anything."

'And then a lot of comrades started coming. They told me that we must go to the camp, so we went there, my sister and her husband and my husband together with myself, and when we arrived there my husband said to them, "I've lost my child." They asked the name, and my husband told them. They asked him, "What was he doing?" and he told them he was at school, and they said, "Please, come this side," where they had put the people and then after a while my husband said, "Please, come." As I appeared there I saw my child and then I found that he was already cold. On the side of his face was a dark mark, and when I touched him I found that the bones were broken, it looked like he had been hit by a bar, and there was a bullet wound on the side that I can't exactly remember if it was the left or the right side.

'That's how the whole thing ended. He had beautiful dreams, I'm still

## TESTIMONY TO THE TRUTH COMMISSION

'I STAND before you today neither in shame nor in arrogance, but deeply conscious of my responsibility...to be open, frank and helpful...to stand by those who served under me...to admit that which was wrong, to defend that which was right and to continue to build bridges in our quest for reconciliation...

'The National Party is prepared to admit its many mistakes of the past and is genuinely repentant...and we have gone down on our knees before God Almighty to pray for His forgiveness...

Those who fought on the side of the government believed that they were defending their country against what they perceived to be the aggressive expansion of Soviet Communism... The great majority of those who served in the security forces during the conflict were honourable, professional and dedicated men and women. They were convinced that their cause was just, necessary and legitimate...

'In dealing with the unconventional strategies from the side of the government, I want to make it clear from the outset that, within my knowledge and experience, they never included the authorisation of assassination, murder, torture, rape, assault or the like...responsibility should be attributed to...individual ministers for all the decisions taken by them personally in their ministerial capacity, including authorised actions and operations.

'Reconciliation...cannot be achieved unless there is also repentance on all sides... No single side in the conflict of the past has a monopoly of virtue or should bear responsibility for all the abuses that occurred. Nor can any side claim sole credit for the transformation of the country. The transformation belongs to us all.'

*F W De Klerk, National Party leader, Cape Town, 21 August 1996*

very sad about this. He had already impregnated a girl, and this girl gave birth to a baby boy, so I asked the mother to give me the child so that we could bring up this child. This child will soon be five years old.' ❑

*Priscilla Gama, Johannesburg, 2 May 1996*

## MAGGIE FRIEDMAN

# 'Bring the criminals to justice'

'It was the 1st of May, 1989, seven years ago this week, and it was a public holiday. David and I left the house early in the morning with our two dogs to go running in David's *bakkie* [van]. We returned about 10 o'clock. David was driving. He parked the car in the street in front of our house and he got out of the car to go round to the back to let the dogs out of the car and I was getting out more slowly on the passenger side and I was aware of a car coming down the street and then I heard what I thought was a car backfiring as it accelerated down the street and it was only afterwards that I realised that something was wrong when I saw that David was staggering and he was holding his chest in the front and he said to me, "I've been shot by a shotgun, get an ambulance." David obviously saw his killers, he saw the weapon. And then he fell down on the pavement and he died about half an hour later...

'There were a lot of investigations and inquiries that touched on David's death. The first was the police investigation by the murder and robbery squad. After that there was an investigation in 1989 commissioned by the minister of justice, Magnus Malan, and the minister of law and order, Adriaan Vlok, and headed by the attorney-general of the Orange Free State to look into the issue of hit squads. Almost at the same time there was an internal military inquiry [into] the existence of the Civil Cooperation Bureau (CCB). This was conducted by Witkop Badenhorst, who reported to Magnus Malan and Adriaan Vlok, and to my knowledge the outcome of that inquiry has never been made public.

'And then there was the Commission of Inquiry into certain alleged murders by Judge Louis Harms — that was early in 1990 — which was followed by a Commission of Inquiry into alleged irregularities in the security department of the city council of Johannesburg. There was then an inquest investigation which looked specifically at David Webster's death presided over by Judge Stegmann. And then as well as those there were investigations by lawyers, by journalists, by the independent board of inquiry and a lot of other organisations and individuals; and from all these a huge body of documentation has been assembled, piles and piles that I can make available to this Commission, except for the inquest documentation, which has been destroyed at the Supreme Court. Apparently they are already destroying stuff from only three years ago, and the only copy that I know of is with the attorney-general.

'Through all these investigations, nobody has been prosecuted, and no prosecutions are envisaged by the state arising out of the investigations, and each and every one of them is inconclusive and leaves the frustrating impression that the answer is there but has been allowed to slip past under cover of a morass of disinformation and conflicting interests...

'The inquest into David Webster's death was severely undermined by the gross and public intimidation of the key witness, one Willie Smit, who was testifying to the fact that Freddie Barnard told him that he had committed the murder, as well as to the extent of the CCB's involvement. In one of the tea breaks he was approached by Barnard's brother and after the tea break he withdrew all the evidence that he had testified to under oath before the break. The judge didn't take up the issue; he simply allowed the testimony to be refuted. To my knowledge Willie Smit was not charged with perjury. There was an astounding amount of conflicting evidence heard at the inquest from members of the CCB, the police and the military, and it seems to me that it was a co-ordinated attempt to spread a series of lies and half-truths in such a way that a positive finding could not be made, and that is what Judge Stegmann said at the end, that he had heard so much conflicting evidence that he couldn't distinguish truth from lies. And I feel that from the time that suspicion first fell on the CCB this was a deliberate tactic used by the perpetrators.

'The subsequent attempt to identify the perpetrators and planners of this can't be seen in isolation, nor viewed as an individual incident. I believe that the assassination of selected opponents of the apartheid state formed part of a carefully planned strategy and was based on a set of conspiracies within a number of state institutions. These conspiracies included carefully implemented plans to hinder investigations, to sow disinformation, and protect those individuals and institutions responsible for planning and implementing assassinations and related acts.

'The chain of command, and hence the responsibility for these illegal acts and conspiracies, reached high into the structures of the state and government and certainly included cabinet ministers, military intelligence, the CCB, the police, the state security council. Additionally, other institutions associated themselves with these conspiracies by suppressing information, hindering investigations, and failing to fulfil duties and tasks which they were legally bound to undertake.

'Arising from all the investigations, I believe that David Webster's murder was ordered and planned from within state structures. Many employees of the state and many institutions were involved or had knowledge of his assassination; that state resources were used in its execution; and the state apparatus was used and manipulated in such a fashion as to prevent its exposure...

'I've thought a bit about what I want from the Truth Commission, and the first and most important thing for me is the truth about why David was killed. I want to know why David in particular was killed, the reasons why somebody decided he should be killed; I want to know who it was who made that decision. I'm a lot less interested in the people who were in the car and who pulled the trigger, and I think anyway we know something about those people.

'The second thing I'd like is for the perpetrators of the murder to be brought to justice. I don't believe that anyone has applied for amnesty for David's assassination, although some of the people I've mentioned may have applied for amnesty in respect of other offences, and I think they will only be applying for amnesty when they feel they are in danger of prosecution. Under those circumstances I can't feel that amnesty should be open to them. However, I would appeal to those who were directly involved to come forward and make disclosures now because for them this is the best moment from which to dissociate themselves from their superiors who are the ones who must accept the brunt of the responsibility. I'm so sure that there are many people who know something about the case being too afraid to talk about it, and I appeal to those people to come forward now to the Truth Commission which has the ability to protect them from those they will be exposing.' ❏

*Maggie Friedman, Johannesburg, 3 May 1996*

# GERRIE HUGO

# Confession of a torturer

**Gerrie Hugo, former intelligence officer, joined the South African Defence Force (SADF) in 1974. He describes to James Brittain his involvement in a typical 'anti-terrorist' action launched in 1986, his reservations on the Truth Commission and the need for accountability at the top**

'WHAT I want to talk about to the Truth Commission is one specific operation, Operation Orpheus, which was launched in 1986 to coincide with the second state of emergency pronounced at the end of 1985. You have to understand that the military was politically a lot stronger than the police at that stage in South Africa and, in effect, this country was under a military dictatorship, there's no other term for it. There was a joint management system of which the military was the senior partner; there was a kitchen cabinet where the military was in control. Even politicians can't get around this one.

'So we got the order. I got called in to my immediate superior's office. He showed me a signal on the enemy situation which spelled out that the mass democratic movement, the United Democratic Front (UDF), the alternative form of government, was now becoming a serious threat to the security of South Africa, and we have to launch a combined operation — the SADF and police — to neutralise the leadership of the mass democratic movement-UDF.

'This operation took place mainly at night. The modus operandi was people wear overalls — Port Elizabeth principality overalls — so as not to be connected to any security forces; balaclavas, to hide the faces for identification parades, etc etc. And we would go into the surrounding township at night and abduct, kidnap people, take them to complexes and interrogate them, and any form of interrogation went, up to the third degree... Half drownings — the favourite term was 'tubing', which is you take the inner of a car tyre and you just put it there on his head until he almost suffocates and then give him a split second to get his breath back and you do it again; electric shocks and various psychological scares — using superstition and stuff like that. That was the norm. Not that it cannot be described as gross human right violations, because that's what it was, but that was the norm.

'I organised the places, I organised the rations — I was the co-ordinator of this operation. I wasn't *per se* an operator. I had my police contingents and I had my military contingents. I went and visited them often which was expected of me — I had to do that. I saw certain things happen, I knew the way they operated, I left them largely to their own designs, because it was effective. At the end of the day I got the product that the initial order tasked me to get.

'I wasn't scared about what happened there until the first week of the Truth Commission hearings. I'm not discounting the fact that gross human right violations took place, because they did, but to us that was the norm. My fear is now [since] I heard Joe Mamazsla [former Vlakplaas policeman] — or saw footage of him — describing what one person did to one of the Pebco Three, picking up the iron bar and beating him to death. The penny just dropped. I said, for Christ's sake, this person worked for me six months after he could have done this. I left them up to their own designs, but what happened that I did not know about? That's where

*28 August 1985: police attack marchers demanding release of political prisoners*

my fear comes in. I now have to go on record and say we did launch this operation. I have to mention names. And I cannot turn around and say I am not accountable because I don't know what they did. So accountability cannot stop with me. I got the order, and I was left to my own designs. So we're sitting with a tricky one here: who's going to be prosecuted: the operator or the one who gave the orders?

'Of course you have your doubts — I mean I had my doubts coming back from Namibia, where there was a clear defined enemy. And you come back to South Africa and all of a sudden everybody is enemy: the population is enemy, and the military is confusing revolutionary activity with a mass of social reform. So you have your moments of self-doubt, but at the given time you are doing your job: it's effective, as regards pumping information back into the system which you've been tasked to get, so what the hell have I got to lose? So what? There's not a hell of a lot of doubt in this. Later on, yes — a sort of distancing oneself more from this operation where I could have played an active role. I can't say that I would have intervened, no, because I would have been hounded or laughed at or probably just replaced, and there would have been question marks around my security clearance, why, how dare I question this. I probably would not have intervened and I probably would have treated somebody that tried to intervene the same way that I saw myself likely to be treated. It was the norm. But I did distance myself. That does not mean that I'm accountable.

'I think the powers that be clearly misread what was happening in this country. They saw massive social reform, coming from the grassroots, as this total Communistic onslaught being organised by a hard core of organisers, agitators, revolutionaries — and that wasn't the fact. The people of this country were sick of a repressive system. And if we go back to basics, apartheid has been wrong from the outset. I mean, that just explains it all. I've still got one view in life, and think that the defenders of apartheid should be prosecuted more fiercely than the ones who tried to change the status quo, because it was a crime against humanity. But that's with hindsight. A lot of people in this country don't believe that — they say we have been in a low intensity war all along. Why don't they perceive once and for all that they've lost the war and they've got to take the rap?

'I'VE got mixed feelings about the Truth Commission. The Truth Commission's got to happen. It's been coming for a long time. It's a healing process. It's got the right people at the top. There's a nice balance between expertise, emotional involvement and competence. [But] I'm worried about the competence of the people. I'm worried that they're not going to look at the overall picture. It's early times yet. They do have a research department. They do have investigators.

'One of my grave concerns is that it's going to look at the individual cases instead of at the overall picture. What's missing in the Truth Commission, for instance, is where's the military expert that's got inside knowledge? Or who can speak Afrikaans fluently or understand military jargon and read between the lines, understand the system? Who can take one part of the security forces and say that there are some documents missing — and can put that kind of picture together? I think that expertise is seriously lacking.

'I think the attitude [of my superiors] is going to be one of keep quiet for as long as possible, as close to the cut-off date for applications for amnesty as possible. I still talk to old colleagues; the message that I get back is, stay on the bus for as long as possible, don't talk yet, see how effective the Truth Commission is going to be at digging out the dirt on the past, then, when you feel the heat, speak out. Now if I can play a role to facilitate the heat sooner rather than later, I will do that, I will start naming names, I am going to. Because where does accountability stop? In this process of knowing who gave the orders, where does political expendability begin? Who gave the orders and who's going to take the rap? There's got to be a line where they say no, this is too awful, we can't sacrifice this general or sacrifice this politician. You know, it's going to be a healing process, but so far it's been forgiveness, there's been no public apology. There's been no bloody repentance. So how can you have healing by somebody walking up to me and saying I forgive you? I don't know what you did, but I forgive you? I mean what fucking relationship is based on that?

'This is a bit of a farce. Repentance in this regard means some of our individuals have done this, we are sorry, we will help the Truth Commission to root out the perpetrators. Why hasn't the military done this? The police at this stage have said it's fine, we will supply investigators, we will do this, we will do that. The military is still playing mum. And the military is not the untainted partner in the previous conflict. They're not.

'THE MOMENT I spoke out I actively became the enemy. I was depicted as this terminally ill individual dying of AIDS. A guy that ran an office in military intelligence said that for more than a year they concentrated on nothing else but following my movements and handing in reports about me. I've been a victim of a smear campaign. Things like I've got syphilis on the brain, that I'm slowly going mad, that's why I'm fabricating these things. There's too many to think of.

'When I initially spoke out, my father, who is also an ex-military man, said you better shut up, so and so said they're going to take you out. It wasn't only from one side. It would be from police I worked with saying, your old colleagues and friends are putting heat under you, and then a year later you would pick up more information and — well, you've got to disappear for while, pack up, don't be active. It's been quite a campaign, to the extent that the new government believed some of this propaganda.

'I'LL TRY and explain [about accountability]. In February 1990, F W de Klerk unbanned various organisations: the ANC was no longer enemy. He said we are now in a process of negotiation. The military, instead of falling in line with the negotiation, intensified operations against the ANC. The record will prove this. It's proven it in the Ciskei against the Transkei. Now I'm saying that the Truth Commission should look at the low intensity conflicts prior to February 1990 and activities after February 1990. They have to zoom in on them because that was an era of illegal operation.

'The police was immediately part of Codesa talks [the Convention for a Democratic South Africa] as part of the security forces, but the military was left out of this up till the end of 1992. For a decade or longer, under the joint management system, the military, the brigadiers and the generals, were getting used to the idea that they are politicians. All of a sudden February 1990 comes and they are no longer politicians; we now negotiate. They intensify operations until they get pulled into the negotiations at the end of 1992.

'Now de Klerk has two choices. He's either got to say: "I'm in the know that I announced negotiations or reform initiatives but, in the meantime, I've tasked my security forces to weaken the enemy." His other option is to say: "I announced the reform initiatives and my generals didn't follow me, they were out of control and I could not act against them out of fear of destroying my own power base." What other options are there? That's where accountability starts.

'Now we go to the generals, and we say, "which side are you on?" And that's how you go on down the line. Of course the defence is going to be, "he misunderstood," or, "they misunderstood orders." Under the joint management system the norm was that kidnapping is OK, torture to the third degree is OK. They knew that as well as I.

'Accountability doesn't stop.' ❑

© *Interviewed in South Africa by James Brittain for ITN, May 1996*

# NTSIKI BIKO

# Justice first

*For the widow of Steve Biko, father of the Black Consciousness Movement, murdered in detention in 1977, only the trial and punishment of the guilty will begin to heal South Africa's wounds*

*Steve Biko, 1946-1977*

'I HAVE LONG been waiting for justice to come. I did announce this after the inquest, that I needed the case to be reopened so that we could get the actual truth. I don't think there's anybody who can give me that truth except to have those perpetrators taken to a proper court of justice and after questioning, or after the court proceedings, prove that we can get the truth about what happened to my husband.

'If these perpetrators are just let to go to the Commission, definitely they are going to lie there, because they want to get amnesty. And therefore no justice will have been done at all to the families. I'm not talking really mainly about my husband's case. There are so many other cases that need to be heard properly. I don't know what the Commission is going to bring. Nobody has ever been to me to explain what this Commission is all about, and all that I know is that at the end of it we will have to forgive those people. But how can you forgive without proper justice having been done? It's very difficult for me to go again and listen to the lies that I listened to in 1978 during the inquest. I really wouldn't like to listen to such lies. What guarantee have I that the perpetrators are going to tell the truth now? They will tell whatever lies so that they get amnesty.

'To me it is an insult [to be asked to go before the Commission] because all that is needed is to have the perpetrators taken to a proper court of justice. Having gone through the trauma, through the suffering... when I think of my kids, when I've had to bring those boys up from the age of six years and two years till today. It has not been an easy thing. And the perpetrators are comfortable wherever they are. Some of them got top positions in their posts, and they were transferred to various places, and here we are, suffering right through for their deed.

'I know very well how Steve would have wanted to have brought up his sons. I had to do all the work, do the work that he could have done and the work I was supposed to have done as a mother. And it was not easy at all, I must say.

'I wonder if they [district surgeons, police officers, others whose names are already known] will ever come forward. I wonder if they will tell the truth. Starting with the security men themselves: they detained Steve. Being a healthy man, there was nothing wrong with him, but he came out of that prison in Pretoria a ragged man with all dents in his face and body. They are the ones who know what happened. And again, the doctors are equally responsible for his death. Because they never did what they were supposed to do to save the life of a dying man. I would never imagine doctors allowing a man who was so seriously ill to be transported in the back of a Land Rover naked, without any medical facility, from Port Elizabeth to Pretoria. And again, when he got to Pretoria he was never taken to hospital, he was taken to a police cell. Now how can they account for that?

'They can come and say that in a proper court. Because they would have to explain in the first place that there are so many investigations that have been done on Steve in Port Elizabeth, but because they knew that they were in a fix, even the specimens that were taken from him to test if he had a sustained head injury were wrongly labelled. So how can they say they did the right thing? I mean they were also killers. I doubt very much whether they can convince me that this Truth Commission is going to bring us reconciling: one would think of reconciling after justice, but justice must be done first.

'It can never be easy. To me, really, it is just opening the wounds for nothing. Because these people are going to go to the Commission — I suppose they have applied or their names have been taken. But if they go there, are they going to tell the truth? Or are they going to lie so they will get amnesty?'

© *Interviewed in South Africa by James Brittain for ITN, May 1996*

# MARLENE VAN NIEKERK

# Triomf

*[Lambert, an epileptic, is standing in the road outside the municipal dump.]*

JESUS Christ! Suddenly it seems to Lambert the lorries are baring their teeth at him, teeth of dusty, yellow iron; they want to swallow him up. He feels the pain again. No, not that. No, Jesus Christ, help! Not here. Got to hold on. Fucking lorries. They are all over him, inside his fucking head. He can feel the sweat breaking out all over, the blood draining from his cheeks. His mother's not there to take charge, jam a clothes-peg between his teeth. He can feel himself falling.

'Hold on, Benadie, hold on,' he tells himself.

Then everything is on top of him, the lorries roaring, swarming over him, like evil spirits. They seem to swoop down out of the sky, flames spurting from their wheels. He feels someone grab hold of him by the arm. He looks up, but can't see, there's sparks in front of his eyes. He's being dragged across the road, out of the way.

'Sit, sit down, man!'

He obeys. Doesn't know where the hell he is.

'Here, my brother, drink some coke, man.'

Lambert gropes for the bottle. He tries to swallow but his throat is tight. His eyes too feel sore and stiff, his tongue limp, lolling out of his mouth. Fuck, that was close! Fucking close. Thank God, thank Jesus!

Lambert opens his eyes. In front of him he sees a kaffir sitting on his haunches. He has on a grey cloth hat and sunglasses with reflector glass. His face is sharp, scarred, his skin yellowish. He looks rough, a stray kaffir maybe. He's wearing a faded denim shirt with the sleeves torn off at the armpits. There's a piece of green cloth tied around his wrist, a copper bangle higher up on the other arm just above the elbow. His arms are thin. So are his legs, like sticks. Lambert notices a string of beads, red and green and yellow. Almost ANC, he thinks. Almost Inkatha. But not quite. He wonders what's this kaffir's case. He's a different sort. Looks sly. Like he finds something's funny. Christ, what's he find so bladdy funny. He stares at the kaffir's takkies. No socks, no laces. Hell, this isn't just some stray kaffir. This, thinks Lambert, is a tsotsi-kaffir: as thin as a dog; what's he want from me?

He tries to stand up, but can't; he's weak and unsteady on his feet.

'It's okay, my brother I'm looking after you. You feeling better now? You faint or what? Those lorries, they nearly got you. Nearly squeezed you flat as a pancake. But I watch out for you, my man. I pick you up, I bring you here, I give you coke, I'm your friend, man. Don't be afraid.'

'I'm not your friend,' says Lambert. 'I want to go home now.' But he can't get up.

The kaffir retreats. Gesticulates with his hands. 'Okay! Okay! Okay! You not my friend, hey, you are my boss, right. Big boss, yes boss, I'm just a kaffir by the dumps, boss, okay! I catch faint whites here. That's my job, yes? Here a whitey faint, there a whitey faint. Faint left, faint right, faint centre, all day long, I'm the fainting boy, right?'

The kaffir turns his back on Lambert. It looks like he's laughing. Then he turns round again. 'Okay? Relax, my brother, just relax. Boss, king, president, chief, kaiser. Whatever God in heaven, anything you want, I say. Any way you want it. At your service. Excuse me, boss, please, boss, thank you boss, yes boss, no boss! sorry boss that I live boss!' Once more the kaffir turns away. He shakes his head.

'I did not mean that so, man. Thanks for your help, man, thanks very much. I must go home now, that's all. I'm not feeling right, you see.'

Lambert leans back. He realises he must wait. He can still feel the spasms. He must wait for it to go over. Otherwise it'll start again. Probably catch him in the road in front of Shoprite, which would be a hell of a lot worse than here, outside the rubbish dump. He can see the kaffirs gathered on the other side of the road, hands in the air — looking for work. Couldn't care less about him lying helpless in the path of the lorries. Why should they? Yes, he was lucky with this tsotsi-kaffir. If it hadn't been for him he'd still be lying there, having his fit in the road, peeing in his pants and all while the cars and lorries and people they all queued, waiting for him to finish.

'Hey,' Lambert calls the kaffir who still has his back to him. 'I mean it. You saved my life there man! Thank you, man. Thanks again very much.' Adding as an after thought: 'I owe you one.'

The kaffir turns round. 'Okay, okay. That's enough.' He comes and sits down beside Lambert. He begins to roll a cigarette, mixing in with the tobacco some greenish flakes which he empties out of a matchbox.

Dagga, Lambert realises; does this kaffir really think he can sit here in front of him, a white man, and smoke dagga!

The kaffir rolls the cigarette with his long, thin fingers. He licks the paper, concentrating hard. Lambert can see he's had plenty of practice. He folds the paper over, squeezing one end. The kaffir lights the cigarette and inhales deeply. He holds the cigarette toward Lambert. Who shakes his head, no thanks. The kaffir shrugs his shoulders.

Lambert glances across the road at the kaffirs who are now staring at the two of them. Cheeky bastard, this one, he thinks: how does he know he won't tell the police? How's he know he isn't a policeman himself? But then, hell, he doesn't exactly look like a policeman, does he? He glances once more at the kaffir who looks as though he's forgotten all about him: is busy watching the road, this side and that side. Lambert wishes he'd take off his sunglasses. When he's looking at the kaffir he doesn't know where to look. All he can see is his own reflection. He feels the kaffir can see him better than he can see the kaffir. This, Lambert decides, is no chicken kaffir. Nothing frightens him. This is an okay kaffir, this.

'I'll take a pull now, thank you,' says Lambert. Why not. He may as well, seeing as he's just found himself on his arse beside the municipal rubbish dump.

'Sure, man.' The kaffir passes Lambert the butt.

Lambert takes a drag. He hopes this kaffir hasn't got any diseases. But then what the hell. He isn't all that healthy himself. He begins to cough, choking on the smoke.

'Easy,' says the kaffir, 'easy now, my brother.' And Lambert smiles at the kaffir and at all the kaffirs on the other side of the road, who are smiling back at him. The kaffir next to him begins to laugh. He takes back the cigarette from Lambert, slapping him on the back. Lambert, joining in the laughter, gives the kaffir a friendly nudge, sends him half tumbling on the grass.

'Hey, man,' says the kaffir sitting up.

'I say moss, man,' says Lambert. 'Ha-ha-ha-ha-ha-ha!'

'Ha-ha-ha-ha-ha!' Lambert and the kaffir laugh together under the trees by the gate to the rubbish dump. Laugh until the tears flow down their cheeks. Then, when they are finished laughing Lambert says: 'So now, what's your name, hey?'

'Ooooh!' says the kaffir; 'I've got many names. One for every occasion. But to you my friend, I'm Sonnyboy, just Sonnyboy, plain and simple. And what's your name?'

'Lambert... Lambertus Benadie.'

And Lambert is aware of his hand going out toward the kaffir. Yes, it's true. And behind his sunglasses the kaffir smiles at Lambert and Lambert sees in his own reflection how he's smiling back at the kaffir as the kaffir takes his hand. Then the kaffir loosens his grip, grabbing hold of Lambert's thumb, so that Lambert gropes for the kaffir's thumb in turn and gives it a squeeze, whereupon the other lets go, and once more grips Lambert by the hand, shaking his hand vigorously.

Again they begin to laugh: holding their stomachs as they try to stand; grabbing thin air as they mimic the way Lambert clumsily tried to shake the kaffir's hand. Laughing and laughing as they lie there on their bellies, under the trees by the gate outside the rubbish dump.

'So now, where do you live, man?' Sonnyboy asks when they've stopped laughing.

'Just there, other side, in Triomf,' Lambert gestures.

'Triomf.'

'Yes, Triomf,' he tells the kaffir.

'Triomf, I see,' says the kaffir, with a smirk.

'And you?' asks Lambert; 'where do you live?'

'Me? Ho, ho, here, there, everywhere. Sonnyboy live everywhere.'

'I see,' says Lambert; 'a rambling rose.'

Again they begin to laugh.

'I mean, where do you come from?' asks Lambert.

'Where you think, my friend?'

'Well, it's difficult to say.'

'How come, I mean you can tell by just looking, hey boss?'

'Eh, it's not easy.'

'No man, you must explain. You see, me. I'm just a damn kaffir.'

Lambert knows he's being teased. But he doesn't mind. This kaffir is his pal; he likes him.

'Well,' he says, 'You're too yellow and you don't talk like a kaffir.'

'Hear, hear. You see this whitey he can't classify me. Me, I'm a Xhosa from Transkei.'

Suddenly, slipping a zipped pink bag out from behind some rocks, he leans over toward Lambert, as if whispering a secret in his ear; 'Now listen to me, my brother, maybe you want to buy something from this rambling rose, hey, I need the money, man I haven't got a job. I live by my wits, you can say, I'm hungry, man, I haven't eaten fuck all for three days.'

'Shame,' says Lambert: 'that's too bad.'

'Bad, man; fucking bad.'

Glancing round, Sonnyboy unzips the bag and rummages about inside it.

'Fuck!' exclaims Lambert. Wrapped in newspapers and some dirty old rags is a handgun and a pair of binoculars.

'Holy Jesus, where'd you get this stuff?'

Quickly Sonnyboy zips up the bag again. 'You think about it, man: it wasn't easy, I tell you.'

'These things, they're too pricey for me. Hell, look at me.' Lambert points to his worn-out boxing shorts and the holes in his green T-shirt. 'I'm poor too, you know.'

'But you're not hungry, man. You are not hungry like I am,' says Sonnyboy rubbing his belly.

'Well,' says Lambert, and he doesn't really know why he's coming out with this, but there under the scraggy trees, by the rocks beside the rubbish dump, he says to Sonnyboy: 'I'm hungry for love, man, and that's really a bad thing, let me tell you.'

Sonnyboy looks away. 'Really?' Looks back at Lambert. 'Shame, man. Yes, no, really, shame. That's bad, man.'

'But I'm getting a girl, you know.'

'A girl?' says Sonnyboy, sceptically.

'Yes, my father is getting a girl for me for my birthday, for a whole night.'

'Really?' Sonnyboy's smile is one Lambert is unable to fathom. It's because of the sunglasses. This yellow kaffir from the Transkei just better not start laughing at him, here in front of the dump. He better know his place, what he is, who he is, yellow or not, even if he acts like a Cape Coloured.

'Where you get those things in any case?' he asks, trying to put some authority into his voice.

'Oooh,' says Sonnyboy; 'here, there, everywhere, boss.'

'I see,' says Lambert, winking at Sonnyboy. Who winks back.

'How much?' asks Lambert.

'Hundred,' says Sonnyboy.

'Too much,' says Lambert.

'Eighty,' says Sonnyboy; 'have a heart, man.'

'I haven't got 80.'

'What have you got then? Come on, man, let's see.'

'I've got 50,' says Lambert, feeling in his pocket.

'Ag, no man. Are you mad? This stuff is worth a few thousand.'

'Tough,' says Lambert, shoving the 50 rand note deeper into his pocket.

'But a hungry man is a hungry man,' says Sonnyboy.

'Right,' says Lambert; 'and beggars can't be choosers.'

'Don't look for shit now, man.'

'Hey, I've got something else. Six free meals, worth 50 bucks each.'

'What shit is this, man?'

'No, it's true. For the Spur. Six tickets. I won them.'

'Spur, hey.'

'Yes, man, the eatplace, Spur. You can go too. In town. Blacks and coloureds can go too, now. It's the new South Africa.'

'Hmmm. How many did you say?'

Lambert feels in his pocket past the 50 rand note, takes out the packet of tickets and unfolds them. 'See, here's six here,' he says to Sonnyboy as he counts them off. 'That's 50 rands worth of food for one. You can eat for a whole week, man, every day a T-bone. Look, I give you four tickets. Keep two for myself. I also like a T-bone some time. My girl also. I'll take her for a T-bone.'

Sonnyboy laughs out aloud.

'What are you laughing at, hey?' And Lambert gives a nervous little giggle. For a while each sits staring into the distance, thinking over the deal. Lambert notices the shadows are lengthening. Outside the dump the unemployed kaffirs have already left; inside, those working are busy removing their gloves. Soon the gates will be closed. A breeze is getting up. Plastic bags are blowing in the dust. The late afternoon sun casts a golden sheen upon rows of rusty containers.

'Do they work proper, these things you got there?' Lambert asks after a while.

'Sure, man, sure,' replies Sonnyboy; 'I'll give you a demo.'

He unzips the bag once more, pulls out the gun's magazine, spins the gun around his finger. 'Click, Click, Click,' he shoots the empty gun into the pink bag.

'Satisfied,' says Sonnyboy.

'Now the binoculars,' says Lambert.

Sonnyboy takes the binoculars out of the bag, gazes out over the dump. He gives a little chuckle as he hands them to Lambert, pointing. 'See that container there? The one, two, three, four, fifth from this end. Now look there, on its side, number five, what do you read?'

Lambert peers through the binoculars. The dump, the plastic bags, the wire fence, it all swirls in front of him, the sunlight turning everything to gold. Finally he gets his bearings, manages to locate the first container, the second, third, fourth. Close up, through the binoculars, their sides look like aerial photographs of the earth, taken from high up. Lines, scratches, odd fragments: planes and dams and bushes: other countries, golden spraypaint, everything. Then he's at the fifth container. It looks like a mine dump, hills of rubbish in close, compact rows, others strung out loose. It looks to Lambert like the aerial photo of Johannesburg on the Chinese calendar in their living-room.

'Read,' says Sonnyboy; 'read to me what you see there.'

Lambert searches along the side of the container and reads out aloud: 'CTR 517, Municipality of Johannesburg TPA.' The letters stencilled in white.

'Right,' says Sonnyboy. 'Now go down to the right. Just a bit. Now what do you see there? It's small. Do you see it? Now read it my brother, read that thing for me.'

'One settler, one bullet.' Scratched out with a nail on the side of the rusty container.

Lambert lowers the binoculars. This yellow kaffir, he's making a fool of him, that's what he's doing. He's a fucking cheeky, mixed-up kaffir, this one.

'Hey, I'll donner the shit out of you, kaffir!'

Sonnyboy laughs. 'Hey, just relax now my brother, I didn't write that shit there. Sonnyboy's not into politics. I just work the dumps. That shit, you can read it all over Johannesburg man. Kill this, kill that, viva this, viva that, long live this, that and the other. I love the NP. I love Dingaan, I love Tokyo. I love Phama. I love Amy. So much love in this place, it sounds like fucking paradise! I don't care about all that shit, man. I just want to show you this thing works.'

Sonnyboy takes the binoculars, places them back in the bag: zips it up. For a while neither speaks.

Finally Lambert says: 'I don't know; what can I do with it, the binoculars, I'm not a spy.'

'Well,' says Sonnyboy, 'you can show your girl the city, from high places.'

'Hmm. And what shall I do with the gun? I don't have a licence.'

'What do you need a licence for, man? Protect your girl with it. Jo'burg is a dangerous place. She'll feel safe and sound with you.'

THE SUN having set, the light is grey over the dump. In the dark under the trees Lambert and Sonnyboy continue to haggle, until finally they agree on a price. Fifty rand and six Spur tickets. Sonnyboy hands over the binoculars and the gun and another small bag.

'Bullets,' he says, '60. For the hotshot of Triomf Town.'

'Now we're agreed,' says Lambert.

'Greased and oiled,' says Sonnyboy.

'So long,' says Lambert, 'and thanks again for saving my life, hey!'

'Thanks for saving mine,' says Sonnyboy. ❑

*Marlene van Niekerk lectures in Afrikaans and Dutch literature at the University of the Witwatersrand in Johannesburg.* Triomf *won the Noma Award for Publishing in Africa in 1995*

© *Excerpted from* Triomf *(Queillerie Publishers (Pty) Ltd South Africa, 1994)*

© *Translated by W P B Botha*
*Illustrated by Geoffrey Keeling*

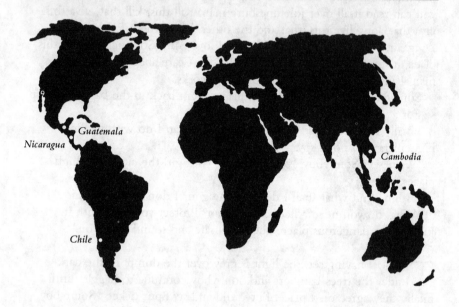

Nicaragua

Guatemala

Chile

Cambodia

## Foul deeds might rise — but who's counting?

CHILE'S six-year investigation into human rights abuses under the Pinochet dictatorship drew to a close in August with the delivery of the Reconciliation and Compensation Corporation's final report. As last chapters go, it was undramatic: a further 899 names added to the official tally of dead and disappeared, still a good deal short of the truth.

More significant than the numbers, however, is that the report's appearance coincided with a bitter debate in Congress over whether or not there should be an annual day of commemoration for the victims of the military regime. The left-dominated lower house says yes, the right-dominated upper house will almost certainly say no. The ruling Concertación coalition, which came together to oversee Chile's transition to democracy, is itself heavily divided on this and other unresolved issues: should it maintain the amnesty for military personnel? Is there a need for further investigations into Pinochet-era crimes? Despite all the reports, commissions, amnesties and reparations, Chile still has not managed to put away its past.

August also brought to light the existence of secret graves in Nicaragua, containing, most likely, the remains of soldiers shot by victorious Sandinista Liberation Front (FSLN) troops during the 1979 revolution. According to the Permanent Human Rights Commission there are many such graves awaiting excavation around the country. But, six years after the end of the Contra war and the fall of the FSLN government, the government of Violeta Chamorro is still performing such a delicate balancing act between the interests of ex-Contras and Sandinistas, that it is reluctant to look too deep into the issue for fear of 'undermining the process of reconciliation'. Foul deeds might rise, but sometimes it is politic to avert one's gaze. In Guatemala, meanwhile, forensic anthropologists have for years been digging up evidence of atrocities committed during its civil war. They continue to receive threats from those — the death squads and others operating with a nod and a wink from the army — who would prefer that the past remained well and truly buried.

Across the globe a ghost is returning to haunt Cambodia, in the vivid form of Pol Pot's former right-hand man, Ieng Sary. Reports of Pol Pot's death might have been greatly exaggerated, but it has definitely served to deepen splits in the already fragile ruling coalition over the best way to deal with what remains of the Khmer Rouge. Each of the country's prime ministers is trying to outdo the other in wooing disaffected members of the guerrilla movement back into the political fold. There is a real prospect of an amnesty for defecting leaders, and a chance that the outright ban on the Khmer Rouge, imposed in 1994, could soon be lifted.

As a result Ieng Sary — known as 'Brother Number 2' during the genocide which killed two million of his compatriots in the 1970s — has hit the comeback trail and is preaching togetherness. 'I agree to the request of the soldiers and people who invited me to lead them...towards a true national reconciliation,' he said in August. ❏

*Adam Newey*

*A censorship chronicle incorporating information from the American Association for the Advancement of Science Human Rights Action Network (AAASHRAN), Amnesty International (AI), Article 19 (A19), the BBC Monitoring Service Summary of World Broadcasts (SWB), the Committee to Protect Journalists (CPJ), the Canadian Committee to Protect Journalists (CCPJ), the Inter-American Press Association (IAPA), the International Federation of Journalists (IFJ/FIP), the International Press Institute (IPI), Human Rights Watch (HRW), the Media Institute of Southern Africa (MISA), Network for the Defence of Independent Media in Africa (NDIMA), International PEN (PEN), Open Media Research Institute (OMRI), Reporters Sans Frontières (RSF), the World Association of Community Broadcasters (AMARC) and other sources*

## AFGHANISTAN

Gulbuddin Hekmatyar, Hezb-e-Islami leader and prime minister, announced special regulations governing radio, television, the press and cinemas in mid-July. Hekmatyar has closed all the country's cinemas and banned music on television and radio, claiming that such entertainment is contrary to Islamic law. The new campaign is seen as an attempt by Hekmatyar, who was restored as prime minister in June, to appear more Islamic than the Taliban, the militant Islamic student group fighting the government. Since seizing control of more than half of the country in the past two years, the Taliban have been harsh in the imple-

mentation of Islamic codes. Kabul residents were said to be angered by the decision to close cinemas. After 16 years of war, only five cinemas remained open in the capital, all of them powered by generators. Since the Mujahedin took power three years ago, films have been heavily censored, with scenes including women or dancing routinely edited out. (SWB, *Guardian*)

## ALBANIA

It was reported in July that the leading independent daily *Koha Jone* has been granted a loan of US$135,000 by the Media Development Loan Fund to save it from bankruptcy. Debts owed to the state printing press had forced the paper to close down for four days earlier in the month. Other papers have complained that the loan has damaged free competition; 16 of them printed a blank page in protest on 26 July. (OMRI)

On 16 July a Tirana court fined four men for taking part in the banned Skanderbeg Square demonstration of 28 May (*Index* 4/1996). Six others were acquitted. No charges have yet been filed against police officers responsible for ill-treatment although seven are reported to have been dismissed from service. (AI)

Greek-language schools are to open in Gjirokastra, Saranda and Delvina, it was reported in August. The Greek government had called for such schools in Greek minority areas as a step to improve relations between the two countries. (OMRI)

## ALGERIA

Cartoonist **Chawki Amari** was given a three-year suspended sentence on 31 July after being found guilty of denigrating the Algerian flag in a cartoon published in the French-language daily *La Tribune*. The paper's director, Kheireddine Ameyar, was given a one-year suspended sentence and editor Baya Gacemi was acquitted on charges relating to the cartoon. The court also ordered that a ban on *La Tribune*, imposed since 4 July, be lifted and its offices, which had been sealed, be reopened. However, the order has not been carried out because the public prosecutor is appealing the decision. (RSF, IFJ)

**Mohamed Guessab**, host of Radio Koran (a religious programme on state radio), was killed on 13 August, together with his brother, when gunmen shot at their car in the Algiers suburb of Beau Frasier. A third brother was wounded in the attack. Journalist **Farida Bouzian**, who worked for a local paper in Tizi Ouzou, was shot dead in a car in Kabylie on 25 July. (Reuter)

## AZERBAIJAN

In early July authorities demanded the addresses and phone numbers of everyone working for the opposition daily *Azadlyg*, and threatened to ban the paper until the information was supplied (*Index* 3/1996). *Azadlyg*'s editor, Gunduz Tahirli, said the demand was an attempt to intimidate his staff and refused to comply. The paper was banned on 31 July. (RSF)

The Russian news agency Interfax reported on 21 July that the government is planning to abolish military censorship in order to enhance the country's chance of joining the Council of Europe. Azerbaijan was granted guest status of the Council at the end of June. Military censorship was introduced in 1993 under a state of emergency, which was lifted in 1995. Nonetheless, the daily *Avrasiya* was suspended by the acting press minister, Nariman Gazanzade, on 2 August because of a series of articles it published on military and political affairs, including a piece about a former Soviet radar station in the north of the country, and a report of a press conference given by the opposition People's Front of Azerbaijan. The paper faces charges under Article 14 of the Press Law. (*Ekspress-Khronika*, SWB)

On 26 July **Metin Yasar Oglu**, a journalist for the newspaper *Mukhalifat*, was arrested while covering a demonstration outside the Russian embassy in Baku. Oglu was detained during the dispersal of the protesters by the local police, who damaged and confiscated his camera equipment in the process. (RSF, CPJ)

### BELARUS

**Andrey Ramasheuski**, vice-chair of the pro-independence **Beer-Lovers' Party**, was given a two-year suspended sentence on 19 July for his part in a May 1995 demon-

stration at which the flag of the Belarusian Soviet Republic was burned. (SWB, Belarusian PEN)

The State Committee for Printing Issues wrote to regional authorities and printing houses on 6 August, reminding them that they must not allow publications to be printed unless they have a valid 1996 publishing licence. There are now 614 registered publications in the country. Before the current round of registrations there were 897. (SWB)

Ministry of Finance inspectors have visited several independent newspapers — among them, *Semida*, *Svaboda*, *Beloruskaya Delovaya Gazeta*, *Belaruski Rinok* and *Svabodnie Novosti Plus* — since 19 August. The Ministry has given no reason for the visits, but observers believe this is part of an official campaign of intimidation against the independent press. (RSF)

### BOSNIA-HERCEGOVINA

TV Srpska threatened on 31 July that it would stop giving airtime to political parties that have criticised state media in Republika Srpska, in particular the Serbian Patriotic Party and the Alliance for Peace and Progress (previously known as the Democratic Patriotic Bloc). Predrag Radic, Serbian Patriotic Party leader and mayor of Banja Luka, was singled out for special criticism by the station. The Alliance has accused state media of operating a 'blockade' of opposition parties in the run-up to the September elections.

(SWB, Institute for War and Peace Reporting)

On 12 August the Republika Srpska Ministry of Communications refused **Free Elections Radio Network** (FERN) permission to broadcast to the Banja Luka area. FERN is reportedly ignoring the ban and Bosnian Serb authorities have not taken action against them. FERN was launched on 15 July by the Organisation for Security and Co-operation in Europe (OSCE) with Swiss finance. (CPJ, Institute for War and Peace Reporting, Media Plan)

On 13 August the OSCE Appeals Subcommittee fined the Bosnian Serb nationalist SDS party US$25,000 for denying humanitarian aid to refugees in the Serb-held town of Doboj unless they agreed to vote from assigned areas. The SDS issued a formal apology on 17 August. The Committee also ruled that voter registration forms had been tampered with in Serb-held Modrica and ordered the local electoral commission chairman to be removed from office. (Reuter)

The homes of three members of parties opposed to the ruling Muslim nationalist SDA were attacked in the town of Cazin on 15 August. No injuries were reported. The following day a coalition of five opposition parties, the **'Joint List BiH'**, issued a statement complaining that Bihac police had confiscated thousands of campaign posters and leaflets the day before. The statement included a signed police receipt which

# WIN NAING OO

## Cries from Insein

*Win Naing Oo was arrested in May 1990 for his work with the All Burma Students' Democratic Front and spent two years in Insein prison*

The prison system of a country reflects the type of government ruling that country. The situation in prisons gives an indication of the situation in the country as a whole. Under the rule of a government which does not respect human dignity, the prison is a place dominated by violations of this dignity, brutal harassment and any kind of ill-treatment that the authorities choose.

There are 36 prisons in Burma, of which Insein prison is the biggest and the most infamous in terms of human rights abuses. It was established in the British colonial period. Almost all well-known political prisoners have stayed in Insein prison at one time or another.

*Position (1) is for the counting of prisoners and for the inspection of prison officials*

Political prisoners reject the fact that they are not recognised as such. They feel this is an insult to their dignity. Even though they have the same status and rights as criminals according to the regulations of the prison, in reality they do not get the rights that the criminal prisoners receive. Political prisoners are even less free in prison than criminal prisoners.

When they sleep they cannot sleep near one another. Visitors and family members who are allowed to visit are thoroughly searched many times. All conversation between political prisoners and their visitors is monitored by prison warders. If more than five political prisoners gather in a group in the prison, it is regarded as a move in defiance of the prison authorities. Political prisoners are even prohibited from going near the entrance of their cells, as the prison authorities worry about them talking to prisoners in other cells.

Political prisoners want to read books, newspapers, and religious material. Even though all books in Burma are strictly censored by the military government, reading material is forbidden for political prisoners. There has always been access to reading material for prisoners

*Position (2) is an emergency position if prison officials pass through*

under every Burmese government except the SLORC [State Law and Order Restoration Council].

On behalf of the political prisoners in Burma, I would like to make it clear that all we sought was freedom, justice and personal security — fundamental rights enjoyed by any civilised society. What we were given was imprisonment, torture and death.

Even during the British era, cases of prison authorities denying water to political prisoners on hunger strike were unheard of. Yet, during the BSPP [Burma Socialist Programme Party] and SLORC period, water pots have been broken into pieces or seized, and the weak hunger strikers beaten again and again. We have heard this many times and now I have seen it with my own eyes. In some cases, prisoners have had to drink their own urine because, during the hunger strikes, the prison authorities seized the water pots.

The world we live in is becoming smaller and smaller day by day. In this modern era a civilised man is one who considers not only his safety and security but also that

*Position (3) is for walking through and standing in front of the prison officials*

*Position (4) is used for punishment. Prisoners were always beaten and kicked in this position*

of other people. We believe man has an unwritten duty to protect, and to promote, peace, culture and the intellectual advancement of all mankind. Is it not an insult to man's conscience and intelligence when, in one corner of the world, a handful of people are arbitrarily committing atrocities against millions of innocent people? Is it not also a challenge to peace and culture of mankind? We want the whole world to know that we, the Burmese people, are experiencing unspeakable suffering under the military regime in this corner of the world.

*From* **Cries from Insein: A Report on Conditions for Political Prisoners in Burma's Infamous Insein Prison** *(All Burma Students' Democratic Front, 1996)* stated 'content against ruling party' as the reason for the seizure. (Reuter)

On 21 August the UN warned that voters supporting parties opposed to the Muslim nationalist SDA party in the Bihac area might be so frightened of reprisals that they might not vote in the 14 September elections. UN monitors in the area received a letter from one of the local opposition parties accusing nine police officers and eight SDA supporters of intimidation. (Reuter)

Recent publication: *To Bury My Brothers' Bones* (AI, July 1996, 26pp)

### BOTSWANA

Journalist **Professor Malema** appeared in court on 19 August on charges of disclosing information about an investigation by the Office of the Directorate on Corruption and Economic Crime (DCEC). No information may be published about DCEC investigations while they are under way. The charge relates to an article Malema wrote for the *Botswana Guardian* in July 1995, concerning local government corruption. On 26 August, however, the charge was temporarily withdrawn, apparently to allow time to lay charges against the editor in charge of the paper at the time of the article. (MISA)

### BULGARIA

On 26 July the official Bulgarian Orthodox Church said it would 'anathematise' **Metropolitan Pimen** (*Index*

3/1996) who was elected Patriarch on 3 July by followers who do not recognise the official Patriarch Maksim. Declaring someone anathema irrevocably severs them from the Church. (Reuter)

On 1 August President Zhelev sent the recently adopted media law back to Parliament for further debate. One of the disputed provisions is the creation of a National Radio and Television Council with the power to cancel programmes and suspend broadcasting licences. Zhelev said the Council's composition threatens the objective coverage of state institutions. (OMRI)

### BURMA

In late June the state-controlled press urged a ban on publications using the name 'Burma' rather than 'Myanmar', the name adopted by the govenment in 1989. The English-language *New Light of Myanmar* said the title 'Burma' is an insult to the nation. (*International Herald Tribune*)

Aung San Suu Kyi's private secretary, **U Win Htein**, and seven other NLD members were sentenced to seven years' imprisonment on 16 August. They were convicted, apparently under a special Emergency Powers Act, of participating in a 'video conspiracy' which 'fabricated the poor situation' of Burmese farmers. Win Htein was one of more than 250 NLD members arrested prior to the party's congress on 26 May (*Index* 4/1996). Twenty other NLD members remain in

detention. (Reuter, Melbourne *Age*, *International Herald Tribune*)

Recent publications: *Renewed Repression* (AI, July 1996, 20pp); *Human Rights Violations Against Ethnic Minorities* (AI, August 1996, 14pp); *Fatal Silence? Freedom of Expression and the Right to Health in Burma* (A19, July 1996, 128pp); *Appeal Cases* (AI, September 1996, 12pp)

### CAMBODIA

On 28 June the Supreme Court upheld the one-year prison sentence and fine against **Samleng Yuvachan Khmae** (Voice of Khmer Youth) editor **Chan Rotana** for defamation (*Index* 2/1995, 6/1995). Rotana, who was convicted in August 1995 of writing a satirical article about premiers Hun Sen and Norodom Ranariddh, was released after one week at the intervention of King Norodom Sihanouk. (Reuter, CPJ, AI)

The League of Cambodian Journalists reported three cases of press intimidation in early July. Five armed men visited the home of **Lip Ratana**, editor of *Sathearanakroat*, on 9 July but were seen off by police. On 15 July the editor of *Reaksmei Angkor* received three threatening phone calls and, on leaving his office, was chased by armed men on motorcycles. Also on 15 July the editor of *Sangkroah Cheat* was followed by a group of uniformed men. (SWB)

On 17 July information minister Ieng Mouly announced a

ban on the creation of new radio or television stations in Phnom Penh. The ban follows a series of attempts to block opposition parties from setting up broadcast stations and will effectively muzzle the opposition in the capital. On 18 July Mouly issued a directive suspending indefinitely the establishment of new newspapers. (RSF, Reuter)

Sieng Sophearak, former editor of *Samleng Yuvachan Khmae*, was convicted of spreading disinformation on 6 August. Charged with collecting anti-government leaflets from the border town of Poipet last year, Sieng received a suspended sentence along with seven other defendants. (Reuter)

Hen Vipeak (*Index* 2/1995), former editor-in-chief of the paper *Serei Pheap Thmey* (New Liberty News), was sentenced to a year in prison and fined US$2,500 on 23 August, when the Supreme Court upheld an earlier conviction for libel. Vipeak was charged under a law brought in by the United Nations during its administration of the country from 1992-93. The charges arose from an article about corruption published in February 1995, entitled 'Country of Thieves'. (RSF)

The first prime minister, Norodom Ranariddh, said on 22 August that he will ask the National Assembly to rescind the ban on the Khmer Rouge in order to assist the current negotiations between the government and a breakaway Khmer Rouge faction. (Reuter)

### CAMEROON

Pierre Essamba Essomba, the editorial director of the state-run daily *Cameroon Tribune*, was arrested and detained for a day on 14 August following publication in the 12 August edition of an article criticising justice minister Douala Moutome and transport minister Issa Tchiroma. (RSF)

Vianney Ombe Ndzana, director of the independent newspaper *Génération*, was attacked by a group of armed people as he was leaving his offices on 20 August. He narrowly avoided a similar attack on 29 July after receiving advance warning. (RSF)

*La Détente* journalist Gaston Ekwalla was sentenced to five months in jail for defaming a member of Parliament, Albert Dzongang, in an article in the 18 August edition which alleged that Dzongang was involved in the distribution of fake diplomatic passports. (RSF)

### CANADA

In July a Royal Commission of Inquiry into the behaviour of Canadian soldiers during the peacekeeping mission to Somalia in 1993 accused military staff of impeding their investigations. Many newspapers led their front pages on 6 July with a photograph showing the army chaplain, Captain Mark Sargent, standing smiling over a group of bound and blindfolded Somali children with signs pinned to them that read 'I am a thief'. When the corporal who took the photograph tried to hand it to the

Royal Commission he was arrested by military police and confined to barracks for leaving his post without authority. (*Times*)

### CHILE

The final report of the Reconciliation and Compensation Corporation, published on 22 August, has added a further 899 cases of people who died or disappeared during the dicatatorship of General August Pinochet (1973-1990), bringing the official tally of victims to 3,197. Of those, 2,095 are known to have been killed; the remaining 1,102 are classified as disappeared. The interior minister said the government is considering setting up a permanent human rights commission and that a special unit will be established to help trace the bodies of the disappeared. (Reuter)

### CHINA

In a circular issued on 20 June the Ministry of Radio, Film, and Television called for increased censorship of broadcasting: programmes should 'follow the correct orientation and help promote reform, development, stability'; 'vulgar' programmes and those with 'unhealthy tendencies' are forbidden; and all stations must submit work to the Ministry for prior censorship. (SWB)

From 1 July film directors wishing to co-produce films with foreign studios must apply for state approval before filming begins. Directors who fail to comply will face heavy fines and possible criminal charges. Illegally made films will be seized and any earnings confiscated. (*Guardian*)

In an effort to curb copyright piracy the Press and Publications Administration announced new regulations on the book trade in early July. Wholesalers and distributors are to re-register with local administrative departments by the end of September. (*Bookseller*)

Labour activist **Liu Nianchun** (*Index* 4/1996) has been ordered to serve three years in a re-education through labour camp, it was reported on 5 July. Liu, a signatory to the 1995 pro-democracy petitions, was detained on 21 May 1995. Dissidents **Chen Longde** and **Wang Donghai**, who were detained on 28 May this year, were also sentenced to re-education on 30 July for three years and one year respectively. Wang has since been released on bail to serve his term at home. Re-education through labour, an administrative punishment imposed by the police, is increasingly used to remove activists from circulation without recourse to judicial trials and the attendant publicity. (AI, Reuter)

Six people were found guilty of copyright infringement and selling pornographic materials in Guangdong province on 19 July. In an intensified crackdown on piracy and pornography, 213 factories and stores were raided and 530,000 items seized in the first six months of 1996. (Reuter)

Writer **Bai Hua** was released

from detention on 30 July, two months after he disappeared in Wuhan, Hubei Province. Bai, a liberal intellectual who provoked Deng Xiaoping's fury with his script for the 1982 film *Bitter Love*, is reported to have been detained for a 'lifestyle problem'. (*South China Morning Post*, SWB)

Four periodicals and a newspaper were criticised at a national conference in July for committing 'serious political mistakes', such as publishing commentaries that were 'out of tune with central guidelines', reports on the Taiwan issue, and praising Mao Zedong. The publications — *Dushu* (Book Reading), *Dongfang* (The East), *Zhanlue Yu Guanli* (Strategy and Management), *Chuantong Yu Xiandai* (Tradition and Modern Times), and *Zhonghua Gongshang Shibao* (Chinese Industrial and Commercial Times) — are all liable to closure. A number of books were also singled out for censure at the conference, including *Setting Sun*, democracy activist **Mou Chuanheng**'s series on negotiating techniques, **Liang Xiaosheng**'s novel *Fear*, **Wei Yahua**'s trilogy *Sheep's Eye*, *Arrogant Look* and *Cat's Eye*. Liang and Wei were condemned for the 'pornographic' content of their work. Over a dozen publications have been closed or restructured this year for publishing articles or photographs deemed unsuitable. They include a foreign trade department journal (which printed a photo from Hong Kong featuring a protest banner) and two magazines associ-

ated with the People's Liberation Army (for articles and photos which gave away classified information). (SWB, *South China Morning Post*)

**Yuan Hongbing**, a former law lecturer detained for 'counter-revolutionary activities' in early 1994, is being held under 'indefinite detention' according to relatives and friends. Yuan, who still receives a salary from Beijing University, is believed to have provided legal advice to the underground trade union movement. In late July he was moved to the library of an academic institution in Guiyang, where he is confined to the premises. (*South China Morning Post*)

Recent publications: *The Cost of Putting Business First* (HRW/Asia, July 1996, 34pp); *At Least 1,000 People Executed in 'Strike Hard' Campaign Against Crime* (AI, July 1996, 7pp); *Religious Repression in China* (AI, July 1996, 41pp); *Women in China — Detained, Victimized but Mobilized* (AI, July 1996, 41pp); *Eighteen Layers of Hell — Stories from the Chinese Gulag* by Kate Saunders (Cassell 1996, 254pp, £14.99)

## COLOMBIA

A Zenú indigenous leader, **Saúl Baltazar**, was killed on 2 July in the village of Carretal by five hooded armed men. The killers entered his house, forced him outside and shot him dead in front of his wife and children. Baltazar was the regional director of the Colombian Indigenous Movement (MIC), whose members have received constant threats from paramilitary groups in recent years. (AI)

President Ernesto Samper has threatened legal action against anyone openly questioning the vote in Congress absolving him of financing his election campaign with money from the drug cartels. A statement issued by Samper's office said that a team of lawyers had been instructed to take legal action 'including any lawsuits that are deemed necessary to demand total respect for the good name' of the president and his family. (Reuter)

The National Television Committee imposed stringent reporting restrictions on journalists covering clashes between protesters and security forces in the coca-growing region of Caqueta on 23 August, in which at least four people died. The restrictions bar the broadcast of any information from unofficial sources or of 'images that reflect situations of extreme human suffering'. Several reporters have been injured while covering the violence: on 29 August Luis Gonzalo Vélez of the television news programme *Colombia 12.30* was badly beaten by several soldiers after refusing to hand over his videotapes. President Samper's supporters in Congress are currently seeking to alter the rules on the allocation of news broadcasting licences, which critics see as a reprisal for the way in which television stations covered the corruption allegations against Samper. (Reuter, IAPA)

Amparo Jímenez and José

Coronada of the television station QAP Noticias were briefly detained by police in Pelaya on 22 August, shortly after covering violence between farm workers and landowners nearby. The journalists refused to hand over their film but, soon after being released by the police, they were stopped by armed paramilitaries who confiscated their equipment and threatened them with death. (RSF)

## COTE D'IVOIRE

Detained journalists Abou Drahamane Sangare, Freedom Neruda and Emmanuel Kore (*Index* 2/1996) have refused to write to the president asking for clemency, according to an article in *Le Républicain Ivoirien*. To gain clemency they would have to renounce their appeal but have 'refused to submit themselves to humiliation', the paper reported in August. (SWB)

## CROATIA

On 1 July Croatian TV reportedly dropped without explanation the popular late-evening news programme *Slikom na Sliku* which covered foreign news and stories critical of the authorities. It was the only programme to cover the slander trial of *Feral Tribune* journalists Vikto Inacic and Marinko Culic (*Index* 4/1996). Television authorities later said changes to the summer schedule necessitated the programme's merger with another news programme. (CPJ, OMRI)

A bomb went off close to the

holiday home of Helsinki Committee for Human Rights president Ivan Zvonimir Cicak on the island of Brac on 18 July. The Committee is openly critical of Croatia's human rights record and Cicak had recently brought a private prosecution against the state-controlled daily *Vjesnik* which published an article accusing him of having been a secret police agent under Communism. Defenders of human rights in Croatia are frequently subject to attacks and harassment. (SWB, AI)

## CUBA

Following the expulsion of CPJ researcher Suzanne Bilello in June (*Index* 4/1996), Jacques Perrot of RSF was denied entry to Cuba on 12 July. Immigration officials told him that his passport was not in order, even though he had the correct documents to enter the country. An Interior Ministry agent later said that Perrot was 'undesirable' on account of a previous visit to Cuba when he met with independent journalists. On 15 July Néstor Baguer (*Index* 4/1995 p133), head of the Cuban Association of Independent Journalists (APIC) and Mercedes Moreno, a reporter with the Bureau of the Independent Press in Cuba (BPIC), were summoned to the offices of state security police and interrogated about their work as well as about Bilello's visit. (CPJ, RSF)

Two Cuban journalists were refused exit visas to attend a conference in Puerto Rico at the beginning of August.

Pedro Martínez Pires, sub-director of **Radio Havana Cuba** and **Francisco García Hernández**, director of the state television network, had been invited by the Association of Professional Journalists of Puerto Rico (ASPRO) to participate in a forum on Caribbean journalism. (CPJ, RSF)

On 30 July **Juan Antonio Sánchez**, a journalist for the independent news agency **Cuba Press**, was apprehended by state security agents as he was leaving a currency exchange booth, having changed US$700 that he had received from RSF. Sánchez was told to hand over the money and sign a statement saying he had received the money from the US government to finance counter-revolutionary activities. Sánchez refused to sign and was released. The money was not returned. (RSF)

Members of the independent news agency **Patria** have been subjected to threats and harassment in recent weeks. On 2 August the agency's chief correspondent, **Ramón Alberto Cruz Lima**, was detained and interrogated for eight hours. Journalist **Bernardo Fuentes Camblor** was arrested on 12 August, as were **Magali Pino** and **Jorge Enrique Rives**. All three were held incommunicado before being released on 23 August. No charges were brought but all were interrogated and reprimanded for having contact with foreign human rights organisations. (AI, CPJ)

Recent publication: *Dissidents Imprisoned or Forced into Exile* (AI, July 1996, 22pp)

## CYPRUS

On 7 July **Kutlu Adali**, editorial writer for the Turkish Cypriot daily *Yeni Düsen* (New Order), the organ of the Turkish Republican Party (CTP), was shot dead outside his home in Nicosia. A caller who telephoned the editorial staff of the newspaper *Kibris* (Cyprus) to claim responsibility for the killing said it was committed on the orders of a far-right group known as the Turkish Revenge Brigade. (RSF, PEN, Reuter)

Recent publication: *Proposal to the United Nations to Establish an Effective Commission of Inquiry to Investigate 'Disappearances', 'Missing' Persons and Deliberate and Arbitrary Killings in Cyprus* (AI, August 1996, 11pp)

## EGYPT

The Ministry of the Interior ordered the confiscation of the book *A Psychological Analysis of the Prophets*, by **Abdallah Kamal**, after the Artistic Censors' office upheld a complaint by the Islamic Research Academy at Al Azhar Islamic university. The author, an editor at the weekly tabloid *Rose Al Youssef*, and the publisher are under investigation by state prosecutors for 'defaming Islam'. This is the second time that confiscations have been undertaken after a complaint by Al Azhar and without a court order: in early June police raided an Alexandria bookshop and confiscated copies of *The Truth of the Veil* by **Said al-Ashmawi**. (*Middle East Times*)

The script for the film *Farewell and Panic*, a romance about an Egyptian man and an Israeli tourist who meet at the Red Sea resort of Taba, was banned in July. (*Independent on Sunday*, *Variety*)

On 5 August academic and writer **Nasr Abu Zaid** was ordered to be divorced from his wife, **Ebtehal Yunes**, following the decision of the Court of Cassation to uphold a Court of Appeals ruling of June 1995 that Abu Zaid is an apostate and thus cannot be married to a Muslim woman (*Index* 4/1996). The court called on Abu Zaid to repent and return to Islam. (Egyptian Organization for Human Rights)

Authorities reportedly confiscated 10,000 copies of the Cyprus-based, Arabic-language monthly *al-Tadamun* on 27 August because of an editorial entitled 'A Chronic Mental Illness', which demanded that all Arab leaders undergo psychiatric tests. (Reuter)

Recent publication: *Indefinite Detention and Systematic Torture — The Forgotten Victims* (AI, July 1996, 20pp)

## EL SALVADOR

On 26 June an underground far-right group, the Roberto D'Aubuisson Nationalist Force (FURODA), sent a communique to various media outlets in San Salvador accusing several journalists, priests and politicians of trying to undermine the government of Armando Calderón Sol. 'We warn all of you that your time is up and that as of this date you have become an additional target to destroy,' the communique said. On 3 July the group released another statement threatening radio and television stations as well as foreign correspondents. On 12 July **Francisco Elmas Valencia**, editor-in-chief of the paper *Co-Latino* who was named in the first communique, was briefly detained on defamation charges for refusing to reveal his source for an article on government corruption. On 26 July, during an international meeting of left-wing parties and movements in San Salvador, another threatening communique was released, stating that the detention of Elmas was 'only the beginning' and that everyone listed in the first communique would be killed. FURODA is named after the late founder of the ruling ARENA party, Roberto D'Aubuisson, but the government has denied having any links to the group. (AMARC, RSF, AI)

### ETHIOPIA

On 9 July the editor of monthly magazine *Tobia*, Mulugeta Lule (*Index* 2/1996), was ordered to report to the Central Criminal Investigation Department for questioning. He was interrogated and charged in connection with an article published in December 1995 about a surgeon who operated on the former speaker of Parliament, Admassie Zeleke. He was also charged in connection with the fact

that *Tobia* does not currently have a deputy editor. The press law of 1992 requires publications to include a list of editorial staff but does not state that it is mandatory to have a deputy editor. Lule was freed on bail of US$1,600 and is currently awaiting trial. (CPJ)

**Binyam Tadesse**, publisher and manager of *Agere*, was released on bail on 8 July, after having been detained since 10 January. (CPJ)

### FRANCE

On 5 July François Mitterrand's doctor, **Claude Gubler**, was given a four-month suspended jail term for breaching medical secrecy in his book *Le Grand Secret*. In the book Gubler reveals that Mitterrand misled the public about the state of his health for 11 years (*Index* 2/1996). (*International Herald Tribune*)

On 9 August the government suspended a decree issued by the far-right mayor of Orange, Jacques Bompard, which banned the handing out of leaflets in the streets of the southern town. Bompard's political rivals claimed that the decree was intended to prevent them campaigning. The suspension of the decree followed a government-commissioned report which found that in July Bompard had refused the purchase of certain books for a new municipal library. The mayor's office said it had only withdrawn books that 'offended good morals'. Among the books were a collection of African short stories for children and a history of

World War II. Orange is one of three southern towns in which the National Front won control in last year's municipal elections. (*Daily Telegraph*, Reuter)

On 21 August the interior minister, Jean-Louis Debré, asked the highest administrative court, the Council of State, to review the country's immigration laws and, in particular, an apparent contradiction which means that some immigrants cannot either be expelled or granted rights of residence. This followed a politically damaging row over hunger strikers, part of a group of 300 African immigrants, who occupied the Church of St Bernard in Paris on 28 June to demand the right of residency. Fifteen thousand immigrants have been deported from France since last year's elections. (*Independent*, *Times*)

### GAMBIA

On 16 August the country's three main political parties were banned from taking part in presidential and parliamentary elections set for 26 September and 11 December respectively. The ban came two days after a two-year ban on all political activity had been lifted. The country's military ruler, Yahya Jammeh, has since launched his own party, which will be allowed to campaign in the elections. (*Guardian*, *International Herald Tribune*)

### GEORGIA

The Tbilisi-based independent television station **Rustavi-2** was ordered off the air by the

Ministry of Communications on 17 July. There has been a long-running dispute over the station's licence, but the move is reported to be contrary to the latest judicial ruling in the affair. (CPJ)

## GERMANY

**Gary Lauck** (*Index* 4/1996) was sentenced to four years in prison in Hamburg on 22 August for exporting neo-Nazi material to Germany from his base in Nebraska. (*Independent*, Reuter)

The former president of Iran, Abdolhassan Banisadr, told a Berlin court that the murders of three exiled Iranian Kurdish dissidents and their translator had been ordered by Ayatollah Ali Khameini, with the approval of President Rafsanjani (*Index* 1/1993). The four men, members of the **Iranian Democratic Party of Kurdistan**, were shot dead on 17 September 1992 as they sat in a restaurant in Berlin. Banisadr was testifying in the trial of five men — one Iranian and four Lebanese — charged with carrying out the killings. (Reuter)

## GUATEMALA

**Otto Leonel Hernández**, a key witness in a kidnapping and murder case, was abducted in Quetzaltenango on 21 June. He was found alive five days later near Quetzaltenango airport. He had been tortured and was taken to hospital for treatment but on 3 July was transferred to Totonicapán prison where, despite orders to the contrary, he is being confined with other inmates. (AI)

Anthropologist **Carlos Federico Reyes López** has twice been threatened with death recently because of his work with the **Guatemalan Forensic Anthropology Team** (EAFG), a non-profit, non-governmental organisation which is documenting, analysing and identifying human remains in mass graves, most of them dating from the most intense period of the civil war during the 1970s and 1980s. EAFG is amassing evidence which will be used in trials of people accused of committing massacres and extrajudicial executions. Further mass graves were discovered at the start of August in Chimaltenango department. (AI, AASHRAN)

## GUINEA

Radio France International correspondent **Serge Daniel** was detained without charge on 2 July and subsequently deported to Cote D'Ivoire. Two other journalists, **Thiernio Sadou Diallo** and **Siaka Kouyate** of the newspaper *Citoyen*, are currently in detention on charges of defaming President Conte and publishing false information. (Reuter)

## HONG KONG

**Emily Lau Wai-hing**, **Elizabeth Wong Chien Chi-lien**, **Albert Ho Chun-yan**, and **Lee Cheuk-yan** of the **United Front Against the Provisional Legislature** were refused travel visas for their planned protest trip to Beijing at the end of June. Eight other members of the group flew into China on 1 July to deliver a 60,000-signature petition but were barred from disembarking and summarily returned to Hong Kong. In addition, their travel documents were confiscated and their petition refused. Elizabeth Wong was barred from China for a second time on 15 July when her invitation to an Internet conference at Beijing's Qinghua University was withdrawn because of a supposed error in her visa application. (*South China Morning Post*, *Guardian*, *International Herald Tribune*, Freedom House)

On 24 July five labour activists were convicted of 'disorderly conduct' and fined US$65 each. The activists — **Wong Ying Yu** and **Christopher Mung** of the Hong Kong Federation of Trade Unions, **Leung Lik**, **Leung King Tsuen**, and **Leung Kwok Hung** — were arrested on 10 January after security guards broke up a peaceful protest against the international toy industry outside the Toys and Game Fair at the Convention and Exhibition Centre. (Hong Kong Coalition for the Safe Production of Toys)

Internet service providers (ISPs) complained in late July that government proposals to monitor the network unfairly penalise them. According to proposed legislation, ISPs will be legally responsible for the content of material on their servers. (*South China Morning Post*)

A ban on prisoners receiving newspaper racing pages (*Index* 1/1996) was reimposed by the Court of Appeal on 31 July. The rights of prisoners, the court ruled, may be restricted in order to maintain prison discipline. (*South China Morning Post*)

A slide of Édouard Manet's 'Le Dejeuner sur L'Herbe' has been removed from a projected slide show at the Arts Centre, after the Television and Entertainment Licensing Authority branded it indecent in early August. Its depiction of nudity, said a spokesman, rendered the work unsuitable for children. (Reuter, *South China Morning Post*)

Recent publication: *China's Challenge — Freedom of Expression in Hong Kong* (A19/Hong Kong Journalists' Association, June 1996, 48pp)

## INDIA

At the beginning of July a New Delhi judge, aiming to stem the 'cultural pollution' of India, banned the showing of adult movies on state television, and made it compulsory for all programmes, including advertisements, to obtain a 'universal' certificate from the censor board. (*South China Morning Post*)

On 8 July 19 Kashmiri and foreign journalists were kidnapped at Anantag, 50km south of Srinagar, by gunmen of the Jammu and Kashmir Ikhwan, a militia group reputed to be backed by the Indian authorities. Reporters **Gulzar Ahmed** and **Abdul Qayoom** of *Uqab,* **Masood Ahmed** of *Wadi-ki-Awaz,* **Shujaat Bukhari** of *Kashmir Times,* **Zahoor Shair** of *al-Safa* and photographer **Maqbool Sahil** of *Chattan* were told they

would be killed unless the editors of Srinagar's major daily papers appeared before the Ikhwan commander. The editors had ignored a 'ban' the Ikhwan had ordered the week before. The Ikhwan accused the Srinagar press of not giving them enough coverage. The editors ignored the Ikhwan's summons. The Ikhwan said the 13 other journalists could leave but they insisted on staying until their colleagues were released. All journalists were released after seven-and-a-half hours through the intervention of the Indian authorities. (CPJ)

**Ashraf Shaban,** editor-in-chief of *al-Safa,* was abducted from the newspaper's offices on 1 August by three unidentified men. He was released the next day. The previous editor of *al-Safa,* Shaban's father, was murdered in April 1991. (CPJ, Reuter)

Recent publication: *Assam — The Killing of a Human Rights Defender* (AI, June 1996, 6pp)

## INDONESIA

On 3 July the government announced that it will not allow the pro-Megawati faction of the Indonesian Democratic Party (PDI) to contest the 1997 parliamentary elections (*Index* 4/1996). Only three political parties — the ruling Golkar, the PDI, and the Muslim-oriented United Development Party — are permitted to take part in Indonesian elections. One hundred and thirty supporters of the ousted PDI leader are believed to have been detained in the aftermath of

riots in Jakarta on 27 July. Activists continue to be harassed, including members of the newly outlawed People's Democratic Party (PRD) which the government accuses of orchestrating the riots. **Muchtar Pakpahan,** general secretary of the unofficial Indonesian Prosperity Trade Union, was detained on charges of subversion on 29 July and 10 PRD members, including the leader, **Budiman Sudjatmiko,** were detained on similar charges on 11 and 12 August. Banned writer **Pramoedya Ananta Toer** and **Sukmawati Soekarnoputri,** Megawati's sister, were also called in for questioning on 13 August. Activists have been detained in East Java, Medan and Bali. The government has refused to release details of those imprisoned, injured and killed during the riots and relatives, journalists, and human rights monitors have been prevented from investigating casualties and fatalities. (AI, HRW, *South China Morning Post,* Tapol)

Journalists covering the Jakarta unrest were also subject to restraint. On 28 July General Syarwan Hamid advised Jakarta-based editors and bureau chiefs to support the government's stance while General Amir Syarifudin told news organisations that the military were 'drawing a line' between 'friends' and 'enemies' in the local media and threatened the large national dailies, *Kompas* and *Merdeka,* with closure. Also threatened were radio stations **Ramako** and **Sono,** which attempted to report the seizure of the PDI headquarters live on air.

# MEGAWATI SOEKARNOPUTRI

## A forum for freedom

*Megawati Soekarnoputri led the opposition Indonesian Democratic Party (PDI) until a pro-government faction of the PDI met in Medan in June and voted to replace her. The subsequent police takeover of the PDI headquarters in Jakarta in July led to widespread rioting*

Since the very beginning I have repeatedly tried to get the message across to the government that something was going to happen. It started at about 7.30 in the morning, when my maid told me the [PDI] headquarters were under attack. I tried to call the headquarters but it was very difficult. So I immediately got changed and another call came in. I told them I was on my way, but they said, 'Ibu,' [a term of respect in Bahasa Indonesia meaning 'mother'] 'please don't come. The situation here is critical.'

So I started calling other members of the PDI Central Board. They already knew about the attack. They told me not to come because the whole area was flooded with military and police and I had no chance of reaching the office. Then at 8.30 another call came. Someone in the office said the central Jakarta police chief wanted to talk to me.

I took it and asked, 'Who are you?' He said: 'This is police chief Abubakar. And who are you?' 'Ibu Mega. What is the purpose of our conversation?' He said he wanted me to 'agree to the status quo'. I asked him what the status quo was. He said those who are inside the office should stay there, behind a police line, and those who are outside the office should not attempt to go in. I told him I would give the order to my commandant in the office.

But the commandant was out in the compound. He was very difficult to find. So I told the guy on the line to give the order to the commandant. But before I'd finished speaking he said: 'Ibu, we're under attack again.' It was extremely noisy and that was my final contact. It was around 9 o'clock.

Journalists at both stations were subsequently temporarily removed from the newsroom by the management. Reporters were barred from covering the riots and many of those who attempted to do so were injured. **Cecep Sukma**, photographer with *Ummat*, was beaten for refusing to hand over his film to soldiers, **CNN** was prevented from reporting at all, and film belonging to **Associated Press**, *Asiaweek*, and the **Australian Broadcasting Corporation** was confiscated. Three Japanese and one Dutch journalist were detained in central Java on 2 and 3 August, accused of planning to disseminate PRD documents abroad. In Surabaya two journalists, **Subechi** of *Surabaya Post* and **Adi Sutarwijono**, were detained by police during a rally on 28 July and reportedly tortured at Surabaya military command. When they were finally recognised as reporters they were released and given *uang damai*, or 'peace money'. (Institute for the Studies on Free Flow of Information, RSF, IFJ, CPJ)

I have said many times that the unconstitutional Congress in Medan was the cause [of the riots]. Prior to that Congress on 20 June nothing violent happened with either the PDI members or my other supporters. They conducted their protests with discipline and with order.

After the 20 June incident, I sent delegates to the Jakarta military commander, asking him to give us a place where my supporters could channel their emotions. We finally agreed to set up the free speech forum. But now they are trying to corner me with the free speech forum, saying that people used the forum to discredit the government. That is slander. The forum was open to the public. It was a medium for political education where people could express their views on democracy.

Since the riots I have not been allowed to leave the house. I assume the riots occurred because of general frustrations within society and particularly because they witnessed what had happened to the PDI headquarters. As the PDI chair I said repeatedly: 'Don't take our office by force because it will provoke anger.' Could we block anger? Could we ban feeling? They are unorganised and who can control an unorganised crowd?

If [breakaway PDI chair] Suryadi really is a democratically elected leader, which he claims to be, why doesn't he come to the PDI office? If he has the support of the majority, why didn't he just go to the headquarters and politely ask me to hand it over? Why would he ask the military to take it over?

There's a lot of work to be done now establishing the number of victims. I am also having trouble with efforts to link me with the Communists. They allege that I have contact with a former Communist leader, Sabardi Rewang Parto, whom I do not know. I was still a teenager in 1965 [the year of the attempted Communist coup against Megawati's father, President Soekarno] and do not remember that name clearly.

This generation were mostly born after 1965. It was 30 years ago. The younger generation, unlike their parents, live under this government with all of its economic stability. They do not know what happened in 1965. I believe we should ask what this government has achieved if, as they say, the power of their nemesis is still so great?

*Interview by Andreas Harsono*

Prihadi Beny Waluyo, a lecturer at Duta Wacana Christian University, was detained in early August and accused of sending e-mail messages relating to the Jakarta riots to Holland. Waluyo has since been released but is being kept under strict surveillance and ordered to report regularly to the district military command. (HRW)

Fuad Muhammad Sya-fruddin, a journalist with the Yogyakarta-based daily *Bernas*, died on 16 August of injuries after being attacked at his home on 13 August by two unidentified people. A few days before the attack Syafruddin had filed reports on alleged government corruption involving Bantul regent, Sri Roso Sudarmo. His work was reportedly discussed by Sudarmo at a local government meeting on 13 August. (Institute for the Studies on Free Flow of Information)

Catholic priest **Father Ignatius Sandyawan** was charged on 20 August with publicly showing hatred to President Soeharto. He faces three further charges — of insulting the authorities in writing, showing enmity against the authorities, and harbouring three members of the PRD, including the leader, Budiman Sudjatmiko. Sandyawan is secretary of a team of volunteers set up to assist victims of the riot. He faces a six-year prison sentence if found guilty of expressing hatred. (Reuter)

Recent publications: *Muted Voices — Censorship and the Broadcast Media in Indonesia* (A19, June 1996, 24pp); *The 1965 Prisoners — How Many More Will Die in Jail?* (AI, July 1996, 6pp)

## IRAN

In early July **Ataollah Mohajerani**, one of President Rafsanjani's deputies and managing editor of the weekly *Bahman*, was banned from all press work for a year for 'causing public anxiety'. The publication started in January and, after coming under immediate attack from conservatives, closed down in April. Mohajerani lodged an appeal on 23 July. In early August the directors of two other publications were fined: **Ahmad Safaifard** of the daily *Akhbar*, who is also a Rafsanjani aide, was fined US$1,700 and removed from office for six months after being found guilty of 'disseminating falsehoods', disturbing public opinion and promoting prostitution; and **Rahim Said-Danesh** of the weekly *Azarmehr*, was suspended from his post for one year and fined US$330 for 'disseminating falsehoods' about the Majlis elections in March.

(Reuter, *Middle East Economic Digest*)

In August Lida Fariman became the first Iranian woman to compete in the Olympic Games since the 1979 revolution. Fariman also carried the Iranian flag at the opening ceremony. Coverage of most women's events was censored by Iranian television, however. (*Times*, Reuter)

## IRELAND

On 17 July the soft-porn magazine *Studio* was banned by the Censorship of Publications Board. It is the first Irish magazine to be banned since 1975. Although *Studio* had pictures of genitalia blanked out, the Board still found it 'indecent and obscene'. The Board also imposed bans on three books: *Cockers Folly* by **Janine Edwards**, *Slackhurst* by **Hilary Chale** and the anonymous *Through the Hoops*. (*Irish Times*)

## ISRAEL

Three Palestinian cameramen were attacked on 19 July while filming clashes between Israeli settlers and Palestinian villagers in Kariot on the West Bank. Worldwide Television News cameraman **Abdel Rahman Khabisa** was beaten by settlers who also smashed his camera. The settlers then turned on **Hassan Titi**, cameraman with Reuters TV, who was filming the attack on Khabisa. Associated Press cameraman **Abdel Rahim Qusini** was also hurt in the clashes. Israeli soldiers present did not intervene to prevent the attacks. (Palestinian Media

Monitoring Centre, IFJ, RSF)

**Bashar Tarabieh**, a consultant with Human Rights Watch, was detained on 19 August while on holiday in the Golan Heights. Tarabieh, who is resident in the USA, is being held in Jalameh prison near Haifa and interrogated about his human rights work. His captors have reportedly threatened to confiscate his travel documents to prevent him from leaving the country. (HRW)

Recent publications: *Unlawful Killings During Operation 'Grapes of Wrath'* (AI, July 1996, 27pp); *Israel's Closure of West Bank and Gaza Strip* (HRW/Middle East, July 1996, 60pp)

## JAPAN

Nagasaki's Atomic Bomb Museum (*Index* 3/1996) bowed to official pressure once again in late June when it replaced a picture of the Nanjing Massacre on the orders of the mayor. Nationalist concerns have also reached the prime minister, who has instructed the Foreign and Education Ministries to investigate whether photos of Japanese military aggression in museums around Japan are real or fabricated. (*International Herald Tribune*)

Public broadcaster NHK cancelled a planned feature on the 'comfort women' in early July, after admitting secretly filming a conversation between the producer and a Ministry of Justice official. The Ministry has refused to make public records of war criminals involved in sex slavery, suggesting that their records have not been properly verified. Political pressure is believed to have been brought to bear on the programme makers, whose previous work on the subject brought angry reactions from right-wingers. (*Far Eastern Economic Review*)

## JORDAN

**Nasser Kammech**, editor of the weekly *Sawt al-Maraa*, was imprisoned on 20 July for two weeks for 'attacking Jordan's image' by publishing articles on drug use in Amman. He faces a three-year sentence under Article 9 of the press law. **Tawfik Kiwane**, editor-in-chief of the weekly *Akhbar al-Ousbouh*, was remanded in custody for 'spreading false news' on 24 July, following an article about a bank robbery in Zarqa which, it was claimed, was 'completely made up'. And on 20 August four staff members at *al-Bilad* — publisher **Nayef Tawarah**, editor **Khaled Kasabeh**, and journalists **Taha Abu Riden** and **Rakan Sa'aideh** — were arrested on charges of 'sowing discord' and 'publishing false information'. The newspaper had reported that a girl had died during violent protests against bread price increases in southern Jordan. **Fouad Hussein**, a journalist with the daily *al-Aswaq* and member of the Arab Socialist Baath Party, was arrested on 19 August, apparently on suspicion of taking part in the riots, which King Hussein has publicly blamed on Iraq and pro-Iraqi Baathists. (PEN, RSF)

## KAZAKHSTAN

On 17 July the Russian paper *Komsomolskaya Pravda* was ordered to print an apology within a week for its article 'Conversations with Alexander Solzhenitsyn' (*Index* 4/1996). On 18 July the paper ran an editorial in which it expressed regret at the distress caused by Solzhenitsyn's comments, but insisted that it had not incited ethnic enmity. Although short of a full retraction, the expression of regret was sufficient for the prosecutor to drop the charges against the paper and permit it to circulate again after a four-month hiatus. (CPJ, OMRI, SWB)

Recent publication: *Ill-Treatment and the Death Penalty* (AI, July 1996, 26pp)

## KENYA

Police ordered *Sunday Standard* reporter **Waite Mwangi** to accompany them to Nyeri on 15 July, so that he could identify a group of criminals he had written about the previous day. When he said he was too busy, he was given until 4pm the following day to comply. The police chief claimed that people were no longer going out at night in Nyeri owing to fear generated by the article and that Mwangi had to 'show me where the thugs hide so that I can discharge my duties by arresting them.' (NDIMA)

On 18 July armed police broke up a festival in Nairobi organised by the group Release Political Prisoners. About 30 policemen ordered the meeting to disperse on the grounds that it was unlicensed. (NDIMA)

On 26 July the High Court rejected an application by **Koigi wa Wamwere**'s lawyer to have wa Wamwere and his two fellow activists released on bail pending appeal against conviction by a lower court (*Index* 2/1996). (NDIMA)

**Mwangi Geita**, a journalist with the *Nation*, was attacked by 10 local government councillors in Nyeri on 30 July after being accused of filing 'negative' stories about council chairman Hezekiah Waithanje. Geita was forced to flee the Forest Inn Hotel after the councillors threatened to 'teach him a lesson'. (NDIMA)

In mid-August the foreign affairs minister, Kalonzo Musyoka, said that he would no longer be granting interviews to the print media owing to their reporting of the debate on constitutional reform. A cross-section of opposition leaders has called for a review of the constitution before the 1997 elections, with little result. (NDIMA)

## KUWAIT

Several editions of the British daily *The Times* were banned in July for reporting the case of Robert Hussein, a Kuwaiti businessman who converted from Islam to Christianity. An Islamic court denounced Hussein as an apostate and, under *sharia* law, any Muslim who kills an apostate incurs no penalty. In Kuwait, all papers are subject to censorship, but it is unusual for entire editions to be banned. (*Times*)

## KYRGYZSTAN

The Constitutional Court approved amendments to Article 5 of the constitution, granting Russian the status of an official language, it was reported at the start of July. Article 5 had specified Kyrgyz as the only state language, granting equal rights for the free development of other languages, without conferring special recognition on Russian. (OMRI)

**Yrsbek Omurzakov** of the independent weekly *Res Publika* was sentenced to two years in a penal colony for slandering President Akayev, it was reported on 11 July. It is unclear what he said or wrote about Akayev. Omurzakov was released from prison on 6 August, however, after his appeal was granted. (OMRI)

## LEBANON

Journalist **Ali Dia** (*Index* 4/1996) was released from Kishon prison, Haifa, by Israeli security forces on 18 July and escorted back to his home town, Marjayoun, after a month's imprisonment. (IFJ)

## LESOTHO

**Mamonyane Matsaba** of state-run **Radio Lesotho** was demoted from her position as chief programmes officer on 30 July, in accordance with a ruling by the Public Service Commission which found her guilty of 'disobeying and disregarding' an order prohibiting journalists from broadcast-

ing a statement by a member of an opposition party in November 1995. (MISA)

The government issued a circular on 5 August prohibiting all its ministries, departments, institutions and agencies from placing advertisements in the privately owned, Sesotho-language weekly *Mo-Afrika*, because of 'the negative stance this paper has adopted towards the government'. The government is the largest advertiser in Lesotho, and a crucial source of revenue for newspapers. (MISA)

## MACEDONIA

**Fadil Sulejmani**, rector of the Albanian-language University of Tetovo (*Index* 1/1995, 4/1995), four of his staff and the speaker of the Senate, Milahim Fejziu, were jailed for between three and 12 months in mid-July for their part in founding the university, which is not recognised by the authorities. On 27 August, after widespread protests among the ethnic Albanian minority, Sulejmani was released. (SWB)

## MALAWI

On 16 August President Muluzi was granted an injunction restraining the independent weekly *Tribune* from publishing 'further defamatory articles' about him, following an article in the 13 August edition, entitled 'Skeletons of Muluzi', which alleged the president had fraudulently acquired a piece of land worth US$33,000. Meanwhile, another private paper, the *Statesman*, discontinued its

'Dear Anne' column in July, following a writ for defamation brought by Muluzi's wife, Anne. The column is now titled 'Dear Countryman'. (MISA)

**Hastings Maloya**, a radio journalist with the state-run **Malawi Broadcasting Corporation** (MBC), was dismissed on 26 August for covering an opposition Malawi Congress Party rally in Blantyre. **Francis Chikunkhuzeni**, an MBC editor, was suspended for one month for editing Maloya's report. (MISA)

## MALAYSIA

In early August nine members of the outlawed **al-Arqam** Islamic sect (*Index* 4/1996) were ordered to be detained without trial for two years for 'acting in a manner prejudicial to the security of Malaysia'. Six more remain in detention while three others, including Khatijah Aam, wife of the sect's former leader, have been released and placed under restricted residence orders. (AI)

The Terenggau Umno Youth Movement called upon the religious authorities in early August to ban a book on Islamic history which, it claims, promotes Shi'ism. The book, *Fitnah Terbesar Dalam Sejarah Islam*, by Egyptian historian **Taha Hussain**, was first published by a state-owned press in 1992 and its first print run of 2,000 copies sold out. Sunni Islam is being promoted as the official Muslim faith of Malaysia and the authorities are campaign-

2

**INDEX ON CENSORSHIP**
33 Islington High Street
London N1 9BR
United Kingdom

**BUSINESS REPLY MAIL**

FIRST CLASS PERMIT NO.7796 NEW YORK, NY

Postage will be paid by addressee.

**INDEX ON CENSORSHIP**
708 Third Avenue
8th Floor
New York, NY 10164-3005

ing to curb the influence of Shi'ism. (*Straits Times*)

In a speech to the Commonwealth Broadcasting Association on 27 August, the deputy prime minister, Anwar Ibrahim, criticised his government's 'over-zealous censorship and tight control of the airwaves'. Censorship, he said, is 'not only intellectually unsound, but economically unhealthy.' He also criticised the 'knee-jerk reactions' of some countries to the perceived threat of satellite television and the Internet. Satellite dishes are currently banned in Malaysia. (*South China Morning Post*)

## MAURITANIA

Two July editions of the weekly magazine *Mauritanie-Nouvelles* were confiscated at the printing presses by the Ministry of the Interior, apparently because of an editorial on Franco-Mauritanian relations. *Mauritanie-Nouvelles*, which publishes in Arabic and French, had only recently resumed publication following a three-month suspension. It has been forced to change from daily to weekly publication because of persistent hindrances: the Minstry of the Interior demands to see each edition prior to printing, a procedure that can severely delay production. On 23 July the weekly *La Tortue* was also seized at the printing presses. The reasons for the seizure are unclear. (RSF)

## MEXICO

Since the emergence of a new armed opposition group in Guerrero state, the People's Revolutionary Army (ERP), members of peasant organisations have received threats and ill-treatment by police who accuse them of belonging to the guerrillas. On 3 July **Hilario Mesino Acosta**, a founding member of the **Southern Sierra Peasant Organisation** (OCSS), was arrested and charged with sedition and conspiracy. Four other OCSS members arrested on 8 July and charged with conspiracy have reportedly been tortured and ordered to confess to membership of the ERP. On 9 July four members of the **Organisation of Villages and Communities of Guerrero** (OPCG) were arrested and accused of belonging to the ERP. A demonstration held on 14 July against the arrests was broken up by riot police who arrested seven protesters. About 30 people were wounded and medical personnel were threatened with dismissal if they treated the wounded peasants. (AI, *International Herald Tribune*)

On 17 July heavily armed members of the Chiapas State Judicial Police (PJE) and the paramilitary group Alianza San Bartolomé de los Llanos raided the villages of San Sebastián and Señor del Pozo. The men opened fire on community members and killed **Manuel Martínez de la Torre**. Twelve people, most of them members of the **Emiliano Zapata Peasant Organisation** (OCEZ), were arrested. The day before the attack two OCEZ members were abducted and have not been seen since. (AI)

Intimidation and threats against journalists continue: on 23 June radio reporter **Oswald Alonso** was kidnapped from his home and beaten for 24 hours before being released. He is well known for his investigations into police corruption in Morelos for the radio news programme *Nuestras Noticias*. On 2 July **José Cárdenas**, an announcer for the radio station Informativo Panorama, lost his job for broadcasting a report about the ERP. Cárdenas was ejected from the studio before the broadcast had finished and was subsequently dismissed. On 5 July **Fabiola Cancino de los Santos**, a journalist with the daily *El Universal Gráfico*, was held up at gunpoint by seven men at her home and threatened with death if she continued reporting. On 20 July **Thierry Jonard**, correspondent for the Belgian broadcaster RTBF, and recording technician **Juan Ozuna** were assaulted by around 40 armed men while filming a documentary in Chiapas. And on 12 August **Alberto Flores Casanova** of *El Mañana* was attacked by two men while driving to work in Nuevo Laredo. The men approached him and put a gun to his temple while he waited at a red light. He managed to deflect the gun, however, and was shot in the leg. (AI, CPJ, RSF, FIP)

## NIGER

On 6 July the offices of the radio station **Anfani FM 100** and the newspaper *Anfani* were occupied by soldiers. Gremah Boucar, director of the company which owns the station and the paper, believes the occupation is linked to media coverage given to the political opposition in the run-up to the elections of 7 and 8 July. Prior to the elections the country's military ruler, General Ibrahim Bare Mainassara dissolved the independent electoral commission, banned demonstrations and public gatherings and cut international phone lines. Anfani FM 100 resumed broadcasting on 4 August. (CPJ, RSF)

The interior minister, Idi Ango Omar, strongly criticised the foreign correspondents of the BBC and RFI, offering them a 'last national warning' during a broadcast on National Radio on 13 July. On 30 July **Abdoulaye Seyni**, Niamey correspondent for the BBC and a reporter for the independent newspaper *Haske*, was arrested by the Niger Security Service. (CPJ)

## NIGERIA

**Hassan Anwar**, Nigeria correspondent for the Middle East News Agency, was returned to Cairo on 1 July after being detained in a Nigerian jail for a week. Despite an agreement by the minister of information to accredit Anwar as a foreign correspondent, the security authorities insisted that his work was 'suspicious'. His release was secured only after intervention by the Egyptian authorities. (IPI)

**Gani Fawehinmi**, a prominent opposition lawyer, was released from prison on 19

July after spending over five months in solitary confinement. Fawehinmi was arrested on 30 January, shortly before he was due to address an anti-government rally. (*International Herald Tribune*)

Two editors from the opposition weekly magazine the *News* were detained on 11 August following publication of an article accusing the oil minister, Dan Etete, of awarding government contracts to his family and friends. **Bayo Onanuga** and **Babafemi Ojudu** were taken to the Shagisha prison without charge. Ojudu was detained until 13 August and Onanuga until 17 August. (CPJ, AI)

Recent publication: *Justice for Sale* (Civil Liberties Organisation, 24 Mbonu Ojike Street, Alhaji Masha Road, Surulere, Lagos, 1996)

## NORWAY

It was reported on 18 July that a Norwegian soldier who protested against China's human rights record during a state visit by Jiang Zemin was sentenced to 18 days' detention. **Sten Tetlie**, of the King's Guard Band, disobeyed an order to play in the band during the visit at the end of June. (*Times, Independent*)

## PAKISTAN

Criminal charges of public mischief, cheating and forgery were registered against **MH Khan**, a correspondent for *Dawn*, after the paper's 24 July issue published a photograph showing prisoners in fetters. (Pakistan Press Foundation)

The government lifted the ban on the use of portable phones in Karachi on 14 August. The ban was imposed in July 1995 as a measure to inhibit the Mohajir Qaumi Movement (MQM). (*Financial Times*)

## PALESTINE (AUTONOMOUS AREAS)

The authorities were accused of removing copies of the weekly *Sawt al-Haqq wa al-Hurriyah* from news-stands in Nablus and Ramallah on 16 August. The weekly is a mouthpiece for the Israeli Islamic Movement and had recently published an article comparing living standards among the wealthy in Gaza and the residents of the city's Shati refugee camp. (Reuter)

Two books by the Palestinian academic **Edward Said** — *Gaza-Jericho: An American Peace* and *Oslo 2: Peace Without Land* — were banned by the Palestinian Authority in late August. Said, a professor at Columbia University, New York, is highly critical of the Oslo peace accords and of President Arafat's administration. The books were subsequently confiscated by police from bookshops and distributors. Copies ordered from Jordan by a Nablus bookshop were impounded by the Ministry of Information and Culture and the bookshop's owner, **Daoud Makkawi**, warned not to sell the two titles. Makkawi reports that books by other authors, including the British-Syrian writer **Patrick Seale**, are similarly restricted and that security officials regularly visit the shop to check that banned literature is not on sale. (PEN, Reuter)

## PERU

On 1 August President Fujimori introduced a bill in Congress to create an ad hoc commission to review cases of people unjustly convicted of terrorism and treason. It has yet to be decided whether the commission, which would operate for a period of six months with the possibility of a one-off extension, will review the cases, pardon the convicts or apply a general amnesty. Human rights organisations have come forward with a list of 1,490 cases of unjust convictions that they have monitored in recent years. (Instituto Prensa y Sociedad)

In spite of repeated promises the president of the Supreme Court, Marcus Ibazeta, has still not transferred the case files of journalist **Jesús Alfonso Castiglione Mendoza** to the state prosecutor (*Index* 1/1996, 3/1996) in order to review the verdict. At the end of May, Ibazeta had stated that the process would take no more than three weeks. Moreover, it is estimated that once the case files are transferred, they could be held up for another eight months before the Supreme Court is able to render a verdict. Castiglione has been in detention since 29 April 1993 for allegedly being a member of the Shining Path. (Instituto Prensa y Sociedad, RSF)

Recent publications: *Terrorism, Torture and Human Rights* (Parliamentary Human Rights

Group, 1996, 26pp); *UN Experts Condemn Amnesty Laws* (AI, August 1996, 18pp)

## POLAND

The internal affairs minister, Zbigniew Siemaskiewicz, alleged on 18 July that employees of the post office and the state telecommunications company are regularly used in covert surveillance operations, monitoring private correspondence and phone conversations. The board of Polish Telecommunications, however, has denied the claim. In August the ombudsman, Adam Zielinski, warned that the use of phone taps is not sufficiently open to public scrutiny. He called for the establishment of an independent body to monitor the practice. (SWB)

On 24 July the government approved publication of previously classified documents concerning allegations about ex-prime minister Jozef Oleksey's collaboration with the KGB (*Index* 2/1996). The investigation into Oleksey's activities was wound up in April and a parliamentary enquiry into the conduct of the Oleksey investigation is ongoing. (SWB)

**Jerzy Slavomir Mac**, a journalist with the weekly *Wprost*, disappeared on 27 August after leaving the paper's Warsaw office. Mac is well known both for his investigations into organised crime and for raising the allegations against Jozef Oleksey. He has received several threats this year demanding that he cease his investigative work. (RSF)

## ROMANIA

On 11 July editor **Radu Mazare** and journalist **Constantin Cumpana** of the Constanta daily *Telegraf* were sentenced to seven months in prison for libel. The charges related to their reports in 1992 of corruption in Constanta city council. They were also ordered to pay US$8,200 in damages and banned from working as journalists for one year. On 15 July the attorney-general deferred the custodial sentences until 30 August. (IFJ, OMRI)

The government withdrew permission for Bucharest's main soccer stadium to be used for a three-day Jehovah's Witness convention, expected to attract 40,000 people, on 12 July. The decision was made after repeated objections from Patriarch Teoctist of the Romanian Orthodox Church who accuses the sect of heresy. The organisers instead held the event in the Hungarian capital, Budapest. (*Independent*)

On 7 August a group of employees at the Information and Synthesis Centre of the RADOR news agency, part of the Romanian Radio Company, issued a letter of protest at the dismissal of their editor-in-chief **Mihai Andrei**, and his replacement by a former Communist Party Central Committee activist. The Centre, which was set up by Andrei six years ago, monitors Romanian broadcasts and Romanian-language foreign broadcasts and supplies information to government, NGOs, political parties and news agencies. (OMRI)

# ALINA VITUKHNOVSKAYA

## Assault on the truth

*'Employees and agents of the Federal Security Service! Surely it would have been better to kill me off once and for all, rather than allow this poorly fabricated case to continue.'*

I prepared these lines when I was in prison[*], intending to deliver them in court but, in the 15 sittings that took place, I was given no opportunity to speak. The judge spoke, so did the procurator, and a security service colonel. The public were incredulous, surprised and helpless. The statements made by the prosecution were so incoherent, unlikely or absurd that I felt a kind of pity for these people making such sad spectacles of themselves. It was obvious that no manipulation of the 'evidence' would help them achieve their goal. The case began to disintegrate at the first court sitting, and soon crumbled into dust. Sensible people would have cast it to the winds long ago. But where *their* power is at stake, there is no room for sense: brute force and unlimited ambition prevail.

On 4 July I arranged over the phone to meet a friend (my telephone is still regularly tapped). I left our block and set off towards the metro station. My route lay across Flotskaya St which was fairly deserted, as usual. The surrounding area was also quiet. I stepped off the kerb and saw a car coming towards me on the other side of the road. It was still some distance away but I decided to let it pass. When it was almost level with me, it turned sharply in my direction, crossing the road on to the side of oncoming traffic, and knocked me down. It then drove back, picked up speed and hit me again.

I was unconscious for about four hours. I awoke in hospital, my legs bleeding. My wounds had not even been bandaged, but the strangest thing was that the doctor who saw me flatly refused to acknowledge that I was suffering from concussion — something the doctors at the Writers' Union hospital later confirmed. They forbade me to move and prescribed complete rest, which didn't prevent the investigator from summoning me for interrogation four hours after the attack. My lawyer went in my place. The investigator threatened to despatch me to prison for my absence.

The driver made no attempt to escape. He had nothing to fear; he was under the

---

**RUSSIAN FEDERATION**

*Russia:* Sergei Fedotov, the soldier accused of killing journalist **Natalia Aliakina** (*Index* 5/1995), was sentenced to two years in prison for 'involuntary manslaughter through negligent use of firearms' by a military court on 16 July. (CPJ)

Poet and journalist **Alina Vitukhnovskaya** (*Index* 6/1995) was injured by a car which deliberately ran her down on a Moscow street on 4 July. (OMRI)

On 29 July **Valery Yerofeyev**, an editor with weekly *Vremya-Iks* (Time-X)

in Samara, was given a 10-month sentence on charges of 'pandering and pornography' in connection with a series of articles on prostitution in the Samara district. Since he has spent 10 months in pre-trial detention, however, he was immediately released. (Globus Press Syndicate) fond protection of the State Traffic Inspectorate (GAI), whose employees refused to give us details of his identity, saying only that he was 'a very good man' and that his 'Volvo' belonged to 'a very respectable organisation'. At first, the GAI representative who interrogated me was very anxious and tried to persuade me not to mention some of the details of what had happened, particularly the fact that arrangements for meeting my friend had been made over the phone. But after a while, having presumably received the approval of higher authority, he refused — unlawfully and with the utmost cynicism — to open a criminal investigation into the attack on me. He suggested instead that I had thrown myself under the car (which, as it turned out, was not a Volvo but a Jeep).

Yet even the most superficial analysis, surely, points to the fault of the driver. Apparently, this 'very good man' from a 'very respectable organisation' is, by definition, not guilty.

With regard to accusations against *me* things are very different. I am guilty only because a 'very respectable organisation' wants to see me so. There are indications once again that my case, supported by evidence forced out of people in prison in exchange for promises of freedom, and heard by a court fearful of taking the responsibility for acquitting me, will be brought to court for a further investigation, following one which has already taken 10 months.

Apparently, the 7th department of the State Directorate for Internal Affairs (where the case is being examined) is of the opinion that it should be closed. There is nothing more to be investigated. But somebody will have to be answerable for the year I spent in prison. This 'somebody' is not a mere policeman but a colonel of the Federal Foreign Intelligence Service. And not only him. Dozens of well-placed figures are caught up in this vile fabrication. People like these are not answerable for anything.

It is clear that in taking the case to court again they cannot avoid further humiliation and failure — if the court is independent and honest. But in this instance, the court merely sings along to those who call the tune. And I have little cause to believe in any kind of justice.

*Alina Vitukhnovskaya was arrested in October 1994 and a held for a year without trial on dubious drugs charges. The case continues*

*Translated by Irena Maryniak*

The chairman of the government's commission for environmental safety, **Aleksey Yablokov**, resigned on 1 August, claiming that attempts are being made to restrict openness on environmental matters in Russia. On 23 August the trial of **Aleksandr Nikitin** (*Index* 3/1996), accused of passing classified information to the Norwegian environmental group Bellona, was postponed again until 6 October. (SWB)

*Chechnya:* **Ramzan Khadzhiev**, the chief of the Northern Caucasus bureau for the Russian state broadcaster ORT, was killed at a military checkpoint by fire from two Russian armoured personnel carriers on 13 August. His death brings the total number of journalists killed in the practice of their profession in Chechnya to 10. (CPJ)

Vehicles clearly marked as

press vehicles and being used by correspondents from **Cable News Network** (CNN) and **Worldwide Television News** (WTN) were fired on by Russian helicopters in separate incidents on 8 August. One of the vehicles was narrowly missed by a rocket-propelled grenade. (CPJ)

### RWANDA

**Amiel Nkuliza**, director of *Intego* and editor of *Le Partisan*, was released on 13 August after spending a week in detention. He was allegedly beaten when he was detained on 6 August and again as he was leaving custody. While in custody he was interrogated about his work and warned that his life would be at risk if he wrote any more 'subversive' articles. He has been ordered to report to the authorities once a week. *Intego* journalist **Appolos Hakizimana**, who was arrested on 30 July on suspicion of being an *interahamwe*, was released on 19 August. Meanwhile *Intego*'s editor, **Isaie Niyoyita**, is in hiding and is sought by the authorities, and the paper has been banned until further notice. (AI, RSF, CPJ)

Recent publication: *Alarming Resurgence of Killings* (AI, August 1996, 17pp)

### SERBIA-MONTENEGRO

*Serbia:* Democratic Party leader **Zoran Djindjic** went on trial for defamation on 2 July, in connection with a January 1995 advertisement published in *Nedeljni Telegraf*, accusing Serbian prime minis-

ter Mirko Marjanovic of fraud. The paper's editor, **Dragoljub Belic**, is also standing trial. (OMRI)

*Montenegro:* On 14 July freelance journalist **Slobodan Rackovic** was taken to a police station in Petrovac and held without charge for 'informative talks' while his house was searched. Rackovic had recently reported on arrests of Bosnian refugees in Montenegro and their subsequent extradition to Republika Srpska, in which the Montenegro public prosecutor, Vladimir Susovic, is alleged to have been involved. Rackovic called on those responsible to be removed from office. (IFJ)

*Kosovo:* On 1 July Kosovo writer **Agim Vinca** was jailed for 15 days for having a three-year-old Albanian stamp in his passport. Before this year Kosovo Albanians were prohibited from travelling to Albania. (SWB, OMRI)

**Agim Muhaxheri**, a reporter with *Rilindja*, was detained by police and interrogated about his work on 1 August. Another *Rilindja* journalist, **Ibrahim Kelmenid**, was assaulted and questioned by police near Peja on 2 August. He required treatment as a result of his injuries. (IFJ)

It was reported on 7 August that **Enver Grajcevi** (*Index* 4/1996) has been released and his case referred to the Pristina district prosecutor for a decision on whether to indict. He could face charges of 'calling for violent change in the constitutional order' under Article

133 of the Criminal Code of Yugoslavia. (AI)

On 10 August **Sali Temaj** was sentenced to 10 days in prison for quarrelling with a Serbian neighbour. (Kosova Information Centre)

### SIERRA LEONE

On 19 July the editor of the *Point*, **Edison Yongai**, was arrested at his office and detained without charge until 23 July, when he was charged with sedition and libel. He was released on bail the following day and then rearrested on 8 August without additional charge after the High Court set bail at a higher level. The charges against Yongai stem from a front-page story published on 18 July entitled 'Corrupt Ministers'. (CPJ)

Police searched the offices of the daily *Expo Times* on 28 August and arrested the paper's editor, **Ibrahim Seaga Shaw**, and news editor, **Gibril Kroma**. The police were searching for documents relating to an article which said that the rebel Revolutionary United Front had decided to end the ceasefire. (CPJ)

### SINGAPORE

On 11 July the Singapore Broadcasting Authority announced a new Class Licensing Scheme to cover Internet content. The new rules, which took effect on 15 July, ban material which threatens public order and national security, satirises religious or racial groups and incites racial or religious hatred, or encourages permissiveness. Internet service and content providers are required to remove websites which contravene the guidelines and organisations that break the rules could have their licence revoked and a fine imposed. They have until 14 September to develop the technical facilities to block out blacklisted sites. The scheme was put into practice in late July when the SBA requested the removal of a posting on the Newsnet newsgroup defaming lawyers at a local law firm. (*Business Times*, *Straits Times*, HRW)

On 26 July the government rejected an application from the opposition **Singapore Democratic Party** (SDP) for a licence to sell a party political video in preparation for the general elections at the end of the year. The SDP have accused the government of abusing the powers of the Film Act and making its decision without viewing the tape. (Reuter, *Straits Times*)

## SLOVAKIA

**Jan Smolec**, an MP for the Movement for a Democratic Slovakia, resigned as editor-in-chief of the pro-government paper *Slovenska Republika* on 27 July. He has 20 prosecutions pending against him, brought by associates of President Kovac. Smolec is a supporter of the prime minister, Vladimir Meciar. (SWB)

## SOUTH AFRICA

Proceedings began in a defamation case brought by businessman Robert Hall against the investigative journal *NoseWEEK* on 5 August.

Hall is suing for US$116,000 over an article published in April 1994, which alleged that he had had illegal financial dealings with the country's reserve bank. *NoseWEEK*'s publisher and editor-in-chief, Martin Welz, has complained that the court has put the burden of proof on him to establish his innocence, accusing the judiciary of 'still having an apartheid mentality' where journalists are concerned. (Freedom of Expression Institute, CCPJ, MISA)

**Moegsien Williams**, editor of the *Cape Times*, **Shaun Johnson**, editor of the *Argus*, **Ebbe Dommisse**, editor of *Die Burger*, and several reporters with the **South African Broadcasting Corporation** and **Associated Press** were ordered to appear in court on 22 August. All had refused police demands that they hand over footage or photographs of the public murder by vigilantes of a notorious gang leader. (CPJ)

The Film and Television Bill was passed by Parliament on 29 August, finally repealing the apartheid-era censorship laws. Bans on child pornography and hate speech, however, are retained. Free speech groups have criticised the fact that the draft law was not published before the vote, and say that is ill-defined and overbroad in its restrictions. The Bill must now be passed by the Senate to become law. (Reuter, Freedom of Expression Institute)

## SOUTH KOREA

**Cho Song-u**, chief policy officer of the National Conference for Independence, Peace and Unification, was arrested on 31 July and charged with engineering an unauthorised South-North contact which took place in Warsaw between 18 and 20 June. Cho is accused of planning the meeting and sending Yi Song-hwan, vice-chairman of the Association of Korean Youth Associations, to Poland as a delegate. (SWB)

Novelist **Kim Ha-ki** was arrested on his return to Seoul on 19 August and charged with violating National Security Law. Kim, who crossed into North Korea from China on 31 July, was detained by authorities in the North for two weeks before being returned to China on 15 August for questioning. Seoul authorities have accused Kim of entering the North on purpose and 'actively co-operating with the North', claiming that during his detention he read a seven-volume memoir of Kim Il-sung, commenting upon it favourably, and that prior to his return to China he visited the birthplace of Kim Chong-suk, mother of Kim Chong-il. (SWB, Reuter)

Riot police ended a seven-day student occupation of Seoul's Yonsei University when they stormed the campus on 20 August, having arrested some 5,500 protesters during the course of week-long raids. The students had gathered to celebrate the outlawed Sixth Unification Festival (marking the 51st anniversary of the division of the peninsula) and to call for reunification with the North. Prosecutors are currently investigating the legal status of Hanchongyon, the umbrella organisation of student councils believed to be behind the Yonsei occupation. (SWB, Reuter, *Guardian*)

## SPAIN

Fernando Alonso and Antonio Murga, two journalists with the Basque separatist paper *Egin* (*Index* 4/1996), were arrested for terrorist activities during the weekend beginning 17 August. It was alleged that Alonso left explosives and weapons in his flat and a list of ETA targets on his desk at work. A government spokesman rejected calls for *Egin* to be closed down: 'The killers are not words, but the pistols these journalists had at home,' he said. (*Guardian*)

## SUDAN

On 13 July the Press and Publications Council ordered the closure of the **Dar al-Ahila** publishing house which publishes *al-Rai al-Akhar* and the tri-weekly *al-Majalis*. The publications are accused of disseminating 'false information and incitement to belittle the country's cultural policy' in connection with reports on an increase in the price of flour and statements attributed to the chairman of the Federation of Trade Unions. (RSF)

## SYRIA

Eight journalists remain in long-term detention: **Faysal Allush, Anwar Bader, Faraj Beraqdar, Ismail al-Hadjje, Samir al-Hassan, Salama George Kila, Jadi Nawfal**

and **Nizar Nayyuf**. Journalist **Rida Haddad**, who was arrested in 1980 and held for 14 years without charge, died from cancer in June, following his release from prison in October 1995. (HRW, RSF, Moroccan Organisation for Human Rights)

## TAIWAN

The Ministry of Finance agreed on 15 July to lift a ban on advertising alcohol in newspapers. Six weeks earlier a similar ban was reversed for advertisements on radio and television. (*Advertising Age*)

On 13 August the Mainland Affairs Council (MAC) announced a three-stage plan designed to promote journalistic exchange between Taiwan and China. For the first time, mainland media will be allowed to send correspondents to Taiwan on a long-term basis, and local media permitted to set up branches in China. Joint newspaper distribution will be the final stage of the plan to be implemented. (*Taiwan Business News*)

## TAJIKISTAN

**Davlat Khudonazarov**, the popular Tajik film director and former opposition leader, was detained for nine hours in Moscow on 25 July. Khudonazarov was apparently detained because his name had not been removed from a computer 'wanted' list after he fled to Russia in 1992 and was branded a traitor for his opposition to the Tajik government. He was released only after the Tajik government sent a fax to Moscow confirm-

ing that he is no longer wanted in Tajikistan. (Reuter)

On 22 August two men were found guilty of the murder in 1995 of local newspaper editor **Zayniddin Muhiddinov**. Over 40 journalists have been killed since the current regime came to power in 1992. This is the first successful prosecution. (SWB)

## TIBET

Broadcasts by the new exile radio station, **Voice of Tibet**, on shortwave from the Seychelles, have been jammed. The broadcasts were first jammed in late June by white noise emanating from Chinese transmitters. Further disturbances were noted in July when China's English-language domestic music service, Easy FM, obliterated the Tibetan programme. (SWB, Reuter)

Two monks from Sera monastery, just outside Lhasa, were detained in mid-July for distributing political leaflets. Since their detention, steps have reportedly been taken to impose further control over shops offering photocopying facilities in the capital. (Tibet Information Network)

Tibet's three main monasteries have been the target of recent efforts to purge dissident monks. Work teams of up to 150 people arrived in Drepung in early August, Sera on 9 June, and Ganden in early May to begin the registration and re-education operation. Monks are required to sign pledges of political compliance denouncing the Dalai

Lama, accepting China's choice of Panchen Lama (*Index* 1/1996), and opposing separatism; in Drepung they have also been made to promise not to listen to Tibetan-language broadcasts on Voice of America radio. Re-education sessions are held first in groups and resistant monks are then given solo sessions. Those who fail to comply face expulsion from their monastery. New regulations have also been announced limiting membership of monasteries to local residents, which is expected to lead to the expulsion of scores of monks from outside the Tibet Autonomous Region. (Tibet Information Network)

## TONGA

**Mike Field**, Pacific Islands correspondent for Agence-France Presse, was refused entry into the Kingdom of Tonga for the Pacific Island News Association convention on 6-9 August. Since 1993 Field, who has written on Tonga's pro-democracy movement and the sale of Tongan passports, has needed a visa to enter the country, even though the island normally allows journalists freedom of access. (CCPJ, SWB)

## TUNISIA

**Khemais Chammari** (*Index* 4/1996) was sentenced to five years' imprisonment on 17 July after being found guilty of 'disclosing a national secret to a foreign power', a reference to information about the trial of Mohamed Mouadda, president of the Social Democratic Movement (MDS). (AI)

## TURKEY

On 15 July police officers beat five photographers and reporters who were covering a protest against police brutality in Istanbul. Eyewitnesses said the police intentionally targeted the journalists, beating them and breaking their cameras. Several reporters took shelter at the Turkish Journalists' Association but were followed by police officers, who forced their way into the office. (CPJ)

**MED TV**, the world's first Kurdish-language satellite television station, started broadcasting again on 16 August, six weeks after being forced off the air. The London-based station lost its place on Europe's Eutelsat on 2 July, after intensive lobbying by Ankara, but has since gained space on the US-owned Intelsat. Turkey's foreign minister, Tansu Çiller, warned on 19 August that 'the necessary steps will be taken' to shut MED TV down. (*Guardian*, Reuter, SWB)

Writer and human rights activist **Erol Anar** went on trial on a charge of 'separatist propaganda' on 22 August in connection with his four-page chapter in the book *Kurt Sorunu* (The Kurdish Question). (HRW)

## UKRAINE

The Hungarian community was refused permission to erect a monument and hold a religious service in the Verecke pass in August. The monument and service were intended to mark the 1,100th anniversary of the crossing of Hungarian tribes through the Verecke pass into the Carpathian basin in the year 896. The Smallholders' Party say the ban is symptomatic of a general deterioration in the situation of ethnic Hungarians in Ukraine. (SWB)

## UNITED KINGDOM

On 9 July the Advertising Standards Authority criticised the oil company Shell for advertisements, appearing after Ken Saro-Wiwa's execution, which tried to justify the company's position after it was attacked for failing to intervene with the Nigerian government on his behalf. The company was reprimanded for using quotes from Saro-Wiwa's daughter out of context and for failing to substantiate claims of Ogoni sabotage to its pipelines. Shell is considering an appeal. (*Guardian*)

In a report published on 23 July, the Institute for Jewish Policy Research called for the Internet to be subject to the same legal controls as book publishing. It wants companies that sell access to the Internet to be treated as the publishers of the material accessed through their services, instead of on a par with telephone companies. The report says: 'The Internet has provided a relatively regulation-free environment for the publication of racist material and the organisation of the activities of neo-Nazi and other far-right organisations.' (*Independent*)

The University of Birmingham suspended a member of staff on 15 July after the manufacturers of the fabric lycra complained that university computer equipment was being used to place pages called 'Gay Lovers of Lycra' on the Internet. Lycra is made in Northern Ireland by the American corporation Dupont, which said the company was acting to protect its trademark. (*Guardian*)

Following a meeting at the beginning of August with the Internet Service Providers Association, the Metropolitan Police launched a campaign, with the backing of the Home Office, to rid the Internet of pornographic material. The police have written to Internet Service Providers (ISPs) in the UK, presenting them with a list of around 130 Usenet newsgroups that they say should be censored. The police say that ISPs must take action to clean up the Internet, or they will intervene under the Obscene Publications Act. (Newsbytes News Network, *Independent*)

The government won a court injunction barring distribution of a video showing close-up footage of surgery on 25 August. The 53-minute video, *Everyday Operations*, was due for release on 26 August. The government says that the video could breach patients' right to confidentiality, but EduVision, the company which made the video, says that it sought permission from the patients involved. (Reuter)

On 16 July the International Commission of Jurists said that the administration of the death penalty in the USA was 'arbitrary and racially discriminatory'. The Commission, which is made up of legal experts from around the world, stated that the US system of capital punishment was deeply flawed and was in violation of international human rights and anti-discrimination treaties. (*International Herald Tribune*)

CIA director John Deutch said on 17 July that he 'would not rule out' using journalists for intelligence-gathering in cases where American lives were threatened. This is a reversal of a policy held since 1977 and has been roundly condemned by press advocates. (*Guardian*, World Press Freedom Committee)

Internet Service Provider America Online reversed its English-only policy in July after complaints from users and accusations of discrimination. (*Media Daily*)

On 31 July the government said that it will appeal to the US Supreme Court against the 12 June decision ruling the online decency provisions of the Telecommunications Act unconstitutional (*Index* 4/1996). (Reuter)

Princeton University officials advised students and staff in August that its computer network must not be used for 'political purposes...especially in this year of a presidential election'. The university's not-for-profit status bars it from engaging in political activities, but this does not govern the behaviour of staff and students. (Newsbytes News Network)

The Federal Communications Commission voted unanimously on 8 August to ratify new children's television regulations that would ensure that broadcasters air at least three hours of educational programming each week, despite industry claims that it could lead to future incursions against broadcasters' free speech. (Reuter)

President Clinton announced strict rules to control tobacco sales and advertising on 23 August in an attempt to cut under-age smoking. The measures include requiring proof of age to buy cigarettes, restricting vending machines, and banning cigarette merchandising and advertising near schools. The Freedom to Advertise Coalition said on 21 August that it will challenge the regulations in court. (PR Newswire, Reuter)

On 23 August the judge in the OJ Simpson civil trial, Hiroshi Fujitsaki, ordered a complete ban on television and radio coverage, saying he did not want a repeat of the 'circus atmosphere' that surrounded Simpson's criminal trial. He also left in place the gag order preventing lawyers, witnesses or anyone else connected to the case from talking about it in public. (Reuter)

Recent publication: *Modern Capital of Human Rights? Abuses in the State of Georgia* (HRW, July 1996, 214pp)

Opposition leader Willy Jimmy complained in mid-July that the government is routinely censoring news on the state-owned **Radio Vanuatu**. Press releases and advertisements from the opposition have also been banned, he reported. (SWB)

## VIETNAM

On 24 July the Interior Ministry's Investigation Department confirmed its decision to prosecute the daily *Hanoi Moi* (New Hanoi), and the weekly *Tien Phong* (Pioneer) and *Kinh Doanh Van Phap Luat* (Business and Law). All three papers are published by the Communist Party or state organisations and have been charged with disclosing state secrets in articles about the aviation and oil industries published earlier this year. (RSF, Reuter)

## YEMEN

On 11 July **Arafat Mudabish**, a journalist with the opposition weekly *al-Thawri*, was assaulted and threatened by parliamentary guards. He was subsequently detained by security forces but released six days later. (IFJ, RSF)

The opposition weekly *al-Tagammu* resumed publication in late July after the state-owned 14 October Printing Press agreed to continue printing it. The paper was effectively banned on 17 June after it tried to run an article about clashes between citizens and the security forces in the city of Mukalla (*Index* 4/1996). The paper's editors refused a government request for changes to the article, after which the press refused to print it. (IFJ)

## ZAMBIA

On 11 July armed police searched the home of **Brian Malama**, a reporter with the *Post*. The police refused to identify themselves or say what they were looking for. The paper's managing editor, Bright Mwape, described the raid as 'part of the ongoing victimisation of the *Post* and its journalists'. (MISA)

**Samson Mujuda**, a photo-journalist with the *Post*, was assaulted and had his camera broken by plainclothed police on 14 July. The attack took place during the Bastille Day celebrations at the French ambassador's residence after Mujuda photographed a man who had collapsed. The man was later identified as a friend of the police officer who carried out the assault. (MISA)

*Post* editors **Fred M'membe, Bright Mwape** and **Masautso Phiri** appeared in court in Lusaka on 14 August and pleaded not guilty to charges of 'receiving and possessing classified information' (*Index* 2/1996). The trial is due to begin on 18 October. (MISA, *Southern Africa Report*)

## ZIMBABWE

For the second year running the Zimbabwe International Book Fair (ZIBF) has been the focus of a freedom of speech furore, as the government again attempted to prevent the **Gays and Lesbians of Zimbabwe** (GALZ) from having a stall at the fair (*Index* 5/1995). GALZ fought the banning order in the High Court which on 31 July upheld their claim that the order was invalid. The stall was set up in time for the Fair's public opening on 1 August. The High Court ruling drew condemnation from the University of Zimbabwe's Student Representative Council (SRC), which threatened gays and lesbians with 'public genocide' in the *Herald* newspaper. On the evening of 3 August the GALZ stand at the Fair was ransacked by students from the right-wing student association Sangano Monomatapa. Literature was destroyed but no-one was hurt. (CPJ, Norwegian Forum for Free Expression)

Authorities reportedly ordered state-run media to place a total news blackout on the civil service strike, which began on 21 August. A memo sent to the offices of the **Zimbabwe Broadcasting Corporation** and the **Zimpapers Group** prohibited journalists from reporting anything other than official statements. (MISA)

General publications: *The Draft Optional Protocol to the Convention Against Torture* (AI, July 1996, 25pp); *Abolition of the Death Penalty Worldwide* (AI, July 1996, 18pp); *Writers in Prison Committee Case List, January-June 1996* (PEN, August 1996, 116pp)

*Compiled by: Anna Feldman, Kate Thal (Africa); Kate Cooper, Dagmar Schlüter, James Solomon (Americas); Nicholas McAulay, Mansoor Mirza, Sarah Smith (Asia); Laura Bruni, Robin Jones, Vera Rich (eastern Europe and CIS); Michaela Becker, Philippa Nugent (Middle East); Ian Franklin (western Europe)*

*Satorovici, Bosnia 1992: Muslim women in Serb-held territory*

# Wounded nations, broken lives

Can peoples divided by civil war, torn apart by hatred and mutually inflicted atrocities, made sick by terror and oppression, heal themselves? Can nations, like individuals, be reconciled to their past and cured of their ills by working through traumatic events: by telling and hearing the truth? Whose truth? And what part does justice or the desire for revenge play in the process? *Index* questions the different routes — Truth Commissions, War Crimes Tribunals — countries take in the quest for reconciliation. And asks, can nations cleanse the past and start again? More important, perhaps, can they ensure 'Never again'?

# MICHAEL IGNATIEFF

# Articles of faith

WHAT does it mean for a nation to come to terms with its past? Do nations, like individuals, have psyches? Can a nation's past make a people ill as we know repressed memories sometimes make individuals ill? Conversely, can a nation or contending parts of it be reconciled to their past, as individuals can, by replacing myth with fact and lies with truth? Can we speak of nations 'working through' a civil war or an atrocity as we speak of individuals working through a traumatic memory or event?

These are mysterious questions and they are not made any easier to answer by the ways our metaphors lead us on. We do vest our nations with consciences, identities and memories as if they were individuals. But if it is problematic to vest an individual with a single identity, it is even more so in the case of a nation.

These are mysterious questions, but they are urgent and practical ones too. The War Crimes Tribunal in The Hague is collecting evidence about atrocities in the former Yugoslavia. It is doing so not simply because such crimes against humanity must be punished — otherwise international humanitarian law means nothing — but also because establishing the truth about such crimes through the judicial process is held to be crucial to the eventual reconciliation of the people of the Balkans. In the African city of Arusha, a similar tribunal is collecting evidence about the genocide in Rwanda, believing likewise that truth, justice and reconciliation are indissolubly linked in the rebuilding of shattered societies. In both these instances — Yugoslavia and Rwanda — the rhetoric is noble but the rationale unclear. Justice in itself is not a problematic objective, but whether the attainment of justice always contributes to reconciliation is anything but evident. Truth, too, is a good thing; but as the African proverb reminds us, 'truth is not always good to say'.

In South Africa, Archbishop Tutu's Truth Commission is collecting testimony from the victims and perpetrators of apartheid. In Tutu's own words, the aim is 'the promotion of national unity and reconciliation'...'the healing of a traumatised, divided, wounded, polarised people'. Laudable aims but are they coherent? Look at the assumptions he makes: that a nation has one psyche, not many; that the truth is one, not many; that the truth is certain, not contestable; and that when it is known by all, it has the capacity to heal and reconcile. These are not so much assumptions of epistemology as articles of faith about human nature: the truth is one and if we know it, it will make us free.

Such articles of faith inspired the truth commissions in Chile, Argentina, Brazil that sought to find out what had happened to the thousands of innocent people killed or tortured by the military juntas during the 1960s and 1970s. All these commissions believed that if the truth were known, a people made sick by terror and lies would be made well again. In all cases, the results were ambiguous. First, as Pilate said when washing his hands, what is truth? One should distinguish between factual truth and moral truth, between narratives that tell what happened and narratives that attempt to explain why things happened and who is responsible. The truth commissions had more success in establishing the first than in promoting the second. They did succeed in establishing the facts about the disappearance, torture and death of thousands of persons and this allowed relatives and friends the consolation of knowing how the disappeared had met their fate. It says much for the human need for truth that the relatives of victims preferred the facts to the false consolations of ignorance. It also says a great deal for the moral appeal of magnanimity that so many of them should have preferred the truth to vengeance or even justice. It was sufficient for most of them to know what happened: they did not need to punish the transgressors in order to put the past behind them.

> The function of truth commissions, like the function of honest historians, is simply to purify the argument, to narrow the range of permissible lies

The truth commissions closed many individual dossiers in the painful histories of their nation's past. At this molecular, individual level, they did a power of good. But they were also charged with the production of public truth and the re-making of public discourse. They were told to generate a moral narrative — explaining the genesis of evil regimes and apportioning moral responsibility for their deeds.

The military, security and police establishments were prepared to let the truth come out about individual cases of disappearance. But they fought tenaciously against prosecutions of their own people and against shouldering responsibility for their crimes. To have conceded responsibility would have weakened their legitimacy as institutions. Such was the resistance of the military in Argentina and Chile that the elected governments which had created the commissions had to choose between justice and their own survival: between prosecuting the criminals and risking a military coup, or letting them go and allowing a democratic succession to consolidate itself.

The record of the truth commissions in Latin America has disillusioned many of those who believed that shared truth was a precondition of social reconciliation. The military and police apparatus survived the inquisition with their legitimacy undermined but their power intact. The societies in question used the truth commissions to indulge in the illusion that they had put the past behind them. The truth commissions allowed exactly the kind of false reconciliation with the past they had been expressly created to forestall.

The German writer and thinker Theodor Adorno observed this false reconciliation at work in his native Germany after the war:

'"Coming to terms with the past" does not imply a serious working through of the past, the breaking of its spell through an act of clear consciousness. It suggests, rather, wishing to turn the page and, if possible, wiping it from memory. The attitude that it would be proper for everything to be forgiven and forgotten by those who were wronged is expressed by the party that committed the injustice.'

The dangers of this false reconciliation are real enough but it is possible that disillusion with the truth commissions of Latin America goes too far. It was never in their mandate to transform the military and security apparatus any more than it is in Archbishop Tutu's power to do the same in South Africa. Truth is truth; it is not social nor institutional reform.

Nor is it realistic to expect that when truth is proclaimed by an official commission it is likely to be accepted by those against whom it is directed. The police and military have their truth — and its continuing hold consists precisely in the fact that it is not a tissue of lies. It is unreasonable to expect those who believed they were putting down a terrorist or insurgent threat to disown this idea simply because a truth commission exposes this threat as having been without foundation. People, especially people in uniform, do not easily or readily surrender the premises upon which their lives are based. Repentance, if it ever occurs, is an individual matter. It is too much to expect an institutional order to engage in collective repentance. All that a truth commission can achieve is to reduce the number of lies that can be circulated unchallenged in public discourse. In Argentina, its work has made it impossible to claim, for example, that the military did not throw half-dead victims into the sea from helicopters. In Chile, it is no longer permissible to assert in public that the Pinochet regime did not dispatch thousands of entirely innocent people. Truth commissions can and do change the frame of public discourse and public memory. But they cannot be judged a failure because they fail to change behaviour and institutions. That is not their function.

A truth commission cannot overcome a society's divisions. It can only winnow out the solid core of facts upon which society's arguments with itself should be conducted. But it cannot bring these arguments to a conclusion. Critics of truth commissions argue as if the past were a sacred text which has been stolen and vandalised by evil men and which can be recovered and returned to a well-lit glass case in some grand public rotunda like the US Constitution or the Bill of Rights. But the past has none of the fixed and stable identity of a document. The past is an argument and the function of truth commissions, like the function of honest historians, is simply to purify the argument, to narrow the range of permissible lies.

Truth commissions have the greatest chance of success in societies that have already created a powerful political consensus behind reconciliation, such as in South Africa. In such a context, Tutu's commission has the chance to create a virtuous upward spiral between the disclosure of painful truth and the consolidation of the political consensus that created his commission in the first place.

IN PLACES like Yugoslavia where the parties have murdered and tortured each other for years, the prospects for truth, reconciliation and justice are much bleaker. These contexts, however bleak, are instructive because they illustrate everything that is problematic in the relation between truth and reconciliation.

The idea that reconciliation depends on shared truth presumes that shared truth about the past is possible. But truth is related to identity. What you believe to be true depends, in some measure, on who you believe yourself to be. And who you believe yourself to be is mostly defined in terms of who you are not. To be a Serb is first and foremost not to be a Croat or a Muslim. If a Serb is someone who believes Croats have a historical tendency towards fascism and a Croat is someone who believes Serbs have a penchant for genocide, then to discard these myths is to give up a defining element of their own identities.

Obviously, identity is composed of much more than negative images of the other. Many Croats and Serbs opposed these negative stereotypes and the nationalist madness that overtook their countries. There were many who fought to maintain a moral space between their personal and national identities. Yet even such people are now unable to conceive that one day Zagreb, Belgrade and Sarajevo might share a common version of the history of the conflict. Agreement on a shared chronology of events might be possible though even this would be contentious; but it is impossible to imagine the three sides ever agreeing on how to apportion responsibility and moral blame. The truth that matters to people is not factual nor narrative truth but moral or interpretive truth. And this will always be an object of dispute in the Balkans.

It is also an illusion to suppose that 'impartial' or 'objective' outsiders would ever succeed in getting their moral and interpretive account of the catastrophe accepted by the parties to the conflict. The very fact of being an outsider discredits rather than reinforces one's legitimacy. For there is always a truth which can only be known by those on the inside. Or if not a truth — since facts are facts — then a moral significance for these facts that only an insider can fully appreciate. The truth, if it is to be believed, must be authored by those who have suffered its consequences.

The problem of a shared truth is also that it does not lie 'in between'. It is not a compromise between two competing versions. Either the siege of Sarajevo was a deliberate attempt to terrorise and subvert a legitimately elected government of an internationally recognised state, or it was legitimate pre-emptive defence by the Serbs of their homeland from Muslim attack. It cannot be both. Outside attempts to write a version of the truth which does 'justice' to the truth held by both sides are unlikely to be credible to either.

Nor is an acknowledgement of shared suffering equivalent to shared truth. It is relatively easy for both sides to acknowledge each other's pain.

*Tuzla, Bosnia 1996: survivors commemorate the fall of Srebrenica and the death of 7,000 men*

Much more difficult, usually impossible in fact, is shared acknowledgement of who bears the lion's share of responsibility.

ATROCITY myths about the other side are an important part of the identities in question. Hill-country Serbs in the Foca region of Bosnia told British journalists in the summer of 1992 that their ethnic militias were obliged to cleanse the area of Muslims because it was a well-known fact that Muslims crucified Serbian children and floated their bodies down the river past Serbian settlements. Since such myths do not need factual corroboration in order to reproduce themselves, they are not likely to be dispelled by the patient assembly of evidence to the contrary. This particular atrocity myth used to be spread about the Jews in mediaeval times. The myth was not true about the Jews and it is not true about Muslims, but that is not the point. The point is that myth is strangely impervious to facts.

Aggressors have their own defence against truth, but so do victims. Peoples who believe themselves to be victims of aggression have an understandable incapacity to believe that they also committed atrocities. Myths of innocence and victimhood are a powerful obstacle in the way of confronting unwelcome facts.

To call them myths is not to dispute that one side may be more of a victim than the other; nor to question that atrocities do happen. What is mythic is that the atrocities are held to reveal the essential identity of the peoples in whose name they were committed. The atrocity myth implies an idea of a people having some essential genocidal propensity toward the other side. All the members of the group are held to have such a propensity even though atrocity can only be committed by specific individuals. The idea of collective guilt depends on the idea of national psyche or racial identity. The fiction at work here is akin to the nationalist delusion that the identities of individuals are or should be subsumed into their national identities.

But nations are not like individuals: they do not have a single identity, conscience or responsibility. National identity is a site of conflict and argument, not a silent shrine for collective worship. Even authoritarian populist democracies like Serbia and Croatia never speak with one voice or remember the past with a single memory.

The essential function of justice in the dialogue between truth and reconciliation is to disaggregate individual and nation; to disassemble the fiction that nations are responsible like individuals for the crimes committed in their name.

The most important function of war crimes trials is to 'individualise'

> **Peoples who believe themselves to be victims of aggression have an understandable incapacity to believe that they also committed atrocities. Myths of innocence and victimhood are a powerful obstacle in the way of confronting unwelcome facts**

guilt, to relocate it from the collectivity to the individuals responsible. As Karl Jaspers said of the Nuremberg trial in 1946, 'For us Germans this trial has the advantage that it distinguishes between the particular crimes of the leaders and that it does not condemn the Germans collectively.'

By analogy with Nuremberg, therefore, The Hague trials are not supposed to put the Serbian, Muslim or Croatian peoples in the dock but to separate the criminals from the nation and to lay the guilt where it belongs, on the shoulders of individuals. Yet trials inevitably fail to apportion all the guilt to all those responsible. Small fry pay the price for the crimes of the big fish and this reinforces the sense that justice is not definitive but arbitrary. Nor do such trials break the link between individual and nation. Nuremberg failed to do this: the rest of the world still holds the Germans responsible collectively and the Germans themselves still accept this responsibility. The most that can be said is that war crimes trials do something to unburden a people of the fiction of collective guilt, by helping them to transform guilt into shame. This appears to have happened in Germany. The German novelist Martin Walser once wrote that when a Frenchman or an American sees pictures of Auschwitz, 'he doesn't have to think: we human beings! He can think: those Germans! Can we think: those Nazis! I for one cannot...' This is to say that most West Germans accept the same version of the truth about their past; they take responsibility for it in the sense that they believe it was shameful; and to this degree, therefore, believe the past will not return.

Again, however, it is not clear that Nuremberg itself accomplished this transformation of German attitudes. As Ian Buruma has pointed out in *The Wages of Guilt,* many Germans dismissed the Nuremberg trials as nothing more than 'victor's justice'. It was not Nuremberg but the strictly German war crimes trials of the 1960s that forced Germans to confront their part in the Holocaust. Verdicts reached in a German courtroom benefited from a legitimacy the Nuremberg process never enjoyed.

Nor was coming to terms with the past confined to war crimes trials. It was an accumulation of a million school visits to concentration camps, a thousand books, the Hollywood television series *Holocaust* — a vast molecular reckoning between generations that is still going on.

The German example suggests that it is best to be modest about what war crimes trials can accomplish. The great virtue of legal proceedings is that its evidentiary rules confer legitimacy on otherwise contestable facts. In this sense, war crimes trials make it more difficult for societies to take refuge in denial; the trials do assist the process of uncovering the truth. It is more doubtful whether they assist the process of reconciliation. The purgative function of justice tends to operate on the victims' side only and not on the perpetrators. While it leaves victims feeling justice has been done, the community from which the perpetrators come may feel only that they have been made scapegoats. All one can say is that leaving war crimes unpunished is worse: it leaves the cycle of impunity unbroken and permits societies to indulge their fantasies of denial.

IT IS open to question whether justice or truth actually heals. While it is an article of faith with us that knowledge, particularly self-knowledge, is a condition of psychic health, all societies, including our own, manage to function with only the most precarious purchase on the truth of their own past. Individuals may be made ill by repression of their own past but it is less clear that what holds true for individuals must also hold true for societies. A society like Serbia, which allows well-established war criminals to hold public office and prevents them from being extradited to face international tribunals, may be a distasteful place to visit but it is not necessarily a sick society. For such societies will not see themselves as sick but as healthy, refusing the outside world's iniquitous attempt to turn their heroes into criminals. All societies have a substantial psychological investment in their heroes. To discover that their heroes were guilty of war crimes is to admit that the identities they defended were themselves tarnished. Which is why societies are often so reluctant to surrender their own to war crimes tribunals, why societies are so vehemently 'in denial' about facts evident to everyone outside the society. War crimes challenge collective moral identities, and when these identities are threatened, denial is actually a defence of everything one holds dear.

There are many forms of denial, ranging from outright refusal to accept facts as facts to complex strategies of relativisation. Here one accepts the facts but argues that the enemy was equally culpable or that the accusing party is also to blame or that such 'excesses' are regrettable necessities in time of war. To relativise is to have it both ways: to admit the facts while denying full responsibility for them.

Resistance to historical truth is a function of group identity: nations and peoples tie their sense of themselves into narcissistic narratives which strenuously resist correction. Regimes also depend for their legitimacy on historical myths which are armoured against the truth. The legitimacy of

Tito's regime in Yugoslavia depended on the myth that his partisans led a movement of national resistance against the German and Italian occupations. In reality, the partisans fought fellow Yugoslavs as much as they fought the occupiers and even made deals with the Germans if it could strengthen their hand against domestic opponents. Since this was common knowledge to any Yugoslav of that generation, the myth of brotherhood and unity required the constant reinforcement of propaganda. What is one to conclude, though, from this case? That regimes founded on historical myth are bound to crumble when the truth comes out? Or that the Titoist myth was a necessary fiction, the only lie that stood a chance of holding the separate ethnic traditions of Yugoslavia together in one state? How much truth could the immediate post-war Yugoslavia have stood before it fractured into civil war? The tragedy of Yugoslavia might not be that its ruling myth of brotherhood and unity was false to the history of the civil war in 1941-5, but that this myth was propagated by a Communist party — by one incapable of eventually ensuring a peaceful democratic transition. Democracy is a pre-condition for that free access to historical data and free debate about its meaning on which the creation of public truth depends. The Balkan War of 1991-5 was a continuation of the civil war of 1941-5. Competing versions of historical truth — Serb, Croat and Muslim — which had no peaceful, democratic means of making themselves heard in Tito's Yugoslavia took to the battlefield to make their truth prevail. The result of five years of war is that a shared truth is now inconceivable. In the conditions of ethnic separation and authoritarian populism prevailing in all the major successor republics to Tito's Yugoslavia, a shared truth — and hence a path from truth to reconciliation — is barred, not just by hatreds but by institutions too undemocratic to allow countervailing truth to circulate. It is not undermining the war crimes tribunal process to maintain that the message of its truth is unlikely to penetrate the bell jars of the successor states of the former Yugoslavia. The point is merely that one must keep justice separate from reconciliation. Justice is justice, and within the strict limits of what is possible, it should be done. Justice will also serve the interests of truth. But the truth will not necessarily be believed and it is putting too much faith in truth to believe that it can heal.

When it comes to healing, one is faced with the most mysterious process of all. For what seems apparent in the former Yugoslavia, in Rwanda and in South Africa is that the past continues to torment because

*Montevideo, Uruguay 1984: relatives of the 'disappeared' lay claim to the truth*

it is *not* past. These places are not living in a serial order of time, but in a simultaneous one, in which the past and present are a continuous, agglutinated mass of fantasies, distortions, myths and lies. Reporters in the Balkan wars often reported that when they were told atrocity stories they were occasionally uncertain whether these stories had occurred yesterday or in 1941 or 1841 or 1441. For the tellers of the tale, yesterday and today were the same. When Joyce had Stephen Daedalus say, in the opening pages of *Ulysses*, that the past was a nightmare from which the Irish people were struggling to awake, this is what he meant: as in nightmare, time past and time present were indistinguishable. This, it should be added, is the dream-time of vengeance. Crimes can never be safely fixed in the historical past; they remain locked in the eternal present, crying out for vengeance. Joyce saw that in the identities of both Irish Nationalism and Ulster Protestantism, the past was never safely past; its bodies were never safely buried; they were always roaming through the sleep of the living, calling out for retribution. What is mythic — and hence what is poisonous — about the past in societies torn apart by civil war or racial conflict is that it is not past at all.

This makes the process of coming to terms with the past, and of being reconciled to its painfulness, much more complicated than simply sifting fact from fiction, lies from truth. It means working it through the inner recesses of the psychic system so that a serial sense of time eventually replaces the nightmare of pure simultaneity. We know from victims of trauma that this mysterious inner work of the psyche is arduous. At first, the memory of the trauma in question — a car crash, the death of a child or a parent — returns so frequently to the mind that it literally drives the present out of the frame of consciousness. The victim lives in the past and suffers its pain over and over again. With time and reflection and talk, trauma leaves the order of the present and takes its place in the past. As it does so, the pain begins to diminish and what had become a nightmare, becomes only a memory. In this slow reinstatement of the order of serial time, the sufferer can be said to come awake and recover the momentum of living.

It is perilous to extrapolate from traumatised individuals to whole societies. It is simply an extravagant metaphor to think of societies coming awake from nightmare. The only coming awake that makes sense to speak of is one by one, individual by individual, in the recesses of their own identities. Nations, properly speaking, cannot be reconciled to other nations, only individuals to individuals. Nonetheless, individuals can be helped to heal and to reconcile by public rituals of atonement. When Chilean President Patricio Alwyn appeared on television to apologise to the victims of Pinochet's repression, he created the public climate in which a thousand acts of private repentance and apology became possible. He also symbolically cleansed the Chilean state of its association with these crimes. German Chancellor Willy Brandt's gesture of going down on his knees at a death camp had a similarly cathartic effect by officially associating the German state with the process of atonement. These acts compare strikingly with the behaviour of the political figures responsible for the war in the Balkans. If, instead of writing books niggling at the numbers exterminated at Jasenovac, President Franjo Tudjman of Croatia had gone to the site of the most notorious of the Croatian extermination camps and publicly apologised for the crimes committed by the Croatian *Ustashe* against Serbs, gypsies, Jews and partisans, he would have liberated the Croatian present from the hold of the *Ustashe* past. He would also have increased dramatically the chances of the Serbian minority accepting the legitimacy of an independent Croatian state. Had he lanced the boil of the past, the war of 1991 might not have occurred. He chose not to, of course, because he believed Serbs as guilty of crimes against the Croats. But sometimes, a gesture of atonement is effective precisely because it rises above the crimes done to your own side.

Societies and nations are not like individuals, but the individuals who have political authority within societies can have an enormous impact on the mysterious process by which individuals come to term with the painfulness of their society's past.

The experience of the war in Yugoslavia makes it difficult to conceive of reconciliation, if it were ever possible, in terms of those clichés — 'forgiving and forgetting', 'turning the page', 'putting the past behind us' and so on. The intractable ferocity and scale of the war shows up the hollowness of these clichés for what they are. But reconciliation might eventually be founded on something starker: the democracy of the dead, the equality of all victims, the drastic nullity of all struggles that end in killing and the demonstrable futility of avenging the past in the present. ❏

*Michael Ignatieff is a writer and journalist. He is currently working on a biography of Isaiah Berlin*

INDEX online
ON CENSORSHIP
HTTP://WWW.ONEWORLD.ORG/INDEX_OC/

# ALBERTO MANGUEL

# Memory and forgetting

**Twenty years after the start of Argentina's 'dirty war', the fate of its 30,000 'disappeared' is still a live issue. The victims want the truth followed by justice; the guilty walk free, basking in a government amnesty**

O N 24 APRIL 1995, Victor Armando Ibañez, an Argentinian sergeant who had served as a guard at El Campito, gave an interview to the Buenos Aires newspaper *La Prensa*. According to Ibañez, between 2,000 and 2,300 of the men and women, old people and adolescents such as my college friend María Angélica Sabelli, were 'executed' by the army at El Campito during the two years of his service, from 1976 to 1978. When the prisoners' time came, Ibañez told the newspaper, 'they were injected with a strong drug called pananoval, which made a real mess of them in a few seconds. It produced something like a heart attack. [The injections would leave the prisoners alive but unconscious.] Then they were thrown into the sea. We flew at a very low altitude. They were phantom flights, without registration. Sometimes I could see very large fish, like sharks, following the plane. The pilots said that they were fattened by human flesh. I leave the rest to your imagination,' Ibañez said. 'Imagine the worst.'

Ibañez's was the second 'official' confession. A month earlier, a retired navy lieutenant commander, Adolfo Francisco Scilingo, had confessed to the same method of 'disposing of the prisoners'. In response to his confession, Argentinian President Carlos Menem called Scilingo a 'criminal', reminded the press that the commander had been involved in a shady automobile deal and asked how could the word of a thief be counted as true. He also ordered the navy to strip Scilingo of his rank.

Since his election in 1989, Menem had been trying to shelve the whole question of military culpability during the so-called 'dirty war' that had ravaged Argentina from 1973 to 1982, during which over 30,000 people were killed*. Not content with the deadline for filing charges against the military (which his predecessor, Raul Alfonsin, had set as 22 February 1988), on 6 October 1989 Menem offered most of the military involved in human rights abuses a general pardon. A year later, three days after Christmas, he issued a general amnesty to all involved in the events that had bled the country for nine long years. Accordingly, he released from prison Lieutenant General Jorge Videla and General Roberto Viola who had been successively appointed to the presidency by the military junta, the former from 1976 to 1981, the latter for 10 months in 1981.

In legal terms, a pardon implies not the abolition of guilt but a relief from punishment. On the other hand, an amnesty (such as the military had granted itself *in extremis* in 1982 and which was repealed by Alfonsin) is, in effect, a recognition of innocence that wipes away any imputation of crime. After the declarations of Scilingo and Ibañez, President Menem briefly threatened the military with a retraction of the 1990 amnesty.

Until the confessions of 1995, the Argentinian military had recognised no wrongdoing in their so-called anti-terrorist activities. The extraordinary nature of guerrilla war demanded, the military said, extraordinary measures. In this declaration they were well advised. In 1977, following a joint report from Amnesty International and the American State Department's Human Rights Bureau accusing the Argentinian security forces of being responsible for hundreds of disappearances, the military hired a US public relations company, Burson-Marsteller, to plan its response. The 35-page memorandum presented by Burson-Marsteller recommended that the military 'use the best professional communications skills to transmit those aspects of Argentine events showing that the terrorist problem is being handled in a firm and just manner, with equal justice for all'. A tall order, but not impossible in the age of communication. As if moved by the hackneyed motto 'the pen is mightier than the sword', Burson-Marsteller suggested that the military appeal to 'the generation of positive editorial comment' and to writers 'of conservative or moderate persuasions'. As a result of their campaign, the ex-governor of California, Ronald Reagan, declared in the *Miami News* of 20 October 1978 that the State Department's Human Rights Bureau was 'making a mess of our relations with the planet's seventh largest country,

Argentina, a nation with which we should be close friends'.

Over the years, others rose to the advertisers' appeal. On 7 May 1995, shortly after Ibañez and Scilingo's, an article appeared in the Spanish newspaper *El País,* signed by the prestigious Peruvian novelist Mario Vargas Llosa. Under the title 'Playing With Fire', Vargas Llosa argued that, horrible though the revelations might be, they were not news to anyone, merely confirmations of a truth 'atrocious and nauseating for any half-moral conscience'. 'It would certainly be wonderful,' he wrote, 'if all those responsible for these

Nunca Más: *cover of US edition published in 1986*

unbelievable cruelties were taken to court and punished. But this, however, is impossible, because the responsibility far exceeds the military sphere and implicates a vast spectrum of Argentinian society, including a fair number of those who today cry out, condemning retrospectively a violence which they too, in one way or another, contributed to fan.'

'It would certainly be wonderful': this is the rhetorical trope of false regret, denoting a change from shared indignation at the 'atrocious and nauseating' facts to the more sober realisation of what they 'really' mean, the impossibility of attaining the 'wonderful' goal of impartial justice. Vargas Llosa's is an ancient argument, harping back to notions of original sin: no one soul can truly be held responsible, because every soul is responsible 'in one way or another' for the crimes of a nation, whether committed by the people themselves or by their leaders. More than 100 years ago, Nicolai Gogol expressed the same absurdity in more elegant terms: 'Seek out the judge, seek out the criminal, and then condemn both.'

Using the case of his own country as a history lesson, Vargas Llosa concluded his *cri de coeur:* 'The example of what has happened in Peru with a democracy which the Peruvian people have distorted — because of the violence of extremist groups and also because of the blindness and demagogy of certain political forces — and which they let fall like a ripe fruit in the arms of military and personal power, should open the eyes of those imprudent justice-seekers who, in Argentina, take advantage of a debate on the repression in the seventies to seek revenge, to avenge old grievances or continue by other means the demential war they started and then lost.'

Burson-Marsteller could not have come up with a more efficient publicist. What would a common reader, confident in Vargas Llosa's intellectual authority, read in this impassioned conclusion? After hesitating perhaps at the comparison between Argentina and Peru (where the novelist-turned-politician thunderingly lost the presidential elections), which seems to protest too much, too obviously, the reader is led into a far more subtle argument: these 'justice-seekers' — the seekers of that justice which, according to Vargas Llosa, is desirable but utopian — are they not in fact hypocrites who must not only share the guilt for the atrocities, but are also to blame for starting a war which they then lost? Suddenly the scales of responsibility are tipped ominously on the victims' side. Not a need for justice, not an urge officially to acknowledge wrongs, but an itch for revenge or, even worse, sheer spite, apparently drives these so-called justice seekers. The 30,000 disappeared are not to be lamented; they were trouble makers who started it all. And those who survived — the Mothers of Plaza de Mayo, the thousands forced into exile, the hundreds of tortured men and women who crowd the pages of the 1984 *Report on the Disappeared* with their sober accounts of utterly indescribable sufferings — should not seek redress lest they themselves be called to judgement. And furthermore, the seventies are now so far away... Would it not be better to forget?

Fortunately, there were others, like the Argentinian writer Juan José Saer, who were not as confident as Vargas Llosa. After rectifying a number of important factual errors in Vargas Llosa's piece — calling Isabel Perón's presidency a 'democratic government', ignoring the fact that since 1955 until 1983 Argentina enjoyed barely six years of freely elected leaders — Saer notes that Vargas Llosa's arguments coincide, point by point, with those of the military leaders themselves. Saer also points out that Vargas

Llosa's notion of 'collective responsibility' might place Vargas Llosa himself in a delicate position since, at a time when Argentinian intellectuals were being tortured or forced into exile, the Peruvian novelist continued to publish willingly in Argentina's official press.

Saer responded to Vargas Llosa's role, accusing him of being a spokesman for the military; he dismissed or ignored his arguments which are somewhat obviously based on a number of false assumptions. And yet, since these arguments must stand, thanks to Vargas Llosa's craft, as the most eloquent of those penned by the defenders of a military amnesty, they deserve, perhaps, a closer examination.

• The notion of guilt shared between the military government — come to power by force and using torture and murder to fight its opponents — and the victims — guerrilla fighters, political objectors, ordinary civilians with no political associations — is fallacious. While an argument might be found to oppose, on equal terms, the armed opposition and the official Argentinian army (though, even here, the numbers appear to be in the order of 1:1,000), no argument can find a balance of power between the organised military forces and the intellectuals, artists, union leaders, students, members of the clergy who expressed disagreement with them. The civilian who voices an objection to the actions of the government is not guilty of any crime; on the contrary, vigilance is an essential civic duty in any democratic society. But the repression overflowed even the realm of civilian opposition. The National Commission on Disappeared People, led by the novelist Ernesto Sábato, concluded its report on September 1984. 'We can state categorically — contrary to what the executors of this sinister plan maintain — that they did not pursue only the members of political organisations who carried out acts of terrorism. Among the victims are thousands who never had any links with such activity but were nevertheless subjected to horrific torture because they opposed the military dictatorship, took part in union or student activities, were well-known intellectuals who questioned state terrorism, or simply because they were relatives, friends, or names included in the address book of someone considered subversive.'

• Any government that uses torture and murder as ways of enforcing the law invalidates both its right to govern and the law it enforces, since one of the few basic tenets of any society in which its citizens are granted equal rights is the sanctity of human life. 'Clearly,' wrote Chesterton, 'there could be no safety for a society in which the remark by the Chief Justice that murder was wrong was regarded as an original and dazzling epigram.' Any government that does not recognise this truism and does not hold accountable those who torture and murder can make no claims for its own justice. No government can rightly mirror the methods of its criminals, responding in kind to what it might deem an act against the nation's laws. It must enforce the law with the law, and within the letter of the law. Beyond the law, a government is no longer a government but an usurping power; and as such it must be judged.

• It is the trust in this ultimate power of the law that sustained many of the military dictatorship's victims during those terrible years. In spite of the pain and the bewilderment caused by the legitimised abuses, the belief remained that in a not too distant future these acts would be brought to light and judged according to the law. The wish to torture the torturer and to kill the murderer might have been overwhelming, but stronger was the sense that such acts of revenge would become indistinguishable from the acts that caused them and would become, in some abominable way, a victory for the abusers. Instead, the victims and their families continued to believe in some form of ultimate earthly judgement, of bringing the guilty ones to trial in front of the society that had been wronged and according to the laws of that society. Only on the basis of such justice being done did they believe that their society might have another chance. Menem's amnesty denied them that long-awaited possibility.

• This 'absence of justice' was reflected with ghoulish symmetry in the 'disappearing' tactics employed by the military, by which their victims — kidnapped, tortured, thrown from airplanes, dropped into unmarked graves — became not officially dead but merely 'absent', leaving the anguished families with no bodies to mourn. Another writer, Julio Cortazar, speaking in 1981, described in these words the dictatorship's method: 'On the one hand, a virtual or real antagonist is suppressed; on the other, conditions are created so that the family and friends of the victims are often forced to remain silent as the only possibility of preserving the life of those whom their hearts won't allow them to presume dead.' And he added: 'If every human death entails an irrevocable absence, what can we say of this other absence that continues as a sort of

*Hebe Bonafini, President of the Madres (left) and Juana Pargament address an audience in Madrid*

abstract presence, like the obstinate denial of the absence we know to be final?' In that sense, Menem's amnesty doesn't asepticise the past: it merely prolongs that sickness of the past into the present.

• No deed, however monstrous or trivial, can ever be abolished once committed. It can be pardoned, but the pardon must come from the offended person and from no-one else, if it is to have any emotional validity. Nothing changes in the deed itself after a pardon: not the circumstances, not the gravity, not the guilt, not the wound. Nothing, except the relationship between the torturer and the victims, when the victims reaffirm their sovereignty. Pardon is the victim's prerogative, not the torturer's right — and this Menem's government and his supporters, such as Vargas Llosa, have apparently forgotten.

• The pardon granted by a victim — the dripping quality of mercy — has no bearing on the mechanics of justice. Pardon doesn't grant oblivion. But a trial, according to the laws of the society, can at least lend the criminal act a context; the law can contain it, so to speak, in the past so that it no longer contaminates the future, standing at a distance as a reminder and a warning. In a mysterious way, the application of a society's laws is akin to a literary act: it fixes the criminal deed on to a page, defines it in words, gives it a context which is not that of the sheer horror of the moment but of its recollection. The power of memory is no longer in the hands of the criminal; now it is society itself that holds that power, writing the chronicle of its own wicked past, able at last to rebuild itself not over the emptiness of oblivion but over the solid, recorded facts of the atrocities committed. This is a long, dreary, fearful, agonising process, and the only possible one. This sort of healing always leaves scars.

• Menem's amnesty, bowing to the demands of acknowledged murderers and torturers, has postponed the healing for what appears to be a very long time. As it stands today, Argentina is a country bereft of rights: its right to social justice ignored, its right to moral education invalidated, its right to moral authority forfeit. The need to 'carry on', the need to 'reconcile differences', the need to 'allow the economy to flourish once again' have all been invoked by Menem as good reasons for forgiving and forgetting. Supported by literate voices such as that of Vargas Llosa, Menem apparently believes that history can be paid off, that the memory of thousands of individuals can be left to yellow on forgotten shelves in dim bureaucratic offices, that the past can be recovered without expenditure of effort, without making official amends, without redemption. One wishes that Vargas Llosa would read more carefully the furious epilogue of Vargas Llosa's 1963 novel, *La Ciudad y los perros* (The Time of the Hero). It lays out the consequences of a military system — a military academy — adopting brutally sadistic methods to 'educate' its charges. The novel's warning wasn't lost on Peru's military leaders who had it burned in a public square of Lima.

WHILE waiting for the act of justice now denied, the victims of Argentina's military dictatorship can, however, still hope for another, older form of justice — less evident but, in the end, longer lasting. The maze of a politician's mind has seldom held the promise of redemption, but that of a writer (especially that of a writer of Vargas Llosa's talents and poetic wisdom) is almost exclusively built on such a promise, and it allows no forgetting. The books of those years are being written, or will be written, or have been written and are awaiting their readers. The redemptive power of literature, apparent in every work that readers have called great, infinitely makes these assumptions — or this single assumption, again and again: that the human mind is always wiser than its most atrocious deeds, since it can give them a name; that in the very description of the most loathsome acts something in good writing shows them as loathsome and therefore not unconquerable; that in spite of the feebleness and randomness of language, an inspired writer can tell the unspeakable and lend a shape to the unthinkable, so that evil loses its numinous quality and is reduced to a few memorable words. ❏

*Alberto Manguel is a writer and critic living in Paris. A renowned anthologist, translator and editor, his latest book is* A History of Reading *(Harper Collins, 1996)*

★This figure is the estimation of the National Commission on Disappeared People, quoted in *Nunca Más (Never Again): A Report by Argentina's National Commission on Disappeared People,* edited and translated by Nick Caistor (Faber & Faber and *Index on Censorship*, London, 1986)

## MADRES DE PLAZA DE MAYO

# No truth, no justice

*Just a few blocks from the Buenos Aires' Congress building, where the street narrows again, the Madres de Plaza de Mayo have their office. Tourists pass by without noticing the building with its small brass plaque reading 'House of the Mothers'. Every day the Mothers meet here to continue their 20-year struggle, begun during the military dictatorship (1976–1983), to establish exactly what happened to their disappeared sons and daughters and to demand retribution against those who imprisoned, tortured and killed their children. July this year marked their 1,000th meeting. There are also the Grandmothers, women who lost not only a daughter or son, but also their children's children. Some of these were separated from their mothers and killed, others were given for adoption and, to this day, have no idea of their real parents. Ingo Malcher talked to them for* **Index**

TESTIMONY: NELIDA NAVAJAS (AGE 69)

'WHEN someone disappears, it's as if the earth has swallowed them up. Nobody tells you anything. Cristina had only just got pregnant again [with her third child], and there were others they took who were much further along than her. Our worry was always, what's going to happen to the little things when they're born? So instead of just worrying about our own children, getting them back safely, we started searching for their children as well. But to this day, I've never found Cristina's baby. Cristina disappeared on 13 July 1976. The last we heard about her was in April 1977. I suppose they waited till she had her baby, and then they killed her.

'We haven't had either truth or justice. All we know is the little we have managed to piece together about what happened to our daughters. The government doesn't give us any explanations. Nothing. We know that all of them, all those who took part [in the disappearances] were let off, they were protected by those vile laws, like the *punto final* ('full stop') law. And no-one breathes a word. They won't admit anything, but logically we have to assume, they've killed them.

'All these people who ran the secret detention centres, they're still walking the streets as if nothing had happened. That's why we still go on looking for our grandchildren. We want to track them down and give them the chance to find out their true identity.

'Cristina was an activist with the Revolutionary

*Nelida Navajas*

Workers' Party (PRT). The armed wing was called the People's Revolutionary Army (ERP): very pro-Cuban, very pro-Che. Cristina's brother-in-law was one of the leaders. My son-in-law saved himself, because he left the country 15 days earlier. Naturally, my daughter didn't tell me what was going on. But I had an idea something was up and I was afraid for her. I told her: "Why haven't you gone to Europe too? Why don't you go?" I desperately wanted to get her out of Buenos Aires.

'I told her: "I'm really scared." She said: "No, Mama, don't worry yourself." But I could see: she was worried and frightened. These were her friends who were being disappeared. Then one day she told me, "I'm not going to come back to your house. I'm sure it's being watched." I've never moved house, because I always have this idea that one day Cristina might come back. Where else would she go, but to her mother's house?

'It's our love for our children that keeps us going. Truth we don't have, and justice even less so. Truth and justice are what we want — and an end to impunity.'

*Juana Pargament (right) and Hebe Mascia*

## TESTIMONY: JUANA PARGAMENT (AGE 81)

'THEY TOOK my son, Alberto, on 10 November 1976. He was 31, a doctor, a psychiatrist. After he disappeared that was it, I never heard anything more of him, and I never really found out what happened. It's your worst fear, the most terrible thing for a mother, not to know what's happened to her son. Later we found out that they took them, they tortured them and they killed them. What became of my son, in particular, that we never knew. But I'll tell you this, we Mothers and Grandmothers, we're fighting for all 30,000 of them.

'After they took him, I went and asked the court what to do. They said there was a tribunal I could apply to, I should go and present a *habeas corpus* so that the judges could find out where he was. I waited the 24 hours but he didn't turn up. Then I started to look to my friends, to those who had a bit of influence, and I went to the bishops. I searched all day every day;

morning till night.

'Every week we used to go and see one of the military chaplains, Gracelli he was called. Because he knew very well — he worked with the military after all — and we asked him for some help with finding the children. He was keeping a very complete record. And one day he said to me: "Okay, what's he called, your son?" I told him. He said: "Look, I'm only going to tell you one thing — your son is alive." I asked him how he knew. "Because he doesn't appear here on my list."

'So we went to the government offices. What a joke! The very people who were taking our children had opened an office for "ascertaining the whereabouts of the disappeared". Well, we came out of there, and there was another woman with us called Azucena Villaflor de Vicenti — they'd taken her son and his girlfriend. She said: "You can see that we're not getting anywhere like this. Why don't we go and sit in the Plaza, talking to people and writing letters? And when there are lots of us, we'll take all the letters to the government and get our children back." That was 30 April 1977. It was a Saturday.

'By that Thursday there were more of us; and every Thursday more and more Mothers came along. So the police wanted to know what we were up to. We told them: "We're writing letters, asking for our children back." "Well, you'll have to do it walking around then. There's no other way." So we started to walk, one behind the other, in front of the government building. And as we went we wrote letters. Eventually of course the police came and took us away, but we Mothers weren't afraid.

'Now [President] Menem says he's going to give money for each disappeared person. US$1000,000 he's giving away. We don't want any blood money. If you take the money you've got no more claim. Okay, it's one thing if you get the body back, sign that you've received it and you can give up your search, fine. But we're not going to sell our children's blood. We're not going to forgive. We're not going to forget. We're going to carry on with our fight.

'The Mothers' fight is a political one: we want every family to have a proper roof over their heads, fathers to have work, children to go to college. We want a better country. I mean, that's what our children wanted, and why they took them from us. The 30,000 who disappeared, many of them wanted change, a better life for our people. And the Mothers only discovered this after they lost their children. And that's why we often say they showed us the way.'

## TESTIMONY: HEBE MASCIA (AGE 71)

'THE MILITARY took my daughter and her husband. She was 19, he was 23. They'd been married for six months. They took him first, he was working with his father. Then they started looking for her. She worked at a pharmacy in the centre of town, it's still there today. We never found out what became of her. We looked for her high and low. Araceli Susana Mascia and Edmundo Daniel Szapiro they were called.

It's very hard to live with that loss, the sadness is always there. I had three children but my eldest son was killed by a car when he was 12. There's no comparison with this, though. I've always said that God took my son. But I can't pardon the soldiers who took my daughter. You want to do I don't know what to them, something horrible. Because what happened to her was the worst thing in the world.

'I've been with the Mothers since the beginning of 1976. We formed officially in April 1977. We realised we had to work together to be more effective. I'm naturally a strong person, but the Mothers give each other strength, too. We have something together which is really strong.

'We asked for the return of all of the disappeared. We didn't ask specifically for our own children, but for all of them. It was more powerful that way. If one of them had come back, it would have made all of us happy. But none of them ever did come back.

'The real tragedy is that the murderers are still walking the streets. If they were in prison, we might be able to forgive. We want justice. Right now, justice is only a word, nothing more. The same with democracy.

'We're going to keep up the fight for as long as we have to. We're not going to give an inch. We want to know who, when and why they killed our children. Nobody has ever taken responsibility for this. We don't want the bodies, or the money they're offering. If you take the money, it's like admitting your children are dead.

'One day, victory is going to come, I'm sure of it. We're fighting to make sure the killers are put away. All those who are happily walking the streets. We're going to make them pay. And not just with money.' ❑

*Interviewed by Ingo Malcher*

*Translated by Adam Newey*

GILLES PERESS/MAGNUM PHOTOS

*Cerska, Bosnia 1996: unearthing the skeletons of Srebrenica*

## ANTHONY DWORKIN

# The world in judgement

**Do international war crimes tribunals help or hinder national reconciliation?**

WE ARE ALL citizens of our respective countries, but we are also bound together by our common humanity, and certain crimes are so offensive to the conscience of the world that the international community can hold individuals responsible for them, even when the states to which they belong are unwilling or unable to prosecute. That is the idealistic aspiration embodied in the international tribunals for the former Yugoslavia and Rwanda. For the first time, truly international courts have been set up to try people for atrocities — murder, ethnic cleansing, torture and rape — committed against their fellow citizens in the wreckage of a disintegrating society. It is an experiment that may lead to the creation of a permanent international criminal court — or, if it fails, may undermine for decades the idea that international humanitarian law can be not only written, but enforced.

The challenge for the tribunals is to prove that international justice can contribute to the creation of lasting peace in the aftermath of social breakdown. This is important, because there will always be societies that cannot undertake the process of justice and reconciliation on their own. Indeed, former Yugoslavia and Rwanda illustrate the two main situations where outside involvement is most likely to be needed: societies where those who carried out the majority of the crimes remain in — or allied with — authority; and societies that have suffered such cataclysm that the normal domestic structures of justice are inoperable. It is, of course, in precisely such cases that peace and reconciliation are most likely to be elusive. But the unpunished examples of the Khmer Rouge in Cambodia between 1975 and 1979 and Saddam Hussein's gassing of the Kurds in March 1988 stand as a rebuke to those who say that justice must arise from within a society, or not at all.

The international tribunals, on which so much now hangs, were born in an act of evasion. In the summer of 1992, the first reports of the Serbian detention camps in Bosnia reached the outside world. In the leading western countries, public opinion was already displaying over Bosnia the kind of unfocused moral unease that diplomats disparage as the 'something must be done' syndrome, and that might otherwise be described as a nascent sense of international obligation. Faced with such a potent echo of the Nazi past, there was clear pressure on governments to act, but doubts and divisions stood in the way of any effective military response. A war crimes tribunal had the convenient appeal of suggesting action without, for the immediate future, requiring it. So, in October 1992, the Security Council called for a Commission of Experts to study the matter and, moving with uncharacteristic speed, affirmed the creation of the tribunal in May 1993.

In Rwanda the pattern was similar. Traumatised by the experience of intervention in Somalia, the international community — effectively, the

USA and its allies on the Security Council — looked the other way as over half a million Rwandans were massacred in the course of a few months. Having failed to act as a policeman while the crimes were in progress, the Security Council found it easier to offer its judicial services to punish the guilty: the Rwandan tribunal was established in November 1994.

To look at the tribunals in isolation from this background is to see only half the picture. On its own the judicial process cannot begin to repair the kind of social dislocation that Bosnia and Rwanda have suffered. The first chief prosecutor for both tribunals, Justice Richard Goldstone of South Africa, told me in an interview earlier this year that it was the sheer scale of the crimes that had struck him most in his investigations. The more thoughtful among the tribunals' staff will readily admit that their role is inherently limited. Others outside the tribunals — and this has sometimes appeared to be the unspoken view of the UK government — go further: they claim the rigidities of criminal law have no part to play in the give-and-take of international diplomacy and may stand in the way of the kind of compromises on which any settlement must be founded.

The debate leads back to the central ambiguity of international humanitarian law: its principles are by now well established, yet there has never been a permanent body with the power to enforce them. The basic rules date from the determinedly idealistic period of institution-building that followed World War II: the Nuremberg Principles, endorsed by the United Nations, and the Geneva Conventions of 1949, whose Common Article 3 extends the reach of international law to cover conflicts 'not of an international character'. But the decision at any time to apply these laws is a political decision. Set up by resolution of the Security Council, the current tribunals exist not simply to enforce the law, but to promote the restoration of 'peace and security' — the Security Council's guiding remit under the UN Charter. If the Security Council decides that the tribunals' pursuit of justice no longer promotes peace and security, it has the ability, indeed the responsibility, to close them down. But this begs the key questions: What kind of justice? What kind of peace?

Supporters of the tribunals tend to say their fundamental contribution to reconciliation lies in the notion of individualising guilt. It is an idea as old as Nuremberg: by holding military and civilian officials — even heads of state — responsible for criminal actions as individuals, you remove the stigma that would otherwise attach to the nation in whose name the acts were carried out. Updated to the new world of ethnic conflict, its relevance is even clearer. If Serbs, Croats and Muslims are to rebuild any sort of common society, and similarly Tutsis and Hutus, they must learn not to judge each other guilty merely by virtue of the ethnic group to which they belong. Punishing those who have committed atrocities removes their influence and example from the political scene and makes it easier for voices of reconciliation to be acknowledged.

As far as this goes, it's an attractive and plausible idea. But the argument is more ambiguous than may at first appear. In societies where participation in atrocities was widespread, pervasive even, it's unrealistic to think that an international tribunal could begin to process all such cases, even if it had 10 times the resources that the UN has grudgingly granted to the current ad hoc bodies. In Bosnia, war crimes like ethnic cleansing or the deliberate targeting of civilians appear to have played a fundamental part in the military strategy of the Bosnian Serb forces: these were not, it seems, aberrations from the norm, but rather a deliberate policy of terror. In Rwanda, the level of criminal involvement appears to have been even higher. Government forces have detained around 74,000 people on suspicion of having taken part in the genocide, and many additional suspects have fled abroad.

It is neither practicable nor desirable for an international court to try to prosecute all these cases, not least because of the intrusion into national life it would entail. What international bodies can do is to establish an order of responsibility: go after the ringleaders who organised and promoted systematic violations of human rights. Justice Goldstone and his team recognise this. In a thoughtful talk he gave at a recent conference, Payam Akhavan, a legal adviser in the prosecutor's office, stressed that the Rwandan genocide was the result of 'careful planning and execution under the direction of political elites' and argued that 'the symbolic effect of prosecuting even a limited number of such leaders before an international jurisdiction would have a considerable impact on national reconciliation.' But to say this is to say that effective reconciliation will inevitably depend on the interaction between international trials and the domestic situation. Isolated from a corresponding effort to foster justice internally, the work of international tribunals will remain selective and unsatisfactory, their contribution to reconciliation inevitably frustrated.

This is the danger that, in different ways, now confronts the tribunals for Rwanda and former Yugoslavia. In the case of Rwanda, the tribunal is beginning to lose the confidence of the country it was set up to help. The new Rwandan government initially welcomed the tribunal when it was established in November 1994. Since then, however, frictions have developed, particularly over the complications involved in bringing cases to trial, and, inevitably, over differences in values and priorities. The tribunal has been short of money and resources from the start: 'We're 25 investigators looking into a million deaths,' one legal adviser recently complained to a US newspaper. There are no documents to help build cases, witnesses are afraid of reprisals and most of the major suspects are abroad — in Zaire, Kenya or other countries. Against this background, prosecutors have managed to issue only a handful of indictments though these include a number of significant figures and have less than a quarter of these in custody. The first trials are due to start in the autumn.

Rwanda's own justice system has done no better in trying to sort through the appalling aftermath of the genocide: despite the colossal number of suspects (many being held in dreadful conditions) no cases have yet come to court. Nevertheless, the common difficulties faced by the prosecution teams appear, at least for the government, to be a source of conflict rather than co-operation. Senior government figures have begun to question the length of time the tribunal is taking and, more ominously, to complain about its international character. Precisely those qualities that are supposed to be the distinctive contribution of an international body — neutrality, objectivity, universality — have been attacked.

In particular, there is resentment that the tribunal is based not in Rwanda itself, but in Arusha in Tanzania; that it has priority over domestic jurisdiction; and that it does not impose the death penalty — which the leading figures in the genocide would certainly face in Rwanda. The country's deputy justice minister Gerard Gahima recently told the writer Philip Gourevitch: 'It makes it harder to forgive the ordinary people if we don't have the leaders here to be tried in Rwandan courts before the Rwandan people according to Rwandan law.' Others familiar with the situation in Rwanda deny that relations with the tribunal are as bad as Gahima suggests. But his charges nevertheless go to the heart of the tribunal's *raison d'être*.

It is an anomaly, at the least, that middle-level *genocidaires* will face the death penalty in Rwandan courts while those whose seniority and guilt is sufficient to attract the interest of the tribunal can only face life imprisonment. On the other hand, few would seriously propose that the international community should commit itself to a barbaric penalty rejected by a majority of countries.

The more substantial point is that the tribunal will fail if it doesn't establish its credibility in the country where the crimes were committed. It is hardly surprising that many in Rwanda should want swifter, perhaps looser, and certainly harsher justice than is on offer through the court in Arusha. Yet a tribunal that represents (at least in theory) the impartial judgement of the world cannot endorse a judicial procedure that incorporates any element of revenge.

The challenge of reconciling local norms and universal values has become an overriding issue in many areas of international relations. Clearly the international community will overreach itself if it doesn't observe the principle of letting justice be administered at the lowest possible level. It could be argued that Rwanda is such a case; that the government which overthrew the last murderous regime now has the right to reclaim control over the punishment of its worst offenders. Yet the Rwandan crisis has always been, and remains, an issue of international dimensions both because of the huge number of refugees in neighbouring countries, and the potential for ethnic conflict in Burundi to flare up into a calamity of comparable proportions. Indeed, it is notable that the Rwandan government's attitude to the tribunal has become more hostile at exactly the time when tension between Tutsis and Hutus is again increasing, when there are reports of repression and violations of human rights carried out by the regime. The country's drift away from support for international justice may correspond to a less inclusive view of the potential for inter-ethnic reconciliation.

There are both pragmatic and principled reasons why the international community has a stake in seeing justice done after crimes on a scale, and of a character, like those in Rwanda. The Genocide Convention is based on this obligation but the problem is that we don't recognise such an obligation consistently. Bad enough that the Rwanda tribunal has been given so little money and must therefore work so slowly. Much worse is that the behaviour of the outside world during the crisis itself undercut the ability of international bodies to lay claim to a plausible standard of moral behaviour. Gerard Gahima told Philip Gourevitch, Rwandans see the tribunal as another act of the same international community that stood by and watched them get killed. Who can doubt that there would be more goodwill and respect for the UN court if its troops had shown even a similiar level of engagement?

*Massacre at Nyarubuye, Rwanda 1994: nullity of revenge*

THE PROBLEMS of the International Tribunal for the former Yugoslavia have received much more press attention and are better known. Despite their professed ambition to try symbolic figures with the greatest responsibility for war crimes, the prosecutors have had in practice to be guided by the more pragmatic consideration of who they could get their hands on. The first trial has been that of Dusan Tadic, a local karate instructor whose alleged acts, though murderous and sadistic, form only a small part of the greater picture. The majority of those indicted — and, above all, former Bosnian Serb leader Radovan Karadzic and his millitary commander General Ratko Mladic — remain at large within Bosnian Serb territory, where they appear to enjoy considerable local support and immunity from apprehension by NATO forces.

In a paradoxical way, the tribunal has already disproved the cynical charge that the pursuit of justice would prove to be incompatible with peace. Instead, it has become apparent that it is precisely the continued presence of figures such as Karadzic and Mladic within Bosnian Serb society that is exacerbating divisions and fostering a drive toward ethnic exclusivity on all sides. But the point is not simply that these figures should be arrested and put on trial: it is rather that the entire international presence in Bosnia is based on a conception of the outside world's role and responsibility that is fundamentally at odds with the vision that inspired the development of modern humanitarian law as embodied in the Hague Tribunal. The Dayton Accord remained sufficiently ambiguous to obscure this gap, but in practice it has quickly become clear that what the western powers have committed themselves to is not to remove the sources of conflict, to create a foundation for lasting peace. It is simply a lowest common denominator approach: settle for the minimum engagement that can ensure an end to the fighting. In this way it is misleading to characterise the debate over the Yugoslav tribunal — as the sceptics have done — as a choice between peace and justice. The real choice is between two different visions of peace, two different forms of international engagement.

While the tribunals continue their work, a United Nations committee is slowly preparing the ground for a future conference that will debate the creation of a permanent international criminal court. This body, if it comes into being, would have the brief of prosecuting all breaches of international humanitarian law. The decision to create it would mark a formal acknowledgement that the international community has an interest in all crimes against humanity — not only because of the threat they may pose to peace, but because, in themselves, they are an affront to our common values. The lesson of the ad hoc tribunals is that such a court will be unable to make a real difference unless the international community allows a similar commitment and similar values to guide its actions in other ways. ❏

*Anthony Dworkin* is a senior producer with BBC Radio 4's Analysis

# ADAM MICHNIK

# Testament of lies

**On 3 June 1992, Poland's interior minister, Antoni Macierewicz, sent lists of politicians and officials suspected of being former security police agents to parliamentary deputies. The list was drawn up on the basis of secret police files, with no other evidence against those named. In the bitter row that followed, President Lech Walesa was accused of being an alleged Communist informer. Within days the government was dismissed**

I HAVE participated in a great many public debates about documents from secret police archives. Wherever the subject has come up in the old Communist world, it has created divisions in democratic circles. Yet the most reasonable position, it seems to me, must be: give priority to compassion and let justice follow.

Police archives are the legacy of all dictatorships. They contain material gathered over many years to describe and compromise suspects; they were intended as tools of blackmail. They are a time bomb. When they explode, they destroy. In Poland, Antoni Macierewicz's list of supposed agents has rightly been called 'a grenade hurled into a sewer' — whether it kills or maims, it is bound to spatter everyone with filth.

Is it not better at times to draw a curtain of silence over this swirl of human crisis and torment? Furthermore, are these archives trustworthy? Can we put our faith in documents prepared by Stasi informers, for example? Is their evidence an adequate criterion by which to pass judgement? No-one has convinced me yet that documents from these archives can be uncritically trusted. They were drawn up by people whose profession was falsification for the purpose of ruining others. If they destroy again today, we will be witnessing the posthumous victory of the totalitarian police.

The list circulated by Antoni Macierewicz injected poison into the public life of this country: it brought suspicion, false allegations and slander. It saw the culmination of a power struggle waged by the government against the president and the principle of the rule of law. The debate that followed marked the clash of two political cultures. On one side stood those who thought that only the independent verdict of a court of law should disqualify anyone from holding an official post; on the other, those who considered a minister of internal affairs perfectly well qualified to pass a verdict — provided he came from the same political camp as themselves. The second grouping, which likes to call itself the 'centre' right and has widespread support from the Church, had already demonstrated its political style in its fullest glory.

Earlier, it had given myriad promises of political breakthrough and economic acceleration. There was to be de-Communisation and accounts were to be settled with the guilty. Instead, we saw incompetent government and personalised purges, which struck not at Communists but at representatives of other groupings in the anti-Communist opposition. We witnessed a progressive loss of stability in the army, the collapse of the entire field of home policy and irresponsible attacks on foreign policy.

This was accompanied by a brutal campaign of slander against people holding key positions in the country. We heard declarations from the former minister of defence suggesting that a coup d'état was at hand. This was why de-Communisation was to be indispensable. In fact it proved to be no more than the exchange of one set of generals for another — with similar political biographies, even though differently disposed towards the new leadership. Antoni Macierewicz's revelation was the straw that broke the camel's back. President Walesa's swift reaction was justified: the state was under threat.

All this was the new phase of a war at the top, originally fomented in 1990. That was when the mechanism of false allegations, dishonest accusations and empty promises was set in motion. Then we heard for the first time in public lies about secret deals made during the Round Table talks. The latest revelations were to be the Finale: informers of the secret police (never, in fact, Polish-controlled) were to be outed by men of honour and ideals. Agents of foreign powers were to be unmasked.

As a result, the traditional shape of politics in this country has ceased to exist. There is no solidarity between groupings formerly in the anti-Communist opposition. None of the traditional categories — such as right and left — describe the political divisions in the Polish Parliament. Any subsequent coalitions will serve short-term needs. We can only hope that their overriding aim will be concern for interests of the state.

And the genie is out of the bottle. The public accusations should be fully clarified, just as those responsible for making false allegations must be made answerable for them. The whole issue of secret police agents must be depoliticised immediately. It shouldn't remain accessible as an instrument of political struggle, even in the worthiest of hands. This aspect of contemporary politics is too important to be left to politicians. What is required is a body formed not of political figures, but of lawyers, historians and sociologists who would examine the authenticity of the documents and draw up a report based on their findings. This should expose in full the workings of the entire mechanism of crime and terror, the amorality of some and the suffering of others.

As for the archives, they should remain sealed for 50 years in order that no politician can be in a position to draw on them while fighting his political battles. ❏

**Adam Michnik** *is editor in chief of* Gazeta Wyborcza, *Warsaw*

© *Edited excerpts from articles published in* Gazeta Wyborcza, *6 June 1992 and 19 August 1994. Translated by Irena Maryniak*

# MEDIA ETHICS
## PRIVACY, PUBLIC INTEREST and CENSORSHIP
### 20-21 September 1996

The conference fees are £75 including lunches and light refreshments plus £20 for the Conference Dinner. A fee of £10 will be charged for those with a student card or supervisor's signature. Bed & Breakfast accommodation is available at £22 per night. Details and registration forms are available from: Cornelia Shirley, School of Continuing Education, Continuing Education Building, Springfield Mount, Leeds LS2 9NG. TEL: 0113 233 3233   FAX: 0113 233 3240

UNIVERSITY OF LEEDS

Yorkshire & Humberside ARTS

# TRUTH COMMISSIONS & WAR TRIBUNALS 1971-1996

| COUNTRY | TITLE • DATE • SPONSORING AUTHORITY | DATES COVERED • CIRCUMSTANCES | OUTCOME |
|---|---|---|---|
| UGANDA | Commission of Inquiry into the Disappearances of People in Uganda since 25 January 1971 (1974-1975). Report published 1975. President | 25 Jan 1971-1974. Prompted by international pressure on government. Disappearances | Documented 308 cases. Found security forces guilty. Commissioners victimised and report ignored. Stands as official history |
| BOLIVIA | Comisión Nacional de Investigación de Desaparecidos (1982-1984). No final report. President | 1967-1982. Change from military to democratic rule. Disappearances | Documented 155 cases. Incomplete because of lack of resources. No written report |
| ARGENTINA | Comisión Nacional para la Desaparición de Personas ('The Sábato Commission' or CONADEP) (1983-1984). Report published 1985. President | 1976-1983. Change from military to democratic rule. Disappearances | Documented almost 9,000 cases. Report played key role in prosecution of high-ranking officers |
| URUGUAY | Comisión Investigadora sobre la Situación de Personas Desaparecidas y Hechos que la Motivaron (1985). Report published 1985. President | 1973-1982. Change from military to democratic rule. Disappearances | Documented 164 cases. Did not investigate torture. Effects of report minimal |
| ZIMBABWE | Commission of Inquiry (1985). Report kept confidential. President | 1983. Pressure to investigate repression in Matabeleland where at least 1,500 civilians were killed | Defence minister apologised for killings and torture. Continuing demands for publication of report |
| UGANDA | Commission of Inquiry into Violations of Human Rights (1986-1994). Report published 1994. President | Dec 1962-Jan 1986. Following overthrow of Obote government. Human rights abuses | Found evidence of widespread arbitrary arrests, detentions and imprisonments and recommended the repeal of laws allowing detention without trial. Government accepted recommendations and established a permanent Human Rights Commission |
| PHILIPPINES | Presidential Committee on Human Rights (1986-1987). Did not complete report. President | 1972-1986. Transition to democratic regime. State crimes during period of martial law | Amid continuing political unrest, Commission resigned over killing of civilian protesters, 1987. Work unfinished. No report. No prosecutions |
| CHILE | Comisión Nacional para la Verdad y Reconciliación ('The Rettig Commission') (1990-1991). Report published 1991. President | Sept 11 1973-Mar 11 1990. Change from military to democratic rule. Abuses resulting in death or disappearance during time of junta | Major state support, especially financial. Investigated 2,920 cases. Identified 2,298 victims. Recommendations implemented; Reconciliation and Compensation Corporation set up (*see below*) |

| | | | |
|---|---|---|---|
| **CHAD** | Commission d'Enquête sur les Crimes et Détournements Commis par l'Ex-Président Habré, ses co-Auteurs et/ou Complices (1991-1992). Report published May 1992. President | 1982-90. New government. Killings, torture and illegal detentions during previous regime | Report on 40,000 killings and involvement of US, France, Iraq and Egypt in training of military. Names and photographs of perpetrators published. Chiefly, PR exercise for new government: human rights abuses continued |
| **SOUTH AFRICA** | Commission of Enquiry into Complaints by Former African National Congress Prisoners and Detainees 'The Skweyiya Commission' (1992). Report published October 1992. ANC | 1979-1991. ANC investigation into allegations by former members of human rights abuses in its camps outside South Africa | ANC accepted findings, notably 'staggering brutality' in camps. Against naming or prosecuting individuals. Accusations of bias and lack of due process (*see below*) |
| **GERMANY** | Enquet Kommission Aufarbeitung von Geschichte und Folgen der SED-Diktator in Deutschland (1992-present). Parliament | 1949-1989. Reunification. Human rights violations under Communist rule in East Germany | Established following the opening of the Stasi (secret police) files. Unclear whether prosecutions will follow. Still in operation |
| **EL SALVADOR** | Comisión de la Verdad Para El Salvador (1992-1993). Report published March 1993. UN | Jan 1980-Jul 1991. Ceasefire and peace accords after civil war. Investigation into 'serious acts of violence' | Named over 40 individuals; criticised for inadequate investigation of death squads. General amnesty five days after publication |
| **RWANDA** | International Commission of Investigation on Human Rights Violations in Rwanda (1993). Report published March 1993. Human Rights Watch/ Africa, International Federation of Human Rights, Interafrican Human Rights Union, Center for Human Rights and Democratic Development | Oct 1990-1993. Ceasefire and agreement by rebels and the government to establish commission. Abuses during civil war | Mass graves unearthed. Official welcome by Hutu government, but killings start again immediately commission leaves country. Brought pressure on Belgium and to lesser extent France to cease support for government (*see below*) |
| **SOUTH AFRICA** | Commission of Enquiry into Certain Allegations of Cruelty and Human Rights Abuses Against ANC Prisoners and Detainees by ANC Members ('The Motsuenyane Commission') (1993). Report published August 1993. ANC | 1979-1991. Criticisms of lack of independence and due process in previous commission on abuses in ANC camps | Run like a trial. Report finds severe abuses in camps. Perpetrators named. ANC accepted report but denied systematic policy. Called for wider Truth Commission in South Africa (*see below*) |
| **ETHIOPIA** | Office of the Special Prosecutor (1993-present). Transitional government. | 1974-1991. Overthrow of 'Dergue' military regime. To document abuses under rule of President Mengistu Haile-Mariam and to investigate genocide and crimes against humanity | Government held 2,000 officials of previous regime without trial. Commission secured release of over 1,000, some on bail, some unconditionally. In April 1996 trials opened against 46 former 'Dergue' officials and 25 others *in absentia*, including Mengistu. Still in operation |

| COUNTRY | TITLE • DATE • SPONSORING AUTHORITY | DATES COVERED • CIRCUMSTANCES | OUTCOME |
|---|---|---|---|
| **FORMER YUGOSLAVIA** | International Criminal Tribunal for the former Yugoslavia (1991-present). UN | 1991-present. To judge those thought responsible for grave violations of international human rights including serious infractions of the Geneva Convention 1949, violations of the laws and customs of war; genocide; crimes against humanity | Seventy-five suspects, including Radovan Karadzic and Ratko Mladic, indicted; only seven are in custody. Still in progress |
| **HAITI** | Commission Nationale de Vérité et de Justice (March 1995). Report published April 1996. President | 29 September 1991-15 October 1994. Set up following restoration of President Jean-Bertrand Aristide in October 1994 by US-led multinational force. To establish the truth concerning the most serious human rights violations committed inside and outside the country and to help towards the reconciliation of all Haitians | Only a handful of alleged perpetrators of past human rights abuses were brought to trial; many tried in absentia, some were released from prison in controversial circumstances. Documents needed by the Commission were confiscated by US forces and have still not been returned to Haiti |
| **RWANDA** | International Criminal Tribunal for the Prosecution of Persons Responsible for Genocide and other Serious Violations of International Humanitarian Law Committed in the Territory of Rwanda and Rwandan citizens responsible for Genocide and other such violations committed in the territory of neighbouring states (June 1995-present). UN | 6 April 1994-15 July 1994. Set up by the Security Council following a preliminary report from its Commission of Experts | Ten indictments; first trial begins September 1996. Still in progress. *(see Dworkin p137)* |
| **SOUTH AFRICA** | Truth and Reconciliation Commission (including a Committee on Human Rights Violations, Committee on Amnesty, and a Committee on Reparation and Rehabilitation. (November 1995-April 1998). Parliament under the Promotion of National Unity and Reconciliation Act, July 1995 *(see p38 & following)* | 1 March 1960-5 December 1993. To investigate the causes and extent of gross violations of human rights committed during the apartheid era. To grant amnesties to perpetrators under certain conditions and recommend compensation for victims | In session, receiving testimony. Announced at end of August that it will issue subpoenas against those responsible for human rights violations; De Klerk 'apologises' for 'mistakes of the past' under apartheid *(see p57)* |
| **CHILE** | Reconciliation and Compensation Corporation (1990-1996). Report published 22 August 1996. President | Further investigation into abuses under Pinochet regime, 1971-1990 *(see above)* | Found further 899 cases of people who died or disappeared. Total of victims of political repression 3,197 of whom 2,095 are known to have died and 1,102 are officially classified as 'disappeared' |

Compiled from Hayner '15 Truth Commissions 1774-1994' (HRQ 16, 1994), Rolston Turning the Page Without Closing the Book *(Irish Reporter, 1996)* and other sources

# SVETLANA ALEKSIYEVICH

# The play of war

**'A man lies fallen on the ground, killed by another man. Not by a beast, nature, or destiny but by another man. In Yugoslavia, Afghanistan, Tajikistan or Chechnya'**

JUST OCCASIONALLY, I am struck by a terrifying thought about the mystery of war. Madness has prevailed; but glance around and the world is the same as ever: watching television, hurrying off to work, eating, smoking, patching up its shoes, backbiting, listening to music. Today, carrying an automatic isn't an oddity, but asking a straightforward question is. Why *is* that man lying fallen on the ground, killed by another man?

Remember Pushkin: 'I love the blood and play of war. Death's image warms my soul.' That's the nineteenth century. 'Even if the arsenal which threatens universal death is destroyed, the knowledge of how to build it up again will be retained. There is no turning back to ignorance.' Ales Adamovich. So speaks the twentieth century.

Age upon age, art has extolled Mars, the god of war. We have no means now to strip him of his bloody garments...

And that is a reason for writing about war. Years ago, in our village on *Radunitsa* (Remembrance Day) I see a tiny old woman kneeling on an overgrown hillock — with neither words, nor tears, nor prayers. 'That's nothing to be looking at, dearie,' the women of the village said, leading me away. 'You shouldn't know, no-one should.' But in a village there's no such thing as a secret; a village lives in community. Later I learned that, during the partisan blockade, whilst everyone was hiding out in the forest and the marshes during the punitive expeditions — swelling with hunger, dying of fear — the woman had been there with her three little daughters. One day it became transparently clear that either all would die, or some might survive. The neighbours heard the youngest child pleading in the night: 'Mama, don't drown me, please. I shan't ask for my tea, really I shan't.'

Incisions in the memory...

During one of my trips I met a small woman wrapped tight in a downy shawl despite the summer heat, whispering urgently: 'I can't bear to talk, I don't want to remember. For decades after the war I couldn't bring myself to go to the butcher's and see all those cuts of meat, especially the chicken, it was like human flesh. I couldn't sew in red. I'd seen so much blood. I won't remember, I can't...'

I never liked books about war, yet I wrote three. Living with death, and stories and memories you become mesmerised by questions relating to the bounds of our humanity and what lies beyond. 'There's not much humanity in human beings,' one character in *Zinky Boys* remarks,' that's one thing I did learn among the rocks and stones of Afghanistan.'

To this day we have before us the image of the Great Patriotic War, the soldier of '45. For years we were taught to love the man with the gun. And we did. But, since Afghanistan and Chechnya, war has become something different; and for me it has raised doubts about much that was once written about the subject. I do not exclude my own work. For we observed our own nature with the eyes of the system — not as artists.

An old peasant woman tells me how she sat at the window as a child and saw a young partisan beating the old miller over the head with his gun. The miller didn't fall, he simply sat down on the wintry earth with his head split, like a cabbage. 'That was when I lost my wits,' she said, weeping. 'My mother and father tried to cure me for years, they took me to all sorts of healers. But whenever I saw a young man I'd scream and collapse in a fever, and I'd see that old miller, his head split like a cabbage. I never married. I was afraid of men, especially young ones...'

Or there's that story the woman who fought with the partisans told me. Her village had been burnt; her parents roasted alive in the wooden church. And she'd go and watch the partisans killing the German prisoners, the *polizei*. Her deranged whispers are still with me. 'Their eyes would pop out of their sockets and burst, they gouged them out with ramrods. I would watch and then I'd feel better.'

At war we discover in ourselves things we would never have guessed at. We want to kill, it's fun. It's an aspect of our biological nature we know nothing about; it's absent in our literature. We undervalue it in ourselves, believing too much in the power of words and ideas. And no story, not even the most accurate report can be compared to the reality.

*Herat graveyard, Afghanistan 1988: 'how young and beautiful our sons...'*

OUT THERE in Afghanistan, I heard a young conscript bellow: 'What can you possibly understand about war? A lady novelist. Do people here die like they do in books or films? There they die beautifully. A friend of mine was killed only yesterday. A bullet went through his head. He kept running for another 10 metres picking up his brains. Will you write that?'

And seven years on, that conscript, now a successful businessman who likes to recount his Afghan adventures, called me and said: 'What are your books *for,* exactly. They are too ghoulish.' This wasn't the boy I'd met among the dead, who, at 20, didn't want to die. The tale of one life and destiny incorporates a range of characters who happen to share the same name. But I have spent the past 20 years trying to produce documentaries, albeit in a literary form. Now I no longer know what a documentary is. The only kind of 'pure' document which doesn't raise doubts in my mind is a passport or a tram ticket. What will that tell people in 100 years time? Only that our typography was poor. Everything else is interpretation. Somebody's truth, somebody's passion, somebody's lie, somebody's life.

When my book *Zinky Boys* was put on trial, the document faced the public in earnest. And I understood then what a loss it would be if documents were controlled exclusively by their contemporaries; if, for example, 30 years ago they had been responsible for re-typing the *Gulag Archipelago*, or Shalamov or Grossman. 'Truth is as mysterious as it is inaccessible,' Albert Camus writes, 'and it must be fought for eternally.' Fought to be understood. The mothers of soldiers killed in Afghanistan would come to the courtroom with their photographs and medals. They would weep and cry: 'See how young and beautiful they were. Our sons. And there she is reporting that they killed out there.' And to me they'd say: 'We don't need your kind of truth. We have our own truth.'

The road from reality to word is long and arduous; yet that is what builds the archive of our humanity. There is a sense in which present reality does not exist. We know no present, only past or future, or what Brodsky called 'real time in extension'. Reality is recollection. It vanishes, but remains preserved in memory or words — both imperfect instruments: fragile, treacherous and relative. Hostages of time. And then there is the witness caught between reality and the word. Three witnesses of a single event are three interpretations, three attempts at truth.

When a mother, who has lost her son to the state and got him back in a zinc coffin, cries out ecstatically, prayerfully: 'I love my country! My son died for it! And I loathe you and this truth of yours!' I see once again that we were not just slaves, but romanticisers of slavery. Only one woman out of the hundred I met wrote: 'I killed my own son! Slave that I was, I brought up a slave.'

Communist and nationalist newspapers may be calling people to demonstrate under their scarlet banners; but to suggest that politicians are responsible for everything would be too simple. The bloodshed is behind us; the earth has been dug over countless times. And still there are no tormentors to be found. No admissions of guilt. Everyone is a victim... Some say they love their country and did everything in its name (let her answer for it; isn't that what all those expressions of love are for?). Others say they shed blood for an ideal. And there's no knowing whether there is more fear of repentance or inability to cope with freedom here. To belong, to submit to higher authority, to the state, to be dissolved, to vanish in it: the form of existence characteristic of a religious or martial society. We have been both. So steeped are we in this tradition that we can't even guess to what extent we remain a martial society, or how far we envisage life and death in military terms.

I was convinced, once, that truth had to be followed through to the end. Faced with writing that an Italian landmine the size of a toy can turn a human being into half a bucketful of flesh, I hesitated; but I decided to follow it through. Because, I thought, the simpler and more mundane the killing, the more important human life should be in art. Now I'm no longer sure. Perhaps we have reached a point of no return.

We don't need freedom. We don't know what it is or what to do with it. In our history there isn't a single generation without the knowledge of war and killing: able to get on with life. We have never lived otherwise; we have always lived communally. We don't know how to live apart from each other, how to be answerable for ourselves or our own transgressions.

A man lies fallen on the streets of Grozny, killed by another man, staring into the sky. 'Write about it', they say. But I cannot. Nothing matters more than a single human life. Dead body. Dead bird. Dead building. In the name of what? Russian soldiers washing their boots in the Indian Ocean... Pumping Chechen oil... Are we crazy? Can a sane human being watch murder on television and listen to murder on the radio day after day?

I went to one of those funerals... They were burying a young officer, they had brought the body from Grozny. A tight ring of humanity around a freshly dug grave... A military band... Silence, no weeping even from the women... A general gave the address: the same phrases we heard a decade or a century ago, about the inviolability of our borders, about Greater Russia and vengeance and hatred and duty. Can killing be a duty? A little girl looked into the crimson grave, vulnerable and naive. 'Dad. Where are you, Dad? Why won't you say anything? You promised to come back... I've drawn you lots of pictures. Daddy, where are you?' Not even the military band could deafen her disbelief. And then she is torn away from the crimson grave like a little wild creature and carried off to the car. 'Dad! Daddy! Da...'

A human being among us. But the discourse of adulthood continues according to ancient ritual. An oath. A salute. We are not at war. But the coffins for Russia are on their way, as I write. ❏

*Svetlana Aleksiyevich is a Belarusian writer and journalist. Her controversial writings on feminism, Russian troops in Afghanistan and the Chernobyl disaster earned her the Swedish PEN Centre's 1996 Tucholsky Prize*

*Translated by Irena Maryniak*

# BABEL

## JAMES RON

# Rabin's two legacies

**From Israeli soldiers, testimony to their brutal treatment of Palestinians during Yitzhak Rabin's government**

*Jerusalem, November 1995: Rabin lies in state, Israel reaps the whirlwind*

FOLLOWING the assassination of Israeli prime minister Yitzhak Rabin the Israeli and western media reworked his biography into a seamless web of virtue. The emphasis was exclusively on Rabin, unwavering peacemaker. No-one recalled that when the Palestinian uprising began in late 1987, Rabin, then defence minister, ordered the army to crush the challenge through beatings: to 'break limbs'. The policy spiralled out of control and tens of thousands of Palestinians, according to human rights groups, were affected.

The consequences remain with us today, as each suicide bombing reminds us anew. Although the bitterness runs wide and deep among Israel's neighbours, a concerted Israeli effort to acknowledge its past can help. Rather than coming to terms with their history, however, Israelis have preferred not to remember.

### In the Green Mosque

AMONG 45 Israeli veterans I interviewed in 1993 was Shoni Albeck, a company commander during a January 1988 incident in Hebron. He recalled that one morning a group of Palestinian militants organised a protest during prayer time in what was known as the 'Green Mosque' on military maps. They barricaded themselves inside with hundreds of worshippers, climbed to the roof, and unfurled the Palestinian flag, using a loudspeaker to call for support. Several platoons of Israeli military reservists, backed by paramilitary Border Police, imposed a siege. The militants peppered the troops with stones, and the soldiers fired back with tear gas and .22 rifles.

As daylight ended, Albeck's men stormed the entrance, broke down the doors and burst into the building. Armed with assault rifles and clubs, the soldiers encountered no resistance once inside. 'What could they do?' he recalled. 'We had our guns and they were unarmed.' Albeck ordered a squad to the roof, but the militants faded into the crowd. Albeck ordered the hundreds of Palestinian worshippers to sit on the ground with their hands on their heads.

A senior officer appeared and told Albeck to withdraw. 'He said the Border Police would handle the rest,' Albeck recalled. Albeck walked to his jeep, drank some water, and chatted with his men, gazing at the mosque across the square. Then he saw the wounded begin to emerge.

'They staggered out of the mosque, badly hurt, bleeding, clothes torn. It was sickening. There were many of them, so many, I couldn't count.' Albeck ran back inside, seeing dozens of Palestinians lying on the ground, moaning and whimpering. 'I couldn't believe it. All the people we had taken prisoner, who had given up without resistance, had been clubbed within an inch of their life by the Border Police. For no reason. Some elderly and other normal people were mixed in with the rioters, but they were beaten as well.'

Yotam Levin, another reservist, kept a written account of events. 'Tens of soldiers, completely berserk, stormed the mosque,' Yotam wrote that night. 'There was shooting with live bullets and ammunition. There was a strong, sharp smell of stun grenades in the air.' Yotam wrote that when he tried to help the wounded, he became 'covered with the blood of Arabs whose limbs had been crushed and bent all out of shape... It was impossible to stop the madness. Soldiers beat wounded people on the head, as if completely crazed, and then some of the wounded lost consciousness. I saw one lieutenant stomping on the hand of a wounded person, lying all crumpled up.' Even the middle-aged reservists joined in, Levin wrote, contradicting Albeck's claim that only the ultra-tough Border Police were responsible. 'Most of our own company,' Levin wrote, 'completely lost control and entered into a kind of ecstasy of beating. Our supply sergeant even managed to break his club in half.'

## The professionals

ON 19 January 1988, Colonel Yehuda Meir, then a senior officer in the Nablus military headquarters, handpicked a team of elite soldiers for a job that required substantial professionalism. As opposed to the Green Mosque, Col Meir's operation was orderly and precise, and would later be described as the most careful implementation of Rabin's call to break protesters' arms and legs. At the time, Col Meir believes his operation was a vast improvement on the random beatings most soldiers were engaging in across the occupied lands. For Col Meir, wild, savage incidents such as the Green Mosque were evidence of a policy gone wrong.

Ilan Shani, then a lieutenant, recalled that his company was Col Meir's favourite. 'We played basketball all day,' Shani said, 'and only went to work when Meir needed something special.'

On 19 January, Shani's company were summoned to force stone-throwers off the main road near Beita village. By evening Shani's company had pushed into the village and imposed a curfew. Col Meir soon arrived together with a list of suspected organisers given him by Israel's secret police. Meir ordered Shani's men to find and arrest the suspects and then carefully break their limbs. The operation was complex; Meir needed to be sure that none of the suspects would be killed, and specified that only the best troops should participate.

Shani's men spread out through the village, checked identity cards, and found their targets. The Palestinians, numbering over a dozen, were handcuffed, blindfolded and then loaded on to a bus, lying face down on the ground. They drove to a nearby field and Shani asked for volunteers. There were plenty.

**They staggered out of the mosque, badly hurt, bleeding, clothes torn. It was sickening. So many I couldn't count**

Each Palestinian was led to a squad of three soldiers and an officer, forced to the ground and then clubbed. 'I began the beating each time,' Shani recalled, 'so as to give the men a good example of how it should be done. I wanted to make sure they would only hit the limbs, not internal organs.' Once a squad was sure it had broken the prisoner's arms and legs, they called for the next victim. 'There was a lot of screaming,' Shani said.

Gilad Anat, a soldier in Shani's platoon, remembers that 'when we were driving towards the field they said to make sure you hit the Arabs on the kneecap, since that was the best way to make sure the leg would break.' When it was over the Palestinians were left lying in the field, and the soldiers drove off in silence. 'I was surprised that none of the soldiers protested,' Shani recalled.

Col Meir has no qualms. During the preceding weeks he had led troops throughout the area, breaking demonstrations with rubber bullets, tear gas and, increasingly, clubs. 'We went through three generations of clubs in those first few months,' Meir recalls. 'They kept breaking, so we finally wound up using metal bars.' There were so many arrests that the military prisons were overwhelmed. 'We had no space to put them. The next best solution was to beat them,' Meir explains. The colonel believes the policy he introduced at Beita — selecting specific suspects for beatings — was far better than the massive, random clubbing then going on in the streets.

Shani, however, is now horrified. 'It was an act that Nazis would do,' he said. 'To take people like that, to not tell them what was going to happen to them, and to hit them while they lay bound and blindfolded — that's a Nazi act.'

## The good torturer

THE PAPERS soon filled with stories of beatings and Rabin, concerned with Israel's image, ordered the troops to cut down on street violence. Israel's clandestine interrogation centres, however, were shielded from prying eyes; abuses there continue until today. According to international human rights groups, over one-third of the 100,000 Palestinians arrested between 1988 and 1994 were violently interrogated.

AM, a military reservist, estimates that during a 30-day stint in 1988 he tortured some 300 persons. A tall, heavyset man, AM belonged to a team of six, and figures that together they handled 1,800 prisoners during his tour. The prisoners, mostly teenagers, were accused of waving flags, painting nationalist graffiti or throwing stones. None were real 'terrorists', because senior activists and armed militants were questioned elsewhere.

When AM first reported for reserve duty he was sent to al-Fara'a, an army prison, assuming he would pull guard duty. When he arrived, however, an officer pulled him aside and asked him if he 'wanted to do something special'. AM agreed immediately. Anything to evade the tedium of guard duty, he explains. He was taken to the interrogation section, an area set off from the rest of the prison, where he was told he would have an opportunity to combat terrorists. Formally, his job was 'security guard' in the section; practically, he hit prisoners when they refused to talk. 'The interrogator would sit facing me,' AM recalls, 'and the prisoner sat with his back in my direction. They would talk in Arabic, which I didn't understand. And then, when the interrogator didn't get the answer he wanted, he just looked at me, and I hit the guy.'

The only instructions AM received were to try to not kill. 'Everything else was permitted. I hit them in the face, the balls, everywhere.' He broke 'lots' of bones and smashed many teeth. 'I bet the Arab dentists had a lot of work to do on the prisoners we finished with,' he says. 'If the prisoners fell on the ground, we just kept beating them right where they lay. They started crying from the moment they came in to the room, but they really started to scream during the beatings. The interrogators liked that, because they wanted all the Arabs waiting outside to hear.' With some particularly stubborn detainees, interrogators poured a fiery liquid on to their open wounds. 'It was some kind of burning stuff, maybe astringent, and then they really began to scream. Screams like I've never heard.'

AM grew uneasy when he saw a Palestinian he knew among the prisoners, a young man who worked in a restaurant AM once managed. 'He looked at me, I looked at him, and all of a sudden it felt different.'

He continued until his 30 days were up, but his heart was no longer in it. 'The army always picked me for the dirty jobs because I'm ugly and fat,' AM says bitterly. 'They saw me walk into the prison and said, "That's a torturer for sure!"' AM falls silent for a moment. 'I'm not a monster,' he insists. 'They shouldn't have assumed I would be right for the job.'

Rabin has left us with two contradictory legacies. The most recent and most fragile is one of peace, but the legacy with the strongest roots is one of pain and humiliation. Rabin, unfortunately, is not here to help undo the mess he helped to create. For all his faults, he was one of the few Israelis with enough credibility to convince his countrymen to end the war.

The credibility Rabin enjoyed, however, is itself part of the problem, for he purchased it at the price of tens of thousands of damaged Palestinian lives, with all the subsequent hatred and bitterness. Rabin's successor, Shimon Peres, did not enjoy the same credibility and it cost him the election. The new prime minister, Binyamin Netanyahu, seems bent on going back to the darkest moments of Rabin's past. It is as if none of the lessons Rabin learned were passed on.

Every time a suicide bomber strikes, Israelis shake their heads in wonder. 'Crazy Arabs, how can we deal with such people?' I react differently. I wonder whether he was in the Green Mosque, whether he met Ilan Shani, or whether he was interrogated by AM. ❑

*James Ron, now a research fellow at Columbia University's Institute for War and Peace Studies, was a research consultant to Human Rights Watch and the International Committee of the Red Cross. He has written about human rights and counter-insurgency in Israel, Turkey, Nigeria and former Yugoslavia*

*This article, excerpted from 45 interviews with Israeli veterans in 1993, was made possible by a research and writing grant from the MacArthur Foundation*

# DIARY

## STANLEY COHEN

# No time for reconciliation

**Israeli Jews are too locked in to their own domestic conflicts to care about what happens to the Palestinians. Peace is precarious and 'reconciliation' a long way off**

MARCH 1988. These were the terrible early months of the intifada. No-one had any idea where the stone-throwing and mass demonstrations were leading, how long all this would last, whether it was under anyone's control.

Meantime, the Israeli army was reacting with both controlled and uncontrolled frenzy. Soldiers had been directly ordered by the defence minister, Yitzhak Rabin, to 'break limbs'.

A friend of mine, who had returned to America after living here for nearly 10 years, was visiting for a wedding. She was placed at a table with someone whom neither of us would normally meet: businessman, right-wing Labour, ex-*Palmach*. The talk, as always in Israel, soon got round to 'the situation'. His message was predictable: the uprising would soon be put down; the international media were biased against Israel; the Palestinians were unimportant and the Arab states would never accept Israel's right to exist. The conversation was civil and my friend remained restrained — even after being given the standard condescending line that people who had not been born here could never understand the Middle East.

She then asked a mild enough question: what, then, did he think was the solution to the conflict? Suddenly, his tone turned vicious: 'Only you Americans have this idea that all problems have solutions. Can't you accept that there are conflicts, like this one, which simply have no solution?' Only generations of violence lay ahead.

Variants of this world view are well known. They include the crudest Zionist propaganda about how 'we' have always wanted peace and 'they' will never be reconciled to our existence; stereotypes about the 'Arab mentality'; sophisticated theories of academic Orientalists. At the core was the fixed principle behind Israeli and US policy: a refusal to recognise that the Palestinians were getting ready to compromise.

Even as late as 1988, full assent to the two-state solution — recognition of the PLO, stopping settlements, withdrawal from the Occupied Territories, recognition of Palestinian sovereignty — lay beyond the margins of conventional political discourse. Our wedding guest came from the mainstream. Like everyone else he wanted peace, but only when the Palestinians and Arabs were 'ready' — which meant being ready to make peace without getting anything in exchange. Not 'land for peace' but 'peace for peace' — exactly the same formula announced by newly elected prime minister Binyamin Netanyahu in the American Congress in July 1996. In the meantime, any talk of reconciliation was ignorant or utopian.

SEPTEMBER 1993. On 13 September, the day of the Great White House Signing, I was in Gaza. The occasion was a conference organised by Dr Iyad al-Sarraj from the Gaza Community Mental Health Programme. The conference 'Mental Health and the Challenge of Peace', had been planned a year previously, long before anyone could have guessed the timing of the Oslo Agreement.

The scenes in the streets and alleys of Gaza were unforgettable: truckloads of people waving the Palestinian flag, children holding balloons, cars blasting their horns, posters of Arafat on the walls, rumours of Israeli soldiers being given flowers. The exhilaration was real and not even the most hardened political veteran was ready to discount this as a bad case of false consciousness.

Unclear, though, as the details of the Oslo Declaration of Principles were then, everyone at the conference expressed grave reservations. What could be deduced then is clearer now. On basic principles — land, water, settlements, territorial integrity, Jerusalem, state sovereignty, the return of the refugees — Israel was conceding less than the minimum. Even if not everyone was ready to accept Edward Said's later diagnosis of Oslo as the 'Palestinian Versailles', the mood was visibly more restrained than the rejoicings in the street.

Still, bogus as they sounded from Rabin's lips, words like 'reconciliation' were in the air. Over the next few months, the majority of Israelis — a steady 60 per cent by all polls — showed themselves willing to support the 'peace process'. They wanted to get out of Gaza and make some territorial adjustments in the West Bank. They were ready to recognise the PLO and — remarkably — to adjust themselves to the physical presence of Arafat in Gaza and his transmutation from arch-enemy to a statesman who would police the Palestinians for us.

And on the Palestinian side, even the most sceptical observers could not align themselves with Hamas rejectionism. They had to settle for working within rather than against the agreements. The hope was that stage by stage, without explicit Israeli collusion, the momentum to a Palestinian state was inevitable.

SEPTEMBER 1994. Another conference in Gaza, this one organised by the Palestinian human rights lawyer Raji Sourani from the Gaza Centre for Rights and Law.

Again, there was the contrast between the street outside — relaxed, now completely free of Israeli soldiers — and the mood inside. The feeling of empowerment and autonomy — something extraordinary *had* happened — was matched by a sense of demoralisation, failure, even mourning.

One session was devoted to the subject of reconciliation. In the CNN spectacle that passes for 'news', the Palestinian-Israeli conflict had already slipped into the zone of History. The iconography of the Secret Talks in Oslo, the White House Handshake, back to Oslo for the Nobel Prize...all this appeared alongside the fall of the Berlin Wall and the South African elections. And the human rights community was already being asked how the 'justice in transition' debates (emerging from the collapse of Latin American dictatorships, state communism and apartheid) applied here.

No doubt some 'transition' was taking place — but beyond this, these comparisons looked to us then (and now) as sadly irrelevant or premature. The Israeli government was backtracking on even the Oslo and Cairo provisions; in the West Bank, the human rights violations from the 'old days' were happening on a smaller scale: torture and ill-treatment of detainees (now more often Hamas than Fatah), house-demolition,

*(Right) Occupied Territories, Israel 1988: Palestinian funeral procession in the days of intifada*

restrictions of movement, extrajudicial killings by IDF undercover units. Settlements were blandly being expanded, more land confiscated, the boundaries of Jerusalem extended.

Of course, even in the worst-case projection, this was not the final status. The negotiations, however protracted and one-sided, looked eventually to give more control to the Palestinians. But even in the best-case projection of a viable Palestinian state (a prospect further from the government's mind than the Israeli peace camp wishfully thought) there will be one crucial difference from those other places. This will not be an internal transition, where previous enemies have to live together in the same society, but a separation into two political entities. The analogy is not Argentina after the generals, Poland after the Communists or South Africa after apartheid, but rather decolonisation. The model of the original Zionist movement as colonialist was always a little implausible. But the standard by which the interim and final status agreements should be judged is the decolonisation of the post-1967 territory.

**I find it impossible to imagine the circumstances in which retrospective justice will occur. There will be no political authority to put Shabaq agents on trial for torture**

Even if the internal transition model is irrelevant and decolonisation is a long way off, we tried in Gaza to imagine the justice debate.

First, there is the issue of truth and acknowledgement, 'coming to terms with the past' through such methods as Truth Commissions. In the Israeli-Palestinian case knowledge was and is freely available. The relative openness of Israeli democracy and the Palestinians' own freedom to know and talk, exposed every facet of the occupation to scrutiny. Human rights organisations — Palestinian, Israeli and international — documented and disseminated information to an extent unthinkable in any of those authoritarian regimes. But public knowledge is not official acknowledgement. I find it hard to visualise any future Israeli government setting up a Truth Commission. Note, though, that injustices of the Occupation are far easier to acknowledge than the recent exposures by the 'revisionist historians' about what happened in 1948. That history is the real taboo.

The second issue is justice and accountability, by prosecuting individual perpetrators, disqualification or compensation. Again, I find it impossible to imagine the circumstances in which retrospective justice will occur. There will be no political authority to put Shabaq agents on trial for torture. The prospects for compensation are more realistic — not so much for individuals but as social restitution. Mass payments to the Palestinian Authority, however, are made more to stabilise Chairman Arafat than out of any sense of redress for past injustices.

The third issue is reconciliation itself, a political goal that confronts both sides, whatever the lack of historical symmetry between them. The problem is not how to live together but how to live side by side, with some respect and dignity. After one interim year, this seemed a long way away. On the Israeli side, there was little spirit of reconciliation, whether at the level of official negotiations or the humiliations inflicted by ordinary soldiers at road-blocks. This is a settling of accounts rather than a sense of accountability. Measures such as the amnesty or release of prisoners will result not from the spirit of reconciliation, but from pragmatic political considerations. And as long as terrorism continues, Israelis can hardly be expected to change.

Does any of this matter? One thesis is that no just resolution is possible without honestly confronting the past. Without a full acknowledgement of injustices — including the atrocities inflicted by Palestinians — the ghosts of history will return. The other thesis is that it doesn't matter what goes on in people's heads, hearts or souls. A structure of political and legal compulsion has to be implemented which gives people no choice but to conform.

JULY 1996. There are any number of good explanations about why Peres and the Labour Party lost the May elections. Some of these theories complement, others contradict each other, none is entirely implausible.

Given that the gap was so small — a mere 15,000 people, less than 0.5 per cent of the electorate had to vote the other way — it makes sense to look at proximate, contingent reasons for the right wing's victory. The Labour campaign was terrible; Peres is a loser with no public appeal; the religious parties were bought off; the Russian immigrant vote discounted; Rabin and Peres moved too fast (or too slow) and never prepared public opinion for the deal; too many Israeli Arabs (how ungrateful of them) turned in blank ballots to punish Peres for the cruel invasion of Lebanon.

And, of course, there was the Rabin assassination and the government's fateful error in trying to placate rather than isolate the religious right-wing forces behind the assassin. And finally, perhaps the most powerful reason, there were the appalling Hamas suicide bombings of February and March, leaving behind, justifiably, a sense of deep insecurity in all Israelis.

But behind these proximate causes lie deeper currents. From the end of the 1970s, the Zionist socialist movement's power base has been eroding. They had lost the oriental Jewish working class, the development towns, the religious populations and the new immigrants — lost not directly to the Likud, but to the ethnic religious blocks. The successful institutions of Labour Zionism — the Histadrut, the health funds, the kibbutz movement — were in decay. Begin's right-wing populism has let the genie out of the bottle.

The sociological complexity of this story means that the election results cannot be read as a simple vote 'against peace'. To the Palestinians, however, these complexities might be a little less interesting. They see a simpler message: even the grudging concessions of the Peres government were too much. If we calculate the Jewish vote alone (a simple statistical exercise rather than the right-wing's racism about the power of the 18 per cent Israeli Arab vote) then the ratio becomes something like 56 per cent to 44 per cent for Netanyahu. A grimmer assessment would be to count only the Labour and Meretz voters as supporting anything like reconciliation. This gives only one third of the Jewish vote. When de Klerk held his referendum in South Africa, some two thirds of the white voters supported his direction for change. This one-third/two-third breakdown is the critical ratio.

By this reading, two out of every three Israeli Jews are too insecure to take any chances. More accurately: they are too locked into the internal conflicts in Israeli society — traditional against modern, Ashkenazi against Sephardi, religious against secular — to be bothered about what happens to the Palestinians. Their cognitive map is matched exactly by the public pronouncements of the Netanyahu government. That is: wait till the Palestinians are 'ready to fulfil their obligations' (that is, stop all terrorism and accept Oslo minus); consolidate settlements; refuse to negotiate about Jerusalem — but all the time make enough noise about 'peace' to keep the Clinton administration happy.

Various completely opposite political forces are spreading the theory that the election made little difference. American-orchestrated international wisdom is that Netanyahu is so pliable that he will eventually be pushed into a final settlement not very different from Labour's. Many

Arabs and Palestinians profess to see the Zionist enemy as totally static and homogeneous: Peres is just as bad as Netanyahu. And there are the usual Trotskyist theories that clear repression is better than hypocritically disguised repression; things have to get worse before they get better.

There is no need to romanticise the Rabin-Peres years to understand that such theories utterly underestimate the radically different composition of the new government. Anyone who does not grasp this has no idea what sort of people are in Netanyahu's cabinet.

How the Palestinians will respond is uncertain. Meantime, Arafat desperately consolidates his internal power. During the last year, both Dr Iyad al-Sarraj and Raji Sourani (Iyad's lawyer) have been arbitrarily arrested, detained and maltreated by the Palestinian Authority for daring to criticise Arafat.

On 18 June, an advertisement appeared on the front page of *Ha-aretz*, the leading Israeli newspaper. Sponsored by an unknown group called 'We Will Not Forget', it consisted of a biblical passage from Kings I. This describes how King Ahab obtained a vineyard from a man who did not want to sell it: Queen Jezebel persuaded two men to swear falsely that the owner had committed a capital crime; after he was executed, Ahab took possession of the vineyard. God now sends the prophet Elijah to curse King Ahab: 'And thou shalt speak unto him saying: Thus sayeth the Lord: Hast thou killed and also taken possession?'

The message was obvious: the same people responsible for Rabin's assassination had now reaped the advantage by winning the election. In case the biblical trope was unclear, the advertisement concluded: 'This was placed as a painful reminder to the public and to those who take God's name in vain...upon the swearing in of a new government in Israel, 230 days after the murder of Yitzhak Rabin.

The religious right immediately reacted by calling on the attorney-general to prosecute the anonymous sponsors for criminal incitement. This is where Israeli Jewish society remains: settling its own internal scores, reconciling its permanent contradiction between religious-ethnic exclusivity and democracy. Reconciliation with the Palestinians is not very high on this agenda. ❑

*Stanley Cohen* is professor of criminology at the Hebrew University, Jerusalem, and Martin White professor of sociology at the London School of Economics

# US DIVIDES

## CHARLES GLASS

# Another American, God help us, century

**How stands the Union on the threshold of the last election of the American century? Not well, sir, not well. Time to rewrite the Constitution? Yes, indeed, sir**

*'The US prison population rose to nearly 1.6 million inmates in 1995, double the number of a decade ago, the Justice Department said.' (Reuter, Washington, DC, 18 August 1996)*

IN THE autumn of 1796, General George Washington, 'first in war, first in peace, first in the hearts of his countrymen', urged Americans to preserve their unity and liberty. He was using the occasion of his imminent retirement from public life, near the end of his second term as president, to deliver a Farewell Address to the American People. He proposed this challenge to the young republic: preserve the freedom for which his generation had fought from 1776 to 1783. It would be a more protracted and arduous task than defeating the British in the War of Independence.

Washington saw the foremost threat to liberty in 'the common and continued mischiefs of the spirit of party'. Of party spirit, he warned, 'It serves always to distract the public councils, and enfeeble the public administration. It agitates the community with ill-founded jealousy and false alarms; kindles the animosity of one part against another, foments occasionally riot and insurrection. It opens the doors to foreign influence and corruption...' He counselled the people and their elected representatives, 'promote, then, as an object of primary importance, institutions for the general diffusion of knowledge. In proportion as the structure of a government gives force to public opinion, it is essential that public opinion should be enlightened.' He advised Americans 'to cherish public credit' and to avoid 'likewise the accumulation of debt'. On what would later be called foreign policy, he said, 'The great rule of conduct for us, in regard to foreign nations, is, in extending our commercial relations, to have with them as little political connection as possible.' That object required 'good faith and justice towards all nations' but no 'passionate attachment' to a foreign power. 'Harmony, liberal intercourse with all nations,' he said, 'are recommended by policy, humanity, and interest.'

In that year, 1796, the father of our country prepared to return to his Virginia estate content that the candidates to succeed him were John Adams and Thomas Jefferson.

How stands the Union to which General Washington bade farewell 200 years ago? One measure of America's attentiveness to the general's advice is the choice this year for the office he honoured: 'Bill' Clinton and 'Bob' Dole. If we had listened to him, men like Clinton and Dole would not be considered. Instead, Washington's heirs in the capital that bears his name have dishonoured his legacy. The political parties he despised monopolise the electoral system, and concentrations of corporate wealth dominate the parties. The two largest parties, the Republicans and Democrats, control the executive office and legislatures of the nation and of the 50 states. Worse, even the supposed two-party system became, in the journalists I F Stone's phrase in 1968, 'a one-party rubber stamp'.

Although George Washington advised us that 'public opinion should be enlightened,' Americans have degraded education. In the schools and at home, commercial television has superseded teachers and parents as guardians of instruction. Rather than 'avoiding likewise the accumulation of debt,' as the general counselled, the United States has borrowed more money, trillions of dollars for the military alone, in the last dozen years than in all its previous history. In contrast to Washington's abhorrence of 'passionate attachments' to other nations, the US government allies itself to some foreign states, makes clients of others and damns the rest to international purgatory. It sends ships and soldiers to more than 50 countries each year. American military, intelligence and economic power is the prop of governments whose populations would otherwise depose them as General Washington and his comrades overthrew Britain in North America. Is this what Washington intended when he counselled 'against the mischief of foreign intrigue, to guard against the impostures of pretended patriotism'?

*'I asked Tom if countries always apologised when they had done wrong, and he says, "Yes; the little ones does."'* (Tom Sawyer Abroad, Mark Twain)

WELCOME to the American Century. Its end draws nigh, but American imperium is determined to outlast it under mediocre and callow men like Clinton and Dole. The American Century was in gestation 100 years after Washington issued the warning his country ignored, and its imperial pretensions violate every principle upon which Washington, Jefferson and Thomas Paine stood when they confronted the Red Coats. America's Century, perhaps only the first of many, was conceived in the economic necessity of disposing of more than US$1 billion in manufactured goods the American public could not consume. It formed itself in the febrile imaginations of Alfred Thayer Mahan the naval theorist, Theodore Roosevelt the jingo politician, William Randolph Hearst the press boss, and J Pierpont Morgan and Jay Gould the robber barons. One hundred years ago, in the riotous Gay Nineties, American whites completed their conquest of the North American continent with the final massacre of 300 Sioux men, women and children at Wounded Knee, South Dakota. The Census Bureau declared the frontier closed, and America turned its attention to the world.

The presidential candidates in the last pre-centennial election, in 1896, were William Jennings Bryan and William McKinley. Bryan stood for silver currency, urging Americans not to be 'crucified on a Cross of Gold', and against high tariffs. Anaconda Copper and William Randolph Hearst, both owners of silver mines, supported the Democrat Bryan. The rest of industry, needing tariffs to compete with English manufacturers, went for McKinley, as did the voters.

With gold, high tariffs and a vanquished native population on the reservation, President William McKinley entered the markets of the world through what his secretary of state, John Hay, called 'the open door'. The Republic was to become what the US historian William Appleman Williams called 'an informal empire', achieving dominance and access without the burden of colonies and native administration-empire on the cheap. Another historian, Howard Zinn, observed in his excellent *A People's History of the United States*, 'If peaceful imperialism turned out to be impossible, military action might be needed.' It was needed more often than not. When doors closed, the US Marines kicked them in. Of course, the bigger doors, like those of the British, Dutch and French empires, stayed shut to American enterprise. The State Department troops, as the regular army derisively called the Marines, broke open the smaller doors of banana republics and the crumbling Spanish Empire. It worked. McKinley made Puerto Rico, Guam, Hawaii and the Philippines into colonies of a formal empire. He made the informal empire as well, with America the overlord of Cuba, Haiti, and Central America. He put US troops into China. He and his supporters made America, as Mark Twain lamented, 'a World Power'. A German editorial cartoonist drew Uncle Sam with his arms wrapped around the world, hands struggling to touch, proclaiming, 'I can't quite reach that far, but that may come later.'

*Jefferson assumed we would rewrite the Constitution every 20 years. 'The Constitution belongs to the living and not the dead,' he said. It is time for the living to assert themselves*

Most US intellectuals and journalists supported the murderous battles against the Filipinos and action in China, but Mark Twain worried that the old spirit of Washington was giving way to the new patriotism of Brigadier General Frederick Funston. Funston was a hero of the Philippines war, a Norman Schwartzkopf of his generation. US troops had orders to kill everyone over the age of 10 in some provinces, put 300,000 peasants into concentration camps in another and set fire to the countryside — exploits of which Funston boasted and which were emulated 60 years later in Vietnam. Funston captured the Filipino revolutionary leader Emiliano Aguinaldo by a deception that Mark Twain viciously condemned. When Funston returned to the US, he denounced all opponents of the Philippines War as 'traitors'. Twain wrote in response, 'On these terms I am quite willing to wear that honourable badge & not willing to be affronted with the title of Patriot & classified with the Funstons when so help me God I have not done anything to deserve it.'

Twain joined the Anti-Imperialist Leagues, along with William James, Andrew Carnegie and half a million other Americans who opposed colonising the Philippines. Challenging an imperial America was a duty imposed on him, he believed, by Washington's legacy. 'It was Washington's influence that made Lincoln and all other real patriots the Republic has known; it was Washington's influence that made the soldiers who saved the Union; and that influence will save us always, and bring us back to the fold when we stray.' He contrasted the growing influence of Funstonism and all it represented:

'Then the thing for the world to do in the present case is to turn the gilt front of Funston's evil notoriety to the rear, and expose the back aspect of it, the right and black aspect of it, to the youth of the land; otherwise *he* will become an example and a boy-admiration, and will most sorrowfully and grotesquely bring his breed of patriotism into competition with Washington's.

...Funston's example bred many imitators, and ghastly additions to our history; the torturing of Filipinos by the awful "water cure", for instance, to make them confess — what? Truth? Or lies?... you know about those atrocities which the War Office has been hiding a year or two; and about General Smith's now world-celebrated order of *massacre* — thus summarised by the press from Major Waller's testimony: *Kill and burn — this is not time to take prisoners — the more you kill the better — Kill all above the age of 10 — make Samar a howling wilderness!*'

A new empire deserved a new flag. Twain suggested that 'we can have just our usual flag, with the white stripes painted black and the stars replaced by the skull and crossbones.'

'Today the net worth of the world's 358 richest people is equal to the combined income of the poorest 45 per cent of the world's population — 2.3 billion people.' (James Gustave Speth, administrator UN Development Programme, International Herald Tribune, 23 August 1996)

A NEW century is near, and America is enhancing its global reach by missile, warplane, soldier, business and television. As Mahan and Teddy Roosevelt prepared the ground for US domination in the twentieth century, military and economic planners — many writing in *Foreign Affairs* and *The New York Times* — are setting the stage for our role in the twenty-first. Resistance, often brave and admirable, is insignificant. A rally for democracy in Indonesia, an attack on Israeli occupying troops in south Lebanon, an indian uprising in the Amazon, an attack on oil installations in Africa that pollute the air and water or isolated attempts at economic independence do not tilt the balance. Just as the Filipino rebels were conquered a century ago, their memory has encouraged Filipino democrats ever since. New generations may take inspiration from those who today risk their lives to stop slavery in third-world textile mills, who fight sex tourism by overfed European and US child abusers and who champion the right of the poor to govern themselves and work for fair rewards.

Transnational corporations, government propagandists, the mass media and other institutions of coercion and manipulation so distort democracy and liberty that Americans are expected to believe countless lies. Among them, that the best leader for our country as it enters the millennium is either Bob Dole or Bill Clinton. That our people's only contribution to world culture can be the mass-manufactured hamburger and a cartoon mouse. That big corporations, left to themselves, will protect the air we breathe, the food we eat and the water we drink. That we have the right, and often the obligation, to impose our will on the world by force. That international law should not apply to our actions. That the world is ours to plunder. That the poor in America are robbing the rich. That immigrants, apart from billionaires like the former Australian Rupert Murdoch, are without civil and political rights. That we should erase from the Statue of Liberty the exhortation of Emma Lazarus that has welcomed immigrants since 1886 — 'Give me your tired, your poor,/ Your huddled masses yearning to be free,/ The wretched refuse of your teeming shore,/ Send these, the homeless, tempest tost, to me:/ I lift my lamp beside the golden door.' That we must put the lamp out and enrich our richest.

Perhaps I, as an American living for a quarter century in exile, have no right to criticise my country for turning away from Washington and the principles in the preamble to the Declaration of Independence. When my younger son, Edward, and I crossed the United States last year, we traversed in a few weeks ground our ancestors crossed over two centuries. We began in Baltimore, Maryland, where some Glass exiles from Ireland, probably Catholic slaves or indentured servants, had settled in 1690. We went to Alleghenies, the frontier with the indian tribes of western Pennsylvania when they settled there in 1790. The Glasses, a family called McGuire and Father Demetrius Gallitzin, a Russian prince with a French

Catholic mother who was the first priest ordained in British America, founded a Catholic village in a beautiful forest of pines. They named it Loreto for Our Lady of Loreto. Ancestral tombstones bound us, including my son born in England of an Anglo-Scottish mother, to that land. Later, we walked every foot of the field where the battle of Gettysburg in Pennsylvania decided the fate of the Union in 1863. We moved west, as the sons of those buried in Loreto did, to Chicago, where they joined the Union army in the War Between the States. Then, again following their trail, we made our way west across the Plains and the Rocky Mountains to California and the end of the frontier. We belong to that country, wherever we dwell, and it is part of us.

Moving abroad has not absolved me of the obligations of citizenship and of opposing my country's crimes at home or abroad. I second the words of Carl Schurz, the immigrant, financier and cabinet member, who told Congress in 1872, 'Our country, right or wrong. When right, to be kept right; when wrong, to be put right.' Putting America right may require a second revolution, and I hope it takes place before the powerful put another 1.6 million men behind bars or launch another war in the third world.

*'I like a little rebellion now and then. It's like a storm in the atmosphere.'*
*Thomas Jefferson*

A MERICA has the means for a revolution without bloodshed. We can write a new constitution that restores sovereignty to the people, who have lost ground in two centuries to unaccountable corporate wealth and government power. Jefferson assumed we would rewrite the Constitution every 20 years, but we have yet to produce a second. 'The Constitution,' he wrote, 'belongs to the living and not the dead.' It is time for the living to assert themselves. Article V of the Constitution of 1787 permits the people to call a convention to propose amendments to the Constitution, effectively allowing them to write a new one. It is the constitutional way to stop the empire and save the republic. If not, I fear what the increasing disparities of wealth, and thus of power, mean for my country and the world. ❑

**Charles Glass** *is the author of* Tribes with Flags *and* Money for Old Rope, *both published by Picador*

*Read all about it: Boligee teenagers read the national press on the town's church burnings*

# Burning black

*Black churches are burning again in the South. In the woods outside Boligee, in Western Alabama's 'black belt', where three churches were razed and a fourth narrowly escaped, volunteers from across the USA and from Canada are rebuilding Zion. 'The devil is still around,' says the Reverend W D Lewis, 92-year-old pastor of Little Zion Baptist Church, reduced to ashes in December 1995. Nearby Mount Zion Baptist Church was razed to the ground a month later on the same night as Mount Zoar. Attempts to discount any racial motivation behind the 40 black church burnings in the last 18 months, foundered on the hate mail and graffiti daubed on the churches by their destroyers. Most of those arrested so far are young white males, often with links to the Klu Klux Klan. In June, Congress unanimously passed a bill doubling the sentence for church burning from 10 to 20 years and granting federal funds for rebuilding*

© **Photographs by Betty Press/Panos Pictures**

*Music Festival at Boligee: T-shirt displays map of burnings across the South*
*Documents in the case: Civil Rights hearing examines evidence of racism behind burnings*

*Rebuilding Mount Zion: member of Operation Understanding, multi-racial volunteer rebuilding group*
*The Rev W D Lewis, 92-year-old pastor of Little Zion Church inspects the volunteers' work*

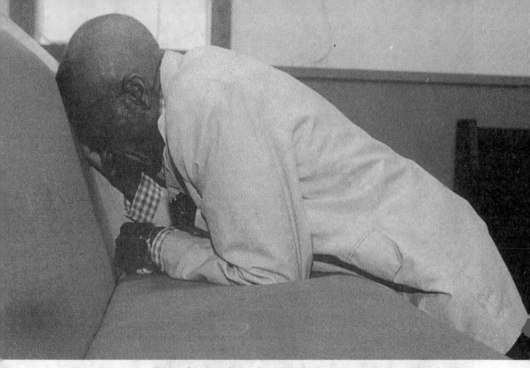

*Prayers for renewal: members of Little Zion Baptist church worship elsewhere*
*Local builder reads graffiti left by volunteers: 'Burned with hate, rebuilt stronger with love'*

# MEDIA

## RAFAEL MARQUES

# Rewards for the unworthy

**Despite the constitution and the Lusaka Ceasefire Protocol of November 1994, both of which stipulate a free press, journalism in Angola remains under fire from all quarters**

NEITHER the MPLA government of José Eduardo dos Santos, president of Angola since 1979, nor Jonas Savimbi's UNITA, who have disputed power since 1975, have much time for the free expression of public opinion, open debate or tolerance of other views. Criticism by the dominantly state-owned media is not appreciated. Journalists who stick their necks out can expect short shrift from the authorities and scant protection from their union or the law. The majority toe the line and are well rewarded by a grateful government.

In a country where moral and social values have broken down; where the economy is in crisis and corruption the most serious threat to reconstruction; where the police in the capital, Luanda, are little more than urban bandits and much of the countryside still disputed between the government and UNITA; and where most citizens, consumed by the daily struggle for clean water, food, education and healthcare — a beer costs US$1 on a teacher's monthly salary of US$5 with yearly inflation running at over 3,000 per cent — have neither money to buy a paper nor faith in the credibility of the media as a whole, the problems of the press corps may seem a small matter.

However, given that most Angolans remain unaware that they have any civil or political rights, the media has a role to play not only in informing them of their rights, but in holding Angola's rulers accountable to its citizens for their record to date and for progress in the reconstruction of the country after 16 years of civil war.

With things as they are, many journalists prefer self-censorship to the prospect of dismissal, demotion or relocation to other jobs by the government. The last few years have seen Vitor Silva, director of the national daily, *Jornal de Angola*, fired in mid-1994 for publishing a cartoon on the ruinous economic management of then prime minister Marcolino Moco; Pires Ferreira, *JA*'s sports editor, dismissed in March 1996 after his series of stories in the Luanda-based newsletter *Folha 8* on corruption and the abuse of power inside the paper. In mid-1995, Carlos Pilartes, a journalist with Radio Nacional de Angola, was dismissed for criticising government economic policy; and in June 1996, 'Opiniao', a popular weekly current affairs programme put out by Televisao Popular de Angola (TPA), was axed by the government following a performance by the minister of agriculture, Isaac dos Anjos, in which he justified a personal bank loan of US$3 million taken to invest in his own business on the grounds that while other ministers didn't need a loan because they were already rich, he did. Urging the government to be more tolerant, the minister also encouraged viewers to express their opinions freely and demonstrate in order to strengthen democracy in Angola.

Journalists in the provinces fare no better. Joao Borges, correspondent of the Angolan news agency, ANGOP, was fired on 19 June 1996 after the governor of Bie Province, Paulino dos Santos, accused him of publishing an anonymous letter in the weekly newsletter, *Comercio Actualidade (CA)*, complaining about the governor's monopoly of commercial ventures in Cuito. The governor had been tipped off by a colleague of Borges on *CA* who saw his way to advancement. The informant got an expenses-paid trip to Cuito; Borges, having resisted the chance of keeping his job and the promise of a car if he revealed the authors of other anonymous letters critical of the governor, remains carless and restricted to Bie Province by on the governor's orders.

The material conditions in which journalists work are every bit as demoralising as state control and the low esteem in which they are held by their public. Salaries are low — between US$10 and US$20 a month at *JA*, the country's leading daily, depending on seniority — and basic equipment like typewriters and telephone lines are in short supply. When *JA*'s journalists went on strike for better conditions from July to December last year, the management refused to negotiate and broke the strike by the age-old practice of bribing a couple of its supporters with trips abroad. Editors involved in the strike have been demoted.

'Loyalty', on the other hand, is well rewarded: permission to divert official funds into private enterprises, access to cars, the chance of overseas reporting trips and access to foreign currency allowances are a few of the plum prizes. Every week, loyal management is rewarded with one crate of beer, one crate of Coca Cola, one bottle of whisky and, on occasion, one bottle of mineral water. At Radio Nacional de Angola and TPA the gifts are better. Journalists who covered President José Eduardo dos Santos' successful re-election campaign in October 1992 were rewarded with cars. Thus is self-censorship encouraged: never mind conformity, feel the benefits.

**Media debate on the social and economic crisis facing Angolans is a means of rending accountable those who have reduced the country to this state — and of educating people in their rights**

A semi-independent media operates alongside the state sector. The four radio stations, Luanda Antenna Comercial (LAC) in Luanda, Radio Morena in Benguela, Radio Cabinda Comercial and Radio 2000 in Lubango, suffer the same intervention as their state-owned counterparts. In 1992, LAC's popular programme 'Recados ao meu chefe', offended government sensibilities with a report on management abuses in public sector corporations. Its producer, Ismael Mateus, was offered a government constituency in the forthcoming elections and, despite his failure at the polls, was subsequently spirited abroad with a scholarship to Portugal. The programme ceased production.

The most popular programme on LAC is the live weekly phone-in, 'Livro de reclamacoes'. In December 1995, a caller demanded the president's resignation. Overnight, he became a national hero and the talk of the town. The producer of the programme, Mateus Goncalves, was immediately warned by the Direcao de Investigacao Criminal that future topics of phone calls must be vetted prior to broadcasting. The police sought the caller in vain: he had left town for a few days.

Two independent newsletters, *Actual Fax* and *Folha 8*, and one mildly critical weekly, *Comercio Actualidade*, circulate in Luanda. *Actual Fax* is the successor to *Imparcial Fax* which closed down after its editor Ricardo de

*Luanda 1992: they won the election for the president — when will they hold him accountable?*

Mello was murdered in January 1995; *Folha 8,* a bi-weekly newsletter, surfs government and other circles for the latest hot gossip in the capital. It is available by fax but at US$50 for 12 issues circulates almost exclusively among foreigners and the local elite. The weekly newspaper *Correio de Semana* claims to be independent but, since the 1992 elections, has published nothing controversial; it relies entirely on *Jornal de Angola*'s facilities — and goodwill — for its survival. Competition among the so-called independent media creates tension among its journalists. Jealousy and betrayal are actively encouraged by the government.

Discouraged by the conditions of work, many of the country's most competent journalists have left the profession. Those that remain fall into four broad categories: the 'loyals', who are often security agents, reporting back on their colleagues to the Servico de Informacao (Sinfo) or management; the 'mercenaries' (a label given by the Ministry of Social Communications) who work as correspondents for the foreign media such as the Voice of America, BBC and news agencies; the 'puppets', the 'yes' men and women who do as they are told; and the 'courageous', those few journalists prepared not to conform who continue to find ways round censorship.

The government's refusal to permit a UN radio station, mandated by Security Council Resolution 976 in February 1995, demonstrates its fear of any change in the media dispensation. Any erosion of its control over the media could prove dangerous: a free press would find President dos Santos at the centre of hostile comment: he has been in power since 1979 and most Angolans blame him equally with UNITA leader Jonas Savimbi for the country's acute social, economic and moral crisis.

UNITA tolerates even less press freedom than the MPLA. Prior to the multi-party elections in 1992, UNITA officials threatened journalists in Luanda that, if they won, they would dismiss them because of critical coverage in the press. UNITA's radio station, the Voice of the Resistance of the Black Cockerel (Vorgan) and its magazine *TerraAngolana*, serve only as crude pro-UNITA propaganda outlets. In February this year, Human Rights Watch observed that journalists working in UNITA-held zones faced even greater difficulties than those working in government-held areas: 'all information is censored and visits by foreign correspondents are tightly controlled and stage-managed.'

Angolans no longer trust their media. During the war, people listened closely to domestic broadcasts on prospects for peace, but for the few with access to short-wave radios, it was the foreign media, especially the Portuguese services of the BBC World Service and the Voice of America, that were the main source of information.

Stories reported on Angola in languages other than Portuguese, make little impact, except when foreign governments take the government to task. Foreign journalists based in Angola like Reuters' correspondent in 1993-1995, Nick Shaxson and the *Independent's* Karl Maier are widely respected for reporting things too dangerous for local journalists even to talk about, such as the November 1992 massacres at cemeteries around Luanda. Angolan journalists working for foreign media also have some latitude but remain vulnerable to intimidation. They often avoid filing stories on controversial subjects such as known cases of senior ministerial and presidential corruption.

If there is to be any change in Angola's media landscape, courageous individuals prepared to push out the boundaries of press freedom are needed in the state media. Investigative journalism is an important tool in exposing and challenging the culture of corruption that has spread throughout society like a terminal cancer. Media debate on the social and economic crisis facing Angolans is a means of rendering accountable the political and military elites that have reduced the country to this state, and of educating people in their rights.

New independent radio stations and newspapers are not the immediate priority: the government has shown its skill in co-opting or paralysing independent press initiatives. Help in raising the standards, quality and resources of the state media is more urgent. Not only will this signal to all Angolans that a new post-war era has truly begun, it could act also as a catalyst for reconciliation. ❏

*Rafael Marques is an Angolan journalist based in Luanda*

Further Reading
*Between War and Peace: Arms Trade and Human Rights Abuses since the Lusaka Protocol* Human Rights Watch, February 1996
*Media em Angola: Relatorio do grupo tarefa do MISA sobre Angola 1 a 8 Dezembro 1993; Actualizado em Fevereiro 1995* Media Institute of Southern Africa, February 1995; *Folha 8* Fax: Luanda 392289

# LETTER FROM ANGOLA

## VICTORIA BRITTAIN

# The longest war

**Angolans have been the victims of civil war since 1975. Children, in particular, have been targeted, boys and girls have been kidnapped to serve in the ranks of UNITA; others, orphaned, traumatised, left to their own devices, hustle a life in the ruins of the cities**

A NTONIO was leaning against the mud and wattle wall of his hut, in the shade, as we approached. He started, looked away, and then as Evangelista from the orphanage went up and touched his shoulder gently, he turned round, his face set and tears in his eyes.

'*Saudades, saudades,*' said Evangelista, meaning: memories, nostalgia, sadness. Eight-year-old Antonio's memories include two years in the orphanage in Cuito in Angola's Central Highlands, during the year-and-a-half siege by UNITA in 1993-4 in which 30,000 people died and survivors sheltered underground and were reduced to eating rats and leaves.

Later, after the ceasefire and the return of government control, his family was traced to the town of Chipeta, 50 miles from Cuito which had been abandoned by peasants on the run as UNITA took it over in a major offensive. Antonio came home to this hut, but found that his mother, father, brother and sisters were all dead. His world disappeared sometime as he cowered with several hundred other lost children in the ruins of Cuito, listening to the crump of artillery and mortars day after day. Evangelista, who was with the children then, is a kind and conscientious woman, but those days and months exhausted her emotions to the core, and her own grief for the dozen members of her immediate family who were killed seems to have been put on hold lest it should overwhelm her. Antonio is beyond her responsibility now. He lives with his uncle, a skinny man with weary eyes who says that perhaps the boy is not feeling well today, there is little to eat and he was too tired to go to school this morning. Antonio has a piece of shrapnel lodged in his temple and Evangelista worries that his headaches are getting worse and perhaps he needs an operation. But there is nothing she can do about it, the prospect of medical attention is extremely remote. There is no doctor or hospital in Chipeta and even in Cuito the state hospital is on its knees with a handful of Angolan and Vietnamese doctors and nurses who have no drugs and who struggle to survive on salaries which are paid months late and are anyway almost worthless in this economy broken by the war. There are tens of thousands of Antonios in Angola — children whose lives have been ripped apart by the multi-faceted social and economic crisis of the war and who are left to grow up without enough emotional support and without an education which could offer the only chance of personal autonomy and choices in life. Only four per cent of Angolan 10-year-olds have a chance of a school place. And these children are the survivors: Angola has the highest rate of infant and under-five mortality in the world: 195 per thousand and 320 per thousand respectively.

Carlinda, an Angolan psychiatric social worker, tells a story from the early days of independence in 1976 when she was living in the Central Highlands province of Bie, where Cuito is the province capital. 'It was dusk when the military truck drew up outside the orphanage and a group of soldiers walked in carrying some children they had found left in a village after a firefight with UNITA. Those soldiers were so sweet with them, so concerned that they should be in a safe place, so unconscious of whether they were UNITA children, I have never forgotten that touching scene. Those soldiers had had very good childhoods of their own. These days I don't believe our soldiers can treat children in the same way, they have all of them lived only in war. And, however much we would prefer not to admit it, the circumstances of life do change your values — this is true.'

Angola's is the longest war of our times. A generation has never known peace or any economic stability. A guerrilla war against the Portuguese colonialists began in the late 1960s. From 1975 civil war sponsored by the United States and apartheid South Africa became the backdrop of every Angolan's life. The war became normal, as Carlinda put it. One of the particularities of this war was the systematic kidnapping of children by

UNITA in its long struggle to form a separate state in the underpopulated east and south of the country. Girls were taken to Jamba, the Potemkin town built by the South Africans in the remotest southeast corner of the country where it was supplied from South Africa and formed UNITA's headquarters to be shown to foreigners. (Only with the end of apartheid did the headquarters move to the Central Highlands town of Andulo.)

Girls were needed as sexual partners for the leadership — Jonas Savimbi himself has several wives — and for the UNITA soldiers, always on the move, which the boys soon became. Women and their children became key to UNITA's social control. Wives and children were kept in Jamba, and still are, as hostages. UNITA students and officials who went abroad were controlled by the knowledge that their loved ones were in Jamba. And the reign of fear in Jamba, which touched everyone associated with UNITA wherever they might be, was reinforced by public rituals in which women were burned alive as witches. Babies were killed in equally brutal fashion. Only after the brief peace in 1992 when dozens of people escaped from Jamba did these stories become generally accepted and acknowledged to be true by those outside this closed world. For two decades they had been denied by the powerful western media as mere propaganda against Jonas Savimbi, held up by his western allies as an example to Africa of a leader committed to democracy.

The children of this society are the most tragically brutalised imaginable. Products of a value system in which men and boys have to prove themselves by aggression and cruelty, and in which total obedience to the leader is demanded, they are depersonalised. The boys, initially broken in spirit by acts of humiliation and violence, are routinely given drugs, especially before fighting, to increase their alienation from themselves. Asked what they would like to do after the war, each one gives the same reply: 'Whatever the commander orders.' UN staff who have worked with UNITA child soldiers brought into the quartering areas in 1996 as part of the UN peace process describe all of them as showing the classic symptoms of Post-Traumatic Stress Disorder. They lie systematically about everything, including their age and where they are from, they have very short attention spans, quick tempers, suffer from nightmares, memory flashbacks, bed-wetting, and an inability to think about the future.

In every orphanage and many families in Angola large numbers of children suffer from the same problems, and many of them carry on suffering from them as adults. It is hardly surprising that one of the things elderly Angolans always say is that children no longer respect adults — one of the cornerstones of traditional African society has been destroyed. There is another kind of Antonio, however, who has learned to cope with the circumstances of war with extraordinary resilience. 'Car wash here', says a roughly lettered sign on a piece of cardboard leaning against a shelter made of plastic bags, boxes, and broken car parts. This is the home of one of Luanda's dozens of gangs of boys, usually aged between 10 and 14, and the hopeful signboard shows how far from passive victims these boys are. Mostly they live by begging, and the prime sites in the car parks outside hotels, apartment blocks, and restaurants used by foreigners are prized and jealously guarded by various gangs. But inside the gangs of anything from 10 to 20 boys is a spirit of solidarity and sharing — they have made substitute families.

During the 1993/4 war after the disastrous UN-run elections, many of these children were from the central and northern provinces overrun by UNITA. Like Antonio in Chipeta, they were later often reunited with at least part of their real family. Today's street children are a different kind of war victim. They are victims of the economic collapse which has made it impossible for their families to feed them. Before they are teenagers they have become little adults, responsible for themselves. Some, like those offering a car wash in a city with virtually no running water and where the children themselves wash from broken sewers, make a life through sheer determination and creativity. The weaker ones, though, often do not. Father Horatio, an Argentinian priest who has worked with the street children in the capital for years, said recently that often he feels so outraged by the state of the children he sees that he will take one who is starving and has open wounds, and put him down outside the president's home or the Palace of Congress. It is not known whether a miracle change of circumstances then happens to these boys.

But there are Angolan children whose life experience has made them believe in miracles. Outside a foreigner's office in Cuito another Antonio was standing in the shade. In perfect Spanish and then hesitant English he asked if I or my friends needed any help. This Antonio had spent eight years at school on the Island of Youth in Cuba and then studied agriculture at Havana University — one of the tens of thousands of Angolan children given an education they could not otherwise have dreamed of. Hearing about the siege of his home town he came back without waiting to finish his course. When the siege ended he travelled to

*Ngiva, southern Angola 1996: battered lives among the ruins*

what had been his home and found that his father, two brothers and only sister had been killed. 'Only my mother is left and a small nephew and now I am caring for them, working for foreigners as an interpreter. There is no job here to use what I learned about agriculture, planning and experimenting. Of course I would go away at once if it were not for my mother having no-one else. Every day I think about my dream: it is to go back to that country and study so that one day when Angola is a normal place I could do good work here — not like now. Just surviving.' ❑

***Victoria Brittain*** *is foreign news editor with the* Guardian, *London*

# INDEX 1995/96: highlights

Rapidly increasing magazine sales and frequent reports and reviews of our work in the national and international media have meant that demand for the unique expertise and services offered by *Index* and Writers & Scholars Educational Trust are more in demand than ever.

*An item from the successful
Index Auction of Banned Books*

• We were nominated for a One World 96/Media Natura Award for our coverage of the UN in issue 5/1995.

• We co-hosted, with the BFI, special showings of banned films to coincide with the publication of our issue on 100 years of film censorship — *The Subversive Eye* (6/1995).

• Our Africa specialist, Adewale Maja-Pearce won a Commendation in the 1996 Foreign Press Association Awards — the only journalist not from a major national newspaper to be so honoured.

• Meanwhile, *Index*'s Internet Website has mirrored the success of the magazine, receiving an average of 10,000 'hits' every week, and numerous awards — including a One World 96/Media Natura Award and a listing as one of WEBDO's 125 Best Websites.

• *Index* articles continue to be reprinted in newspapers all over the world. The *Guardian, Independent on Sunday, Evening Standard, Die Tagezeitung* (Germany) and *Het Parool* (The Netherlands) were among newspapers carrying *Index* pieces.

• We mounted two highly successful fundraising events — the film première of Roman Polanski's *Death and the Maiden* (based on Ariel Dorfman's highly acclaimed play which was first published in *Index*) and the *Index* Auction of Banned Books.

*If you'd like to know more about our work behind the scenes at* Index, *our Annual Report 1995/96 gives an account of the year and is available from Joe Hipgrave at* Index